REVIEWING THE TROPES

David P. Ramsden

Copyright © 2022 David P. Ramsden

All rights reserved

Considering the following is based largely on the work of others it would
be wrong of the author to forbid those who can make use of its contents
from doing so. It is, however, recommended that specialists refer to the
original source. Otherwise any part of this book can be used in general
conversation, verbal, written or electronic, so long as it serves to expose
the inequality, injustice and hypocrisy of the world we currently inhabit.

ISBN- 979878719424

Cover by Stuart Gaunt

'I once read somewhere that the only newspaper that tells you the truth is the Financial Times. Apparently, normal people like you and me don't actually need to know the truth of what is going on in the world, which is why we buy all the other newspapers with supplements that tell us what problems we have and what we need to buy in order to cure them. The people with power and money, on the other hand, who have to know the truth to ensure that they keep hold of their money and power, quietly buy the FT.'
(Dan Kieran - I Fought the Law)

CONTENTS

AN INTRODUCTION

There are many reasons to read, all of them good; for pleasure and entertainment, for education and learning, to develop thinking and for what the Victorians called 'self-improvement'. Reading pleasure runs from light, frothy escapism through puzzle-solving detective novels to heavy classics, and all of it has its place. Reading is a voyage of discovery, we might be in search of particular information, general enlightenment or the development of a philosophy. Close textual analysis is sometimes necessary, but at other times skimming and scanning are more than adequate.

Dave Ramsden clearly has an ability to simultaneously combine these different skills. He obviously enjoys his reading and engages wholeheartedly with the specifics of the subject in hand. However, the reader is never in any doubt that he is reading in order to obtain a greater understanding of our world and those who inhabit it. He uses books to bolster his global outlook and strengthen his desire that the world be changed for the better.

It is fascinating to see the whole reading process taking place and we accompany Dave in his discoveries. His reading is wide ranging and his tastes eclectic, but certain themes emerge and are reiterated throughout, such as his contempt for military adventurism and his hatred of exploitation and oppression. As the essays develop the reader can feel the connections between Dave's experiences and the ideas that his reading encourages.

Most people do some reading, but it is clear that for our author, as for myself, it is an addiction; almost a compulsion. The smart phone has made it possible for us to never be without a whole library of nineteenth century novels, but previously one of my greatest dreads was being stuck somewhere with nothing to read.

It is interesting that of numerous written sources; documents and reports, newspapers, magazines, analyses and assessments, Dave restricts himself to the physical book, which possesses a semi-permanent status as a cultural artefact, as opposed to the transience of other material. The book-lined living room is becoming a thing of the past, but I suspect Dave is contemptuous of new-fangled digital devices and formats.

Whatever else the Victorians achieved, their well-stocked public libraries represented significant cultural advance. Like many great Victorian institutions that cannot be turned into money-spinning enterprises they are now under considerable threat. Perhaps some people even see reading as old fashioned, but if we lose our libraries we will have taken a significant backward step.

As our public services shrink we have much to be grateful to the voluntary sector for, but who would have thought they could become a replacement for libraries? Many of Dave's books are charity shop discoveries. This makes his reading selection even more random, and even more interesting. His writing ably demonstrates why reading is so important to the development of individual ideas and to the cultural capital of society, and why books are items to be cherished, even as technology and society changes around us.

Inspired by his reading Dave writes with verve and passion. He uses language to illuminate even familiar topics. His wide vocabulary and his unadorned writing style enhance his ability to get to the heart of the matter. He has a sharp and unremitting focus on the class struggle, but rather than succumb to writing by numbers agitprop, he takes the trouble to engage properly with the material at hand.

Dave makes no secret of his socialism. Through reading and writing he explores and expresses a consistently progressive perspective, while avoiding the trite jargon-filled polemics of some sectarian writing, and as such is a much more effective ambassador for his view of the world.

Martin Jones

PRELIMINARIES

Two Steps Forward: One Step Back

In the early years of the nineteenth century there was passionate and ongoing debate within the burgeoning British Sunday school movement. It is difficult to believe in today's enlightened times, but the question exercising the minds of the lay and clerical great and good was of whether working class children should be taught to read and write. It seems obvious to us now, and to all but the most backward of the world's rulers, that mass literacy is an intrinsically good thing. But, only half a century into Britain's world-dominating industrial epoch, it wasn't yet obvious to the pseudo-paternalistic hierarchy of the Church and their best friends in business that the greater part of the working class would need to be literate in order to be effectively exploited.

On one side of the controversy were ranged those well-to-do guardians of the gospel who wanted to selflessly share it with the lower orders, that they might feel the Glory of God working his mysterious ways through them. However, even these paranoid paragons recoiled at allowing the lower orders the means of self-expression through writing. In fact, at various times in British history, it has been too much for our betters that working people were allowed even to speak openly to each other without fear of arrest, deportation or execution for sedition or illegal combination.

On the other side were those who believed that keeping their inferiors in complete ignorance was the only means by which they could maintain their own dominance, for even within the holiest of books (Adam Smith's *Wealth of Nations* for example) there are sentiments which, honestly interpreted, might undermine the God-given order of things. There was also the frightening possibility that, once in possession of dangerous literacy, the understandably discontented and abused masses might misuse the little time off they were generously granted to indulge themselves in subversive tracts that advocated such unreasonable concepts as liberty, fairness and justice.

The gift of literacy, being reluctantly conceded in the interests of profit, was not of course bestowed without conditions, and the result was largely rote learning. We should not imagine even today, with all of human knowledge at our fingertips that our children are on an endless voyage of discovery about their own history and place in the world. In a 2017 review of Graham Brown-Martin's *Learning (Re) Imagined* George Mombiot laments the current state of education:

'Our schools were designed to produce the workforce required by 19th-century factories. The desired product was workers who would sit silently at their benches all day, behaving identically, to produce identical products, submitting to punishment if they failed to achieve the required standards. Collaboration and critical thinking were just what the factory owners wished to discourage.'

For an all too brief period in the middle of the twentieth century humanity looked like it might be heading somewhere other than to hell in a handcart. Education took a progressive turn and there were tentative steps toward intellectual honesty, but by a roundabout route we have returned. The neoliberal zealots currently engaged in turning back the clock no more require working people to question their pathological attachment to the free market than did their Victorian counterparts. Those who call for a radical rethink are accused of social engineering, as if all education isn't social engineering, and worse. Historically British education has consisted largely in indoctrination, and it is a tragedy that schoolchildren are still consciously misled by a centrally-imposed Anglo-centric national curriculum. Having obtained one of the undoubted privileges of civilisation they are made to focus on the deeds of wealthy white men, many of them political and physical thugs, at the expense of the universal masses, whose daily efforts produce the means of our comfort and sustenance and whose social movements are the real motor of history. Mao Tse Tung is reported to have said that it could be harmful to read too many books, and so it can, but only to those who would keep us in ignorance.

In *Ghost Train to the Eastern Star* novelist and travel writer Paul Theroux says, 'Writers are always readers, and though they are usually unbalanced, they are always noticers of the world.' I have been noticing the world for some time and generally it does not please me. 'Unbalanced' has more than one meaning (and dissenters are regularly branded mentally defective, as in 'the loony left'), but it will be obvious from what follows that I do not subscribe to liberal cant about impartiality. Those who run the world in their own interests are not neutral, any more than are their lackeys in academia and the media, and no writer is under any obligation to pretend they are, though some find it more convenient to do so, coerced or otherwise, especially where their funding or future careers are concerned. Such threats are indeed among the mechanisms of control. Those not subject to such constraints have a duty to be honest. In a grossly unjust and unequal world fake neutrality becomes a political position. To keep quiet about injustice is to side with the unjust, to remain silent about organised robbery is to side with those who benefit from it.

Anyone who wants to properly understand the world needs a coherent method by which to analyse it. Such an analytical method is known as an ideology; a system of ideas. In the run up to the 2010 general election the historian and classicist Mary Beard appeared on the *Today* program and criticised the main parties' manifestos for their vacuity. She was particularly concerned about the absence of ideology. In response she was informed that an absence of ideology was a good thing and ought to be celebrated. This is a mendacious conceit; to pretend not to have an ideology, especially as a potential government, is to actively support the status quo, which is deeply ideological, on the deceitful (or self-deceiving) assumption that it is natural or neutral, which it most certainly is not.

The reason for the abject lack of ideology in modern political manifestoes is that their writers all share the same hubristic assumption that capitalism has triumphed and there is no alternative. No mainstream political party anywhere in the world proposes to be anything other than a capitalist government, and capitalist ideology is behind their every action. It matters nothing to them that capitalist governments are backed up by the capitalist state, which consists in an unelected bureaucracy and bodies of armed men, whose job it is to ensure, by force if necessary, that the status quo is not undermined.

The ultimate resort to force is backed up by libraries full of books celebrating western civilisation, our famous democracy, our meritocracy, our tolerance and our respect for the law. Most of them should come with a health warning for their deleterious effect on perception. In addition there are millions of books whose authors take for granted the legitimacy of the current economic and political system and thereby sanction and sustain it. It is much rarer to encounter by accident works in which 'entrepreneurs' are unmasked, exploitation is called by its proper name and those who act to preserve it are exposed for the warmongering thieves, liars and charlatans they are.

In exploring totalitarianism George Orwell said that reality is whatever the state holds it to be on a given day and that accepted facts change only as a function of power. He saw the manipulation of the past as an essential part of controlling the future. It is quite clear from the British example that the maintenance of ideological hegemony does not require a police state. Between writing the novels *Animal Farm* and *1984* Orwell produced *Politics and the English Language*, in which he observed that 'Political language… is designed to make its lies sound truthful and murder respectable, and to give an appearance of solidity to pure wind.' In a passage that has lost none of its force he says;

'Defenceless villages are bombarded from the air, the inhabitants driven out into the countryside, the cattle machine-gunned, the huts set on fire with incendiary bullets: this is called *pacification*. Millions of peasants are robbed of their farms and sent trudging along the roads with no more than they can carry: this is called *transfer of population* or *rectification of frontiers*. People are imprisoned for years without trial, or shot in the back of the neck or sent to die of scurvy in arctic lumber camps: this is called *elimination of unreliable elements*.'

This is Derry and Vietnam, it is Afghanistan and Iraq, it is Long Kesh, Guantanamo Bay and extraordinary rendition and it is now. As I write we are in the fifteenth day of a Russian invasion of the Ukraine that, if the rhetoric is to be believed, has brought us closer to World War Three than we have been for some time. While all imperialist aggression, with its inevitable massacre of civilians, is to be condemned it is easy in such a situation to fall for the propaganda of our own governments, to see one side as wholly wrong and the other as wholly right. This is equally true in matters of race, industrial relations, public service provision, criminality and every other facet of existence.

Professor Beard also says that anyone who dares to criticise the actions of NATO troops abroad invariably gets the Wootton Bassett card thrown at them. (Royal) Wootton Basset was the English town through which the bodies of unfortunate British soldiers killed by the Afghan and Iraqi resistance were gratuitously paraded, during the brutal imperialist occupations of their countries. Its essence is essentially that as our brothers and sisters in uniform are fighting and dying in our collective interest it is unacceptable to criticise the military in any way. Leaving aside the question of whether armies act in the interests of anyone but the rich, a version of the Wootton Bassett card is currently being used to stifle proper debate about post-Cold War NATO expansionism as one of the contributory causes of Putin's actions. In this case a critique of the whole western order is disallowed and we are expected to believe that the crisis has no history and cannot be fitted into the recognisable patterns of competing imperialisms.

One of the articles in this book features Hoda Katebi, an Oklahoma born Muslim of Iranian descent. During a TV interview designed to set her up she is told she doesn't sound like a proper, i.e. an uncritical, American. Her answer is illustrative; she says 'That's because I read.' In *Traveller*, a deeply human collection of letters and journal entries, the tears Michael Katakis sheds are palpable as he explains why he is so deeply ashamed of his native America for allowing a profoundly ignorant president to murder thousands of innocent Iraqis on the basis of a pack of lies.

This of course raises bigger questions; 'country' when preceded by a personal possessive is a dubious and debateable concept. 'My country' and 'our troops' clearly have very different meanings to 'my family' or 'my car'. It is one thing to appreciate the landscape and people of a particular landmass and celebrate the attention its administration pays to the welfare of its inhabitants. It is quite another to be belligerently uncritical of the past and present actions of the dominant class within its arbitrary borders, over whom we have no control and no real power to remove. In reality we possess neither the country nor the legal ability to fundamentally alter its direction.

Hence we find ourselves once more at the gates of hell. Against a backdrop of lamentably poor attempts to prevent climate meltdown, post-Cold War promises of peace have proved hollow and economic crisis is followed by badly-handled pandemic and war, as humanity staggers blindly from one crisis to the next. Polls consistently show that faith in blatantly self-aggrandising career politicians is falling. The reputation of their police protectors is in tatters and their imperial adventures have ended in disaster for all concerned, and still they go on, oblivious.

Amid all this we have to live our lives as best we can and books can be an escape as much as an education. Asked by Matt Haig in his book *Reasons to Stay Alive* what kept them going, many members of a self-selecting group of depressives cited their children or their dog. A good number of others said it was books. I feel the same, and for many years I have made notes while I read. Most of the following essays (for want of a better word) are the working up of those notes. It has been said that books are meant to start arguments, not end them, and these are not book reviews in the traditional sense; they are the product of active reading. Occasionally an essay is not based on a book but on a TV program or a talk I gave, and scattered among is some of my unworthy doggerel on similar themes.

Unfortunately I didn't always identify in my notes which words were the original author's and which were my own. I don't want to misrepresent anyone, so I emphasise that the opinions expressed in this volume, whether they coincide with those of the book's author or not, except where the opposite is obvious, are mine and not theirs. I apologise in advance for any remaining plagiarism.

It is the job of any writer who considers themselves progressive to comfort the afflicted and afflict the comfortable. Comfort is of course relative, and being personally comfortable is no substitute for a conscience. My lack of comfort is due to the fact that I don't like where we're going and I don't trust the bastards who are taking us there.

IT'S NOT ABOUT THE CAR

Another Fine Mess – Tim Moore

Another Fine Mess is an American road trip, a sketch on Henry Ford and an attempt to understand why Donald Trump won the presidential election. His victory is alleged to signify the end of the American Dream, but Tim Moore recognises that Trump is a symptom, not a cause. The result was only incredible if you hadn't been paying attention: neoliberalism, scapegoating and right-wing populism were bound to have undesirable consequences.

America is a country with problems; wholesale poverty, an out of control obesity and diabetes epidemic, a raging addiction to prescription painkillers and localised life expectancy rates comparable to Namibia. Alternating TV adverts for junk food and medical aids are 'like a porthole into a decadent, sickly endgame, a vision of consumerism eating itself.' Many of those who aren't self-catheterising or in need of a walk-in bath seem to be armed and dangerous.

The American Dream meant consumerism and it began with the Model T Ford. Its maker was a complex man; ignorant, yet generous, a pacifist, freemason and anti-Semite who said US soldiers were murderers and that he'd rather torch his Detroit factories than turn them over to arms production. He was the richest man in America and still got a thousand fan letters a day. He employed a diverse workforce and paid them properly, fully recognising that mass production required mass consumption.

At its heart of the enterprise was Detroit. Today it is

an ex-city; a freeway separates black from white, wealth from poverty, life from death. Race is a good indicator of voting preference, but so is religion. No nation comes close for conflating God and nation. There are even crucifixes painted with the stars and stripes, but God hasn't done anything about falling living standards. High-school educated American men now earn 40% less than they did in 1970. People at the bottom needed someone to blame and Trump gave them the targets. They voted for him in desperation.

In Alabama Tim Moore struggles to reconcile the gentle, sincere people he meets with their support for one of the shallowest and most insincere men on the planet, but he knows his trip would have been entirely different if he'd been black or gay. In Texas respectable old men hate Barack Obama and Hilary Clinton for being black and female. They say Trump is revenge for four years of a Black president.

In comparison Henry Ford looks like an equal opportunities employer, but he believed his mind-numbing production-line methods suited people with inferior mental capacity, and in the early twentieth century this meant black people. Work in the Ford factory was relentless, monotonous toil, made worse by a regime headed by a man who believed fear was a greater incentive to work than loyalty. Unions were banned and paid informers reported every conversation and complaint.

Ford's social experiment extended far beyond the factory and was backed by armed thugs. He employed two hundred investigators who invaded employee's homes and probed into every aspect of their private lives. Any moral failing could result in dismissal. His revolutionary production practices were achieved at a terrible human cost. Stalin utilised Ford's methods in his five-year plans and the two men shared a long-lasting mutual appreciation. The *New York Times* called Henry Ford 'The Mussolini of Detroit.' His ghost-written autobiography was read enthusiastically by Adolf Hitler, who mentions him in *Mein Kampf* and kept a picture of him in his office. The manufacture of Hitler's Volkswagen Beetle was based entirely on the brutal production methods of Henry Ford.

Time after time Tim Moore meets beautiful people filled with foreboding. They hate and fear the federal government and see Donald Trump as their ally. Texas towns, once home to ten thousand people, are reduced to Republican rumps a tenth the size. Women tell Moore they just wish the media would give Donald a chance.

In Oklahoma and Kansas skilled and semi-skilled men haven't worked for years and aren't going to. Invited to dinner Moore discovers a Trump-supporting family living in poverty and squalor. They exaggerate the Hispanic population, celebrate Trump's border wall and believe Barack Obama was uncritically pro-Muslim. Like a third of all Americans his host says he would never criticise *anything* Trump said. And he loves guns. Moore is disgusted by his own disgust at a fundamentally decent man who has fallen out with life and lost patience with so-called liberals.

There's nothing great about the Great Plains; they're full of dead and dying towns bypassed by interstate highways. Oklahoma never recovered from the 1930s dust storms. Nebraska is overwhelmingly Trump. Hilary Clinton got so few votes in Wyoming it was a waste of time standing.

At Mount Rushmore oversized older people in oversized cars gaze in reverential silence at the symbols of a once great country. It's a pilgrimage to a time when America *was*, and everyone knows it.

What Trump supporters want beyond freedom, guns, God and money is difficult to establish. But what they don't want is change. If America was a smaller place its hate filled, armed to the teeth hillbilly citizens would be far more dangerous. Its vastness means that most of them make their idle threats in fly-infested bars drinking piss-weak beer, driving big pickups and shooting up road signs: for now. But life is going to keep getting worse and Trump is likely to be re-elected, not least due to the Democrat tradition of standing someone almost as bad. [Obviously he wasn't, but that doesn't mean he never will be].

A hundred years of American history is bookended by the ignorant and brutal industrialist Henry Ford and the ignorant and brutal politician Donald Trump. They deserve each other. The American people deserve better than Biden. No establishment politician can deliver what is impossible within the bounds of the system. Humanity needs to radically rethink its direction at a time when the majority of Americans appear to have set their faces against change.

Henry Ford, essentially a make do and mend man, inadvertently created the fickle, fashion conscious consumer. He wanted to make a product that lasted a lifetime and never needed updating, he knew if new models were endlessly offered the consumer's appetite would become insatiable. Like Tories from time immemorial Ford disdained all learning that had no earning power and Donald Trump's contempt of people in low paid bureaucratic positions is something he shared with the industrialist. Ignorance is clearly *not* bliss, but a hundred years later, on a half-destroyed planet, it seems impossible for any politician who urges even minor restraint to get elected.

In South Dakota towns have a tenth of their previous population. The streets are full of closed shops and filling stations, interspersed with seedy, barely surviving motels. Among the wreckage there exists a live free or die mentality and a cult of the military veteran.

In Montana, Idaho and Oregon the Guns, God and Guts philosophy is less obvious, but many Americans are waiting for Armageddon; not the end of America, but its new beginning. Forty percent of Americans think the second coming will occur in the next forty years, and because the apocalypse is coming it doesn't matter about the natural environment because God will sort it out. A quarter of Americans think Obama might be the anti-Christ, a third believe global warming is a federal hoax, more than half think a secretive global elite is plotting a new world order.

After biting his lip for 6,000 miles Tim Moore is asked by a Californian man what people in Britain think of Trump. He says, '...by general agreement in my country, Donald is an embarrassing stain on the fabric of the universe.' The man agrees. Too many Americans don't, and unfortunately Tim Moore doesn't speak for all Britons.

Approaching the west coast the fondness for Trump fades, but his detractors cling to the fact that Hilary won the popular vote, as if by some miracle electing a patronising, warmongering dynast would have checked the slide of the distressed and divided nation. Liberal contempt for the concerns of the marginalised was perhaps the main reason they pressed the fuck-you button. Trump will shit on them just like every other millionaire president has shit on them, but what was the alternative?

By the time Henry Ford became a laughing stock the rot had already set in. During the Depression he blamed the unemployed for not working hard enough, he denounced calls for universal healthcare he had once supported. He never renounced his pacifism, always opposed the death penalty, refused to display a single gun in his massive museum and believed the end of war and a parliament of man was possible. He was also a vicious and relentless anti-Semite who promoted anti-Jewish conspiracy theories in a private newspaper every Ford dealer was compelled had to stock. His vile writings were collated in a book that became a bestseller in pre-Nazi Germany and influenced many others into rabid anti-Semitism. In 1938, at the age of seventy five, Henry Ford was awarded the highest honour available to a foreigner by the German fascist regime. It is quite possible that Adolf would have got on with Donald too, American administrations have had some pretty nasty friends.

THE ELUSIVE SILVER LINING

Born in Buenos Ares – Diana Ferraro

Diana Ferraro was born in in the 1940s in a classically styled Buenos Ares public hospital that served the middle class and now serves the poor. There existed in the port city a tension between the original inhabitants, the many European immigrants, and the darker skinned people of the interior. Power was in the hands of an aristocracy descended from 19th century cattle barons who built a city that imitated Paris. Some inhabitants had tried to change the city and failed, many more simply moved away. Other Argentines and many Latin Americans are suspicious of the port dwellers for their lighter skins and their pretensions to Europeanism, and due to a modern outlook and better educational opportunities the people of Buenos Ares have considered themselves superior to conservative provincials. Buenos Ares has produced good artists and notoriously bad politicians.

Ferraro sees the country's Peronist revolution as only one episode in an unsettled history and herself as a product of a violent, macho society whose better future always seems far away. Like many Argentines of her age Ferraro is the granddaughter of immigrants. Unlike them, who in common with immigrants in general, preferred to keep their heads down, her generation have questioned the nature of Argentine society.

The rolling Latin American resistance to dictatorship in the 1950s turned into a battle of empires between the US and the USSR. In Buenos Ares the enemy was the United States, who already ruled the Argentine economy. An ideological war was fought against the Americans, as proxies for the imperial British, and against capitalism in general. Progressive young port dwellers sided with the native Indians and promoted Spanish as the dominant language. Peronism erased questions of race, but the aristocracy ousted Peron, refusing to countenance access to any kind of democracy by darker skinned inferiors.

By the 1970s a melded Buenos Ares population had lost its ties elsewhere and sought ownership of its own country. After Peron those who sought socialism and those who sought true national liberation coexisted. The automatically successful, rich and intrinsically unfair Argentina ended with Peronism, but it was ultimately unsuccessful in delivering what it promised. For this Diana Ferraro blames 'the hidden and permanent civil war.'

This civil war has been described as being between barbarism and civilisation. In Argentina the barbarism was that of the poor in the provinces. The civilisation was that of wealth and privilege sustained in the city through the usual kind of corruption and fake democracy. Naturally some of the noble advocates of civilisation forswore no method of bringing it about, no matter how many innocent lives were squandered in the process.

Progressive Peronism encompassed in its project not only poor provincials but industrial workers living in the capital. As in many other places, at many other times, this potentially lethal combination unleashed a reactionary backlash from the pro-British ruling class, who resented the very suggestion that they should cease to hold sole power.

Racism is ever the resort of struggling rulers and Argentinean rulers were no different to Donald, Boris and Bolsonaro. The descendants of relatively privileged Europeans were encouraged to see darker skinned people as the usurpers of the kind of sham democracy enjoyed by millions today. The tactic of accusing those who seek equality of acting against democracy is as old as fake democracy itself. It demonstrates only that fake democracy is a mechanism for preventing social, political and economic progress, rather than one for bringing it about. It is a means of keeping power in the hands of those who already have it. Its pinnacle is reached in the US where a series of millionaire charlatans expend obscene amounts of money in order to obtain a mandate from the people to represent the interests of capital, to the people's detriment.

Arguments about what Peronism is and isn't have led to much violence. But whatever it is, the citizens of Buenos Ares have generally been against it, except when a distorted, all-too-modern strain of Peronism advocated the kind of civilisation those who sought to lift the country out of barbarism wanted all along, via the intrinsically barbaric steamroller of neoliberalism.

The civil war, sometimes open, sometimes hidden, has seen cruelties perpetrated by military juntas and the guerrillas who have opposed them. It has destroyed personal, collective and political dreams. Many of these dreams were the dreams of immigrants starting a new life; Jews escaping pogroms, people from Japan, Europe and the Middle East. Buenos Ares has absorbed all these and combined them with the legacy of the conquistadors and the aspirations of the Indians from the interior. Buenos Ares is a melting pot and its people have shared, distinct and overlapping histories. Above all else they long for stability and safety, some see that stability and peace as being elsewhere; they leave, or stay and dream.

The Rio de la Plata divides Argentina and defines Buenos Ares. On one side are the port dwellers, on the other is the inland and its people. The city and its politicians are funded by the interior. Argentina is not a federal state; the city exploits the countryside. The rich have enjoyed the boom times and the poor have endured deep recessions. The people have placed their hopes in charismatic leaders and had them dashed by military dictatorships. Argentina used to be Britain's beef farm, now it is China's farm, growing mostly soy. The country has prospered on the export of grains and the government has spent its income on populist programs. But in these grains are the seeds of future poverty, when the price falls or China goes elsewhere. Those who ignore or are ignorant of the rules of capitalism pretend the good times can go on forever. They don't learn from the past and the people tolerate a government they don't like for fear of something worse.

Argentines have a habit of measuring themselves against the 'first' world. They are not the first world, but the first world isn't the first world anymore either. America has all the problems that Argentina has, and so does Britain. Like Britain, Argentina, and Buenos Ares in particular, has begun to like about itself what the new tourists like; Maradona, Pope Francis and everything in between. Like royal families and otherwise dead British villages the people of Buenos Ares have prostituted themselves for the tourist dollar in a world where further travel is impossible. And they have the internet. They are part of the world and the world is part of them. Like all of us they are everywhere and nowhere, shipwrecked on a sea of emptiness. All of this I discover from Diana Ferraro's book.

WARTS AND ALL

Born to Run – Bruce Springsteen

Bruce Springsteen's heritage is Irish, Italian and Dutch. His father worked at the Ford plant; his mother was a legal secretary who married into poverty and servitude. Raised Catholic by his grandparents he lacked boundaries, was bullied at school and questioned the world early. Mental illness ran in the family and debilitating depression bookends his life. By forty his father was the broken and occasionally violent man universalised in his songs. Aged ten Bruce hit him with a baseball bat for abusing his mother.

Freehold, New Jersey was an ugly, redneck place prone to racism, where long hair was considered un-American. The arrival of Elvis changed everything: music offered an escape and it was all Bruce wanted to do. His drummer joined the Marines and became the first local boy to die in Vietnam. Another acquaintance went missing in action.

It was the time of the Tet Offensive and things were going badly for the US. His manager avoided the draft by cutting off his own toe and eighteen year old Bruce didn't want to go. The war wasn't his business and he planned to act the mentally unstable, drug taking loser. In the end he failed the medical and lived with the guilt of not being one of the 58,000 who wasted their lives in a futile, obscene and destructive cause.

When Bruce's family moved to California he was on his own. At nineteen he left Freehold, though it has never left him. He describes himself as a fake hippy with a blue-collar outlook who didn't take drugs. He knew where he wanted to go; others took too many and some of them died.

Time and again he started over, but never considered making a living any other way than by making music. While writing the semi-autobiographical *Greetings from Asbury Park* album he was penniless and slept on the beach. On its release he'd never received anything but cash, never paid tax and never rented a flat. He'd no credit card, no cheque book and no driving licence. His associates were manual workers and dropouts. He talked big but considered himself a fraud.

The record company correctly predicted his 1973 album, the *The Wild, the Innocent & the E Street Shuffle,* would be a flop. Bruce realised he was never going to be a chart act and personally badgered radio DJs to play his songs. Eventually someone described him as the future of rock and roll and he hit the big-time. The seminal *Born to Run* took six months to write. He sought redemption as only a Catholic could;

'I was a child of Vietnam-era America, of the Kennedy, King and Malcolm X assassinations. The country no longer felt like the innocent place it was said to be… Political murder, economic injustice and institutionalised racism were all powerfully and brutally present… Dread – the sense that things might not work out, that the moral high ground had been swept out from underneath us, that the dream we had of ourselves had somehow been tainted… was in the air. …if I was going to put my characters out on *that* highway, I was going to have to put all these things in the car with them. That's what… the times demanded.'

He made the album he wanted to make. He also wanted to last and knew he'd have to work at it. His writing focussed on issues of identity and what it meant to be American. To the lovers in *Thunder Road* everything is ambiguous, life is full of questions. He made the front covers of *Time* and

Newsweek. Melody Maker raved about him and the *New Musical Express* tore him to pieces. Angry at being over-hyped he took charge rather than allow others to cash in. He theorised his art and psychoanalysed his band to gauge their strengths and weaknesses. The cover for *Darkness on the edge of Town* depicted a troubled young man. Off stage he had no family, no home and no real life.

After the Three Mile Island nuclear accident Bruce committed to Musicians for Safe Energy. In *The River* he wanted an entertaining but interrogative album and recorded every song he wrote until it almost bankrupted him. Two years' work produced a double album that raised questions he and others were asking. His home life had been blighted by excess and he wore his self-restraint like a badge. If any band member transgressed he left or they did.

Devastated by reading *Born on the 4th of July* Bruce was taken by Ron Kovic to meet young men destroyed by war who had returned to ignominy. The band helped launch the Independent Vietnam Veterans of America with a charity concert and in telling their stories he found a social use for his talents. Wanting to honour his family and the people he'd grown up with he read history for himself and his music, seeking to expose the reality behind the American façade.

The *River* tour set Bruce up and the money messed with his self-image. He fantasised about moving back to Freehold, returning on lonely missions to top up his resentment at the lives people were forced to live. The result was *Nebraska*, the heartfelt antithesis of the rock music that had got him so far. He was caught between success and honesty, as his characters were caught between coping and madness. Declining to tour the album he said it would have been like selling tickets for the funeral of the American Dream.

Aged thirty-two Bruce released *Born in the USA* and

people heard what they wanted to hear. Ronald Reagan saw a message of hope in what is actually a cry for reason in a world of empty patriotism. Despite his endless lyrical references to hope and faith they are non-starters. Bruce Springsteen is a man of action. He knew there are reasons for what people endure and he toured the country talking to them. The album is about racism, deindustrialisation and exploitation. He worried that *Dancing in the Dark*, a chart song he'd rather not have included, might dilute the message.

The *Born in the USA* tour proved the E Street Band could fill any stadium they wanted, sometimes six nights in a row, but Bruce was a troubled man. Three days after the tour ended he hit rock bottom. He didn't know what to do next and worked at being married. All his insecurities found their way onto *Tunnel of Love*. His previous worship of the open road seemed empty, but he couldn't believe in the alternative and emptiness still had a nihilistic attraction. During the tour Bruce fell in love with Patti Scialfa. He handled the separation from his wife badly and freely admits he failed her.

In East Berlin Bruce's on-stage speech against the wall was cut from the state TV coverage. For Amnesty International's human rights tour he read up on every country the band visited; Zimbabwe, Cote d'Ivoire, Japan, Hungary, Canada, Brazil, India and Argentina. The black-clad mothers of Chile's Disappeared made him embarrassed by the vacuous questions he was asked by reporters at home. He celebrated his 'little, repressed, redneck, reactionary... crap-heap of a home town,' as somewhere you could speak freely without molestation. Sadly, that has always depended on who you are and what you say, as Paul Robeson or Muhammad Ali would testify.

After a failed attempt at living in New York, Bruce and Patti moved to California and he tried his best to ruin another relationship. Not knowing where he was going personally or professionally he disbanded the E Street Band. In the sunshine state he witnessed desperate poverty and blamed the riots that followed the police murder of Rodney King on the deliberate destruction of society. After an Oscar for *Streets of Philadelphia* he junked another introspective album for a return to social issues with *The Ghost of Tom Joad*, knowing an album featuring those left behind in 1990s America wouldn't be a big seller. The downbeat solo tour emphasised the emptiness of the lives it depicted.

After years of mental illness Bruce's father was diagnosed as a paranoid schizophrenic. He was a deeply troubled man who hated himself for his failings and his dependence on Bruce's mother. The illness held the whole family to ransom and Bruce knew exactly what he had to guard against, even if he didn't always manage it.

In 1999, after a ten year break, Bruce reformed the E Street Band and they enjoyed years more fame and success. Any fears about their reception were dispelled by the hysteria that greeted them in Barcelona at the start of a 133 date tour. For the last date in New York Bruce wrote *American Skin* in response to the forty-one shots fired at African immigrant Amadou Diallo by the police. He tried the song out in Atlanta and the New York police commissioner asked him not to play it. The police union was less diplomatic. The song was received to some booing, and he has continued to experience animosity from police officers for it.

Much has happened since Bruce Springsteen first picked up a guitar at the height of the struggle for black civil rights, but he's still speaking for the underdog, the cops are still killing black people and the Leader of the Free World is encouraging white supremacists.

NOT QUITE THE
SECOND COMING

Christ's Entry Into Brussels – Dimitri Verhulst

Dimitri Verhulst has written stark autobiographies and novels about the fate of asylum seekers within an inhuman system. He is a Catholic and knows that ideology's brand of cruelties. This novel provides an insight into the people of Brussels, and by extension the demoralised and gullible consumption junkies of all 'developed' countries.

Many years ago I was told Belgium was famous for producing lard and harbouring international terrorists. It is also the global leader in the consumption of anti-depressants. Mobile phones have provided the perfect distraction for commuters who avoid interaction in a country with four official languages. Instead they scuttle home to spend the evening dissing each other on social media.

While surfing the net when they should be working these 'oafs' discover that Christ is coming to town. In a largely secular country people have more faith in God than the media, which is full of tittle-tattle, destructive comparisons between different communities and environmental stories beside invitations to buy 4x4s and burn endless jet fuel.

Holy visits have a long history in Belgium, the Virgin Mary visited on spec a dozen times in 1933 and again in the 1970s and 1980s. But this tour by the main man-God is pre-booked and the fickle media is full of it. Talk show hosts hope for interviews.

No one thinks to question the truth of the report. Across society residents make ready to welcome the Christ they cast in their own image. At first no one mentions that His return also entails a great reckoning. Catholics who have been abused by priests are ready to forgive. The Church, which carried out the Inquisition and kept quiet about the Holocaust, fears Christ is coming to judge them. The lapsed Catholic narrator can hardly stop himself making the sign of the cross as he ponders a suitable route for the saviour's progress; perhaps the one taken by numerous protesters who have sought justice and fairness, but he knows Christ could equally go straight to the royal palace.

Traditionally the citizens of Brussels flatter celebrity by dressing up the Manneken Pis. What is good enough for Elvis is good enough for Christ. The famous pissing youth was replaced with a replica in 1965, when Belgium had recovered from WWII and the future looked rosy. But there was a bomb at the Olympics, the police began to look like soldiers, nuclear annihilation loomed, bosses went on the offensive, dole queues grew, hungry Africans got more air time than soap stars and racism returned.

Eventually there was new cause for hope: Apartheid collapsed, the Berlin Wall came down and various velvet revolutions took place. The optimism was dealt a hammer blow by Rwanda, which Belgium was ultimately responsible for, and Srebrenica, which happened while Dutch soldiers looked the other way. Belgians turned inwards and engaged themselves with trivialities. They were lifted once more by the Manneken Pis dressed as Christ. The grey city is enlivened, there is something to look forward to. Hotel prices begin to rise, new bed and breakfasts are founded and campsites are extended.

Some members of Belgium's bloated parliaments are

all too willing to exaggerate disagreements between different cultural groups for their own ends, often enlisting God in their cause. It is difficult to assemble a balanced delegation to welcome Christ. The municipal dignitaries also want to bathe in Christ's reflected glory. The ensuing squabbles obscure concerns about poor services, the high cost of education and the degradation of the environment.

The first task is to find someone who speaks Aramaic. They are even prepared to offer citizenship to someone previously designated unworthy of humanity. An eleven year old refugee, who normally sleeps on the street, is eventually chosen as Christ's interpreter. How better could the people of Belgium show the Son of God that they care about those they have up until now allowed to doss down on cardboard in the red light district?

The responsibility rests heavy on the chosen child. In her dreams she has to show Christ Brussels as it is; Brussels with its poverty and lack of work, Brussels where people can't afford medical treatment. The city, the country and the EU are depending on her to give the best impression, but in her dream she leads Him from the central station past the junk food stalls and the drunks; past the beggars the people of Brussels like to believe are dropped off in cars every morning, picked up every night and make a lucrative living. She'll show him the women trafficked into prostitution, the coarse blankets at the homeless shelters, the slums of the city and the homeless people sleeping under parked cars to feel the warmth of their engines.

The dream turns into a nightmare. Christ turns out to be a government inspector, angry that the eleven year old refugee has shown him the pits and not the palaces. Then he is the devil, which to a homeless refugee is just about the same thing. In the dream, for showing Christ the Brussels she knows, she will be sent straight to a deportation centre.

Belgium is not a particularly confident country and its demise has been often predicted, but Christ is coming on the country's national day. Anti-monarchists decide the king will be upbraided for being useless. Others, while acknowledging his uselessness, think he's basically a decent bloke who won't show them up. The traditional national day parade will be combined with the Son of God's procession. There will be a review of the troops and a fighter-plane flypast in the shape of a cross.

The thousands of early well-wishers camped in the parks have their needs met by opportunist event caterers and a host of overflowing portaloos. Newspapers in Belgium and beyond offer advice on cultural must-sees and where to eat and drink. Neighbours begin to talk to each other across landings and make small talk over drinks and supper. It is as if Christ's whole message was about brotherly love and community and the mere promise of his coming has swept away all base behaviour. Lapsed Catholics rhapsodise with near strangers as a kind of religious revival takes place.

Our narrator isn't a patriot and, though he is proud of some of the things his country provides, he has been disturbed by the recent fashion for flag-waving and the singing of an anthem reminiscent of Belgium's imperial past. It is thoroughly unsuitable for the welcoming of Christ. The search for a welcoming paean is thrown open to the public, who are asked to keep it simple so even the most stupid can understand and it can be translated into the four Belgian languages, as well as Aramaic and Latin. Unfortunately the winning entry focusses on things close to Christ's own heart, and turns out to have been plagiarised from socialist texts.

To clear his deceased mother's flat the narrator invites in the very people she feared; Moroccans, Congolese,

Uzbeks, Afghans, whom he has only previously seen as passing shadows. They express their condolences and sincere gratitude. On the same day it is announced that the city centre will be closed to traffic to make it easier to detect car bombs.

The big day is forecast to be hot. The optimists attribute it to Christ's coming, not pollution and global warming. The rest of Belgium is deserted, as are tourist destinations across Europe; countless thousands are drawn like iron filings to the magnet of The Messiah. Our narrator fears for His safety and that of the crowds. He remembers Heysel Stadium and wonders if it might be better to watch proceedings on TV. A rumour circulates that Christ is already in town; an innocent hippy is mobbed. The night before is quiet. The people don't know why Christ is coming, so they lie awake with only their consciences for company.

Come the big day there are T shirt sellers, folding chairs, crates of beer and disposable barbecues. The great and good are assembled for the parade. First come the freebies tossed to the eager crowd. Then there are the floats of the sponsors and the tourist boards, then actors retelling biblical stories, prisoners, self-flagellating penitents and anachronistic, eye-candy beauty queens. Eventually, surrounded by royal guards comes the young interpreter, raised to the level of princess or demi-god. The crowd want to touch her, to photograph her and bring the sick to be cured by her. On stage she is seated next to the king.

When Christ doesn't turn up she is seized roughly by two guards, to resume her proper status as unwanted immigrant, and the people of Brussels react with their normal indifference. The city has enjoyed a short-lived lie. The possibility of outside intervention lifted them all, made them almost human again, it could have been Elvis, the Pope, Mahatma Gandhi, but most of all it could have been Jeremy

39

Corbyn. When it's all dashed they've only themselves, racism, empty patriotism and a superiority complex left.

GUYS, DOLLS AND
US DOLLARS

Dominicana – Angie Cruz

It's the 1960s and the Dominican Republic feels like a dark and dangerous place. The electricity supply is sporadic and poor people use it sparingly to save money. Men carry guns for protection and propose marriage to eleven year old girls. Local gangsters provide a kind of order, women are kidnapped by soldiers never to return.

A mother's priority is to marry her daughter to a petty entrepreneur who can benefit the family, meaning great things for them all. They are dressed up like prizes and promised to men working in the US who need a country girl to keep them out of trouble. Barely pubescent girls are made to write to much older men promoting themselves as good wives. Men marry into farming families in pursuit of their land for development, but it can mean a family ticket to America.

Parents make their daughters unhappy out of necessity, taking them out of school and packing them off with men they don't love for a life of pretence. Only by making their husbands happy can these young women's families be rescued from poverty and gangsterism. Forged marriage certificates add years onto the lives of underage girls. In some countries their honeymoons would constitute rape.

Transplanted to New York fifteen year olds are awestruck by the city and make grotty apartments into homes, the prisoners of unfaithful men who carry on as if they were still single, while making veiled threats and drunken promises they never deliver on.

They prepare food for men they are afraid of and submit to their drunken animal advances, some of them turn violent and then buy presents out of guilt. Young women pretend because they have to; in the Dominican Republic there is political unrest and their families are in danger. They send home what money they can, but people are dying in the streets. It's not lost on them that people are getting killed in America too, often for standing up to racism.

While playing second fiddle to their husbands' shady dealings these teenagers make pin money from side-lines to send home. In reward, while they are pregnant, they smell the perfume of lovers on their jailers. If they are lucky they learn English. Sometimes the violence forces them to contemplate leaving, but the needs of their families back home make them stay. They wish men dead, but they keep on living. If they leave the family will be shamed. Their mothers may beat them.

Sometimes they do leave, braving the streets and trying to ignore the beggars and the smell of piss in the richest country in the world. And then they go back to curl up in a ball on the floor to protect their pregnant stomachs from men who are as nice as pie in public. The pregnancy clinic nurses can see what's happening, but these women lie. Even having a leaflet about domestic abuse can get them beaten. Once pregnant they aren't just prisoners, they're property.

It could only be worse if America invaded the Dominican Republic. Conforming to type it does. The US is busy fighting the Cold War caricature of communism, and as part of it opposes any and all attempts at progress by ordinary people against established regimes. For the US, essentially a reactionary global force, keeping people poor pays. Were it not for America's interference desperate migrants may not have had to leave in search of decency and fulfilment. US Marines are sent to prop up a government that makes people disappear. All the Dominicans in the US can do is hope that their children will be free to learn English, go dancing and eat hotdogs.

The streets of New York are also dangerous for immigrants, the authorities pounce on workplaces and people are killed every day. For the wives of men who go back home to protect their property the absence is blessed relief. They are left with growing babies as co-conspirators as they take up free English lessons and explore the streets.

In The Dominican Republic the Americans are trying to stop a progressive revolution; the demand for better schools and hospitals somehow threatens their interests. While sending thousands of young Americans to Vietnam, to kill and die, the US still has time and resources to interfere in what it calls its own back yard. The papers carry reports of American successes, which immigrants and indigenous people alike may or may not understand. Women are told it is nothing to do with them: that their husbands only want to protect the land they have earmarked for development. Guns are everywhere and Dominicans, like poor people before and since, live under US helicopters.

Once in the land of the free, Dominican newcomers vie with those who have escaped other 'shitholes' the imperialists have helped create, to debase themselves selling street food and cleaning toilets for people who insult and abuse them. Learning English can seem like a bridge to assimilation but no amount of vernacular can whiten a brown skin. And new arrivals cannot fail to notice that activists among their hosts are fighting the same battles they thought they'd left behind, for an end to war, for fairness and the eradication of racism.

As always for women it is worse: they battle a system *and* men corrupted by that system, men who fool themselves that money is the only measure, men who keep them closeted so they don't become tainted. Morality has, for ever and for all time, meant the morality of women. And to keep them pure they are deprived of education and interaction.

In the Dominican Republic American soldiers roam the country looking for 'communists' and dope to anaesthetise them from the blatant injustice of their task. Among the rationing and the curfews, otherwise normal young Americans meet local girls looking for visas and money. Those who have escaped to a different kind of hell hear of loved ones being shot dead during protests, long before their dreams of going to America could be realised.

Once the Dominican Republic is back in the hands of rich US puppets the American white man's newspapers lose interest, and Dominicans in the US ask what was wrong with asking for more schools and hospitals. The memory of their dead relatives drives them on to succeed within the body politic of their hostile host. While immigration officers shut down factories to the advantage of employers, who have made what they can from their staff, devoted husbands and lecherous philanderers alike are thrown on their own resources.

Leaving a bad man can ruin a family's future, so women live a pretence while Dominican farmland is lost to development in return for airline tickets and forged visas. Families mistake self-interest for goodness, love of money for the love of their daughters. Wives wait on men who eat the food they make and then go to see their lovers. And all the while there's Vietnam running like a dirty film in the background.

Just when they've decided their families are more important than their own happiness, the extended families arrive. Women who have stood tall are reduced to daughters under instruction, men who have taken advantage are made into heroes. Matriarchs are diminished by the city but act like monarchs in overcrowded apartments.

And when loadbearing teenagers give birth to girls they are told by disappointed men that they will try again for a boy. It takes hard lessons for mothers to understand what daughters have sacrificed, even though they sacrificed it themselves. But for all of that, America is their home.

This is the story of contradictions: it is one young woman's escape from a poverty stricken country via an abusive relationship to the land of the free, where racism is rife and poverty is everywhere. It's a migrant, non-white story encompassing life, love and everything. It's quietly spoken context is an America that keeps lesser nations poor and practices racism at home. Most of all it is a feminist story. It is set half a century ago. Thank goodness things have changed.

HOMELAND SECURITY

Freedom Fighter: My War Against ISIS on the Frontlines of Syria, Joanna Palani

Joanna Palani was born in Iranian Kurdistan and grew up in Denmark. Her home life was oppressive and dysfunctional. She was isolated at school by teachers who didn't know how to deal with a girl whose parents wanted her brought up strictly Muslim. Gradually she comes to understand the decades of injustice suffered by her people, and decides she wants to fight for their cause with the Kurdish People's Protection Units (YPG). She says. 'Life for many young Kurds in the Middle East doesn't give you much: a Kalashnikov, a hatred of fascism, a love of freedom and memories of a loved one killed for the crime of their birth.'

The left in the west, says Palani, have had a tendency to idealise Kurdish resistance, but her relatives have been *Peshmurga*, who are not known for their progressive beliefs.

The women who fight with the YPJ (the Women's Protection Units or Women's Defence Units, affiliated to the YPG) aren't just fighting Daesh; they want a new society in the Middle East, in which equality of the sexes is integral. She says that only primitive societies turn their women into servants, but this isn't true; *Kinder, Kuchen, Kirke* was the product of a modern industrial society. The currently incarcerated Kurdish leader Abdullah Ocalan himself says, 'Without the repression of women the repression of the entire society is not conceivable.'

Joanna Palani says the Kurdish women's army is the

armed wing of a much wider cultural and political campaign, aimed at destroying patriarchy, saying 'we fight with weapons as others fight with ideas.' She is critical of the 'false feminism' of the west, decrying makeup and body hair removal as tools of sexual slavery.

The implications for the success of such a movement are obvious: in her sketch on Jane Austen's *Pride and Prejudice* Doris Lessing says; 'The French revolution had unleashed in England not only terrors of revolt and guillotine, but of the unfettered females who yelled for more blood as the heads fell, who rampaged about streets in screaming mobs, giving the world a glimpse of just what manic rebellions were being kept in check by chaperones and corsets.'

Nevertheless, the fight for women's equality is a minority current in Kurdish politics, and Joanna Palani is endlessly confronted by men who aren't with the program, just like women everywhere are when they stand up for their rights. She says every woman is always a lawyer to other women, and that she is fighting for the rights of anyone unfortunate enough to be born a girl; because no one will give them these rights, not even within their own movement.

Whilst undergoing military training worthy of the SAS she is told that no one will help her just because she is female, equality in combat means the equal right to die. She is also told that all men hate all women, and while this may make women necessarily wary of certain situations, it begs the question of how equality can ever be achieved. Surely every progressive man should also be a lawyer for women.

Palani is well aware that anyone having been trained to kill can never go back to the innocent person they were before; and a hundred times more so once they've seen combat. On the front line she compares the stripped naked bodies of dead Daesh fighters with the half-naked men other women ogle on the beach, as a returning soldier might look at his half-dressed wife and think of the massacred civilians he has seen.

Back in Denmark the police, unaware that she has already been fighting, threaten her with the gruesome personal consequences of war. It is a pity no one says this to the gullible young men who join the British army. Knowing that many of her comrades from training have already died she dismisses death as a small price to pay for freedom.

The policeman assigned to her, not least by his inappropriate behaviour, makes her see 'how patriarchy can disguise itself so cleverly within the capitalist democratic system and maintain a position of power.' He only makes her more determined to fight the system that creates men like him. Asked why she went to fight against Daesh in Kobani she asks what makes others see endless suffering on TV and do nothing about it.

For Joanna the YPJ are democrats ready for peace, but first and foremost freedom fighters. She knows that obtaining a Kurdish homeland, as distant a prospect as that seems, wouldn't end either gender or class problems, but insists that a free Kurdistan where women are treated as they are treated now is not their goal. When she acknowledges that women will not always fight for women, and can be just like men in war, one thinks of Margaret Thatcher, Condoleezza Rice and Madeline Albright.

When she is eventually rejected by the YPJ for being unduly westernised she fights with the Peshmurga in Iraq. In writing up her experiences she deliberately avoids the detail of the sexual torture women captured by Daesh endure, on the grounds that the grisly detail would impinge on the survivor's dignity, saying only that when you know what they suffer it changes your feeling towards humanity for ever. Coming across a little girl who had been raped and died with dead and rotting twins inside her, she thinks of all the ways little girls get hurt by men, and of what she went through at the same age, though she grew up in a country where there is peace and stability. She recognises what they have in common: the awful experience of being a girl. Abuse comes in many shapes and forms, but it happens all over the world, every day and every hour.

I once heard a British paratrooper say that the Parachute Regiment were his family, and Joanna Palani talks about her time with the YPJ as if it was the making of her. While keeping her dead friends in one corner of her mind, she says that the camaraderie of combatants is like no other. When you read this you begin to understand how girls from care homes in Rochdale and Rotherham, who had never had any love in their lives, could be taken in by members of grooming gangs.

Should anyone think Joanna Palini relishes the killing, as did the British snipers in Iraq I read about in *Sniper One*, she says she is not a psychopath and that dead Daesh fighters become once more human.

The ultimate indignity is not that her story was doubted, or that she was prosecuted and jailed for fighting on the same side as the western coalition, but that the special Danish police anti-terrorism officer assigned to her case comes from the same mould as the sexists she encounters in the Middle East. She eventually learns that he is being investigated for abusing his power, and entering into sexual relationships with those he was supposed to be mentoring. The female investigator asks if she ever reported him and she says, 'What a preposterous idea. Of course I didn't report him. I wasn't believed the first time I reported a man, or the second time, or the fucking tenth time, so what would have made this time any different?'

The account closes with Joanna Palani suffering from PTSD; the nightmares and visions, short temper, avoiding going to sleep, sleeping rough. She must do what all combat veterans must do; try to rediscover some semblance of normality, after seeing the worst things anyone can ever see, and get her life back on track. It is an almost impossible task.

But what has she learned? She hopes in vain that the international community does not renege on its pledges to the Kurds, saying, 'If the west wants a democratic partner in the middle east, then Kurds must be given their right to self-govern, across the four corners of our as-yet-unrealised nation.' Since she wrote this the Kurds have been betrayed again, and left to their fate at the hands of states who deny their existence, and at the same time categorise them as terrorists.

As I write there's plenty of sexual abuse in the news, including reports of violations against women being compounded by police and courts. But as we lay in bed my partner tells me about women in the Congo who have been gang raped so many times that they are doubly incontinent. A network of hospitals has been set up to repair their ruptured bodies. These hospitals will have plenty of work for the foreseeable future, because there will be no peace in the Congo so long as the insatiable thirst for its minerals continues. In fighting against capitalism Joanna Palani no doubt believed she was fighting for these women too, which is a good job, because no one else is.

A GENTLE GOODNIGHT

On The Beach – Nevil Shute

Friday 7th August 2020

I began Nevil Shute's *On the Beach* as my night-time reading (not intending to write about it).

Saturday 8th August 2020

In *On The Beach*, as the global population is experiencing slow death by radiation poisoning, one woman just drinks and dances. She is told that her problem is that she won't face up to things, she's not the only one, and that's what we're all doing now: not facing up to Covid 19 and its causes, not facing up to neoliberalism and not facing up to climate change. We're putting our heads in the sand, keeping calm and carrying on consuming. All the signs are that we'll keep not facing up to it until they kill us all.

Monday 10th August 2020

I wasn't sure about *On The Beach* at first, but a whole population waiting to die from advancing radiation following a stupid war begun by accident is a good leitmotif not inappropriate for our times. Perhaps we should all live as if our days are numbered, perhaps we are doing. Perhaps overcrowded beaches and wantonness at Wetherspoon's is the beginning of the end time. The writing is dated and clunky and the little wife is a sentimental simpleton prone to irrational hysteria.

Tuesday 11th August 2020

I find it difficult not to make comparisons between the

imminent death faced by the characters in *On The Beach* and the fact that it has been over thirty degrees in the south of England every day for the best part of a week and regular reports that the polar icecaps are melting.

Wednesday 12th August 2020

I read *On The Beach* outside Tesco's waiting for Oades to do the shopping, surrounded by the big shiny cars of ant-like consumers in subconscious denial, and then we walked back in stifling heat and blazing sunshine. It really does feel like the end time.

It can't be an accident that Nevil Shute has a navy commander scuttle his ship in deep water to protect classified gear when humanity is on the verge of extinction. His skill is in pulling the reader into the sordid shambles the end of humanity becomes. The earth is to be wiped and made clean for wiser occupants. Right to the end some people are still in denial. Peter says 'there's some kind of silliness you just can't stop, we liked our newspapers with pictures of beach girls and headlines about cases of indecent assault, and no government was wise enough to stop us having them that way.' He also says that if millions of people decide to drop bombs on each other there's not much we can do about it. Millions of people don't make such decisions: a tiny handful of people do, and we can still do something about them. I'm not a literary expert, but I think *On The Beach* is a remarkable book, a bleak and depressing book, a book for our times. It made me want to go for a long cycle ride tomorrow, while there's still time.

BRITISH THROUGH AND THROUGH

When One Door Closes - Peter Sissons

When the newsreader Peter Sissons died he was featured on Radio 4's obituary show *Last Word*. His memoir sounded interesting, particularly as he was shot in the leg as a foreign correspondent and nearly died, so I ordered it from Amazon, wondering how many other people do that when an author is mentioned on the TV or radio. The hardback ex-library book was fifty pence, the postage three pounds.

Tony Benn was fond of saying about the way broadcasters skew the news that 'bosses plead and unions demand.' The suggestion by Sissons is that, having retired, he is no longer bound by the holier-than-thou false impartially broadcasters claim, and can now lift the lid on bad management and hypocrisy, particularly at the BBC. He seems to be saying that the rules prevented him giving vent to entirely establishment views. What he means by this is clear by page three when he blames the trade unions in the 1970s for inflicting massive damage on the nation. Leaving aside the fact that 'the nation' is a questionable construct, the reader is grateful for this insight and awaits such thoughtfulness with regard to the activities of gambling bankers and parasitic speculators.

Sissons labours under the illusion that his selective grammar school was classless and merely gave its pupils standards, spirit and individuality. As proof of this he cites the

classless careers of Paul McCartney and George Harrison. He is
effusive in his praise of fellow Liverpudlian McCartney, though
it is difficult to see what for, but he manages to demonise
Liverpool councillor and Militant supporter Derek Hatton on
the same page. All three of them attended the school after
passing their eleven plus, as did John Lennon. Not being a
fan (of Hatton or Lennon) I struggle to see this revelation
as any more than name-dropping. Anyway, many of his posh
school pals, rather than joining popular beat combos, joined
the army cadets and he says he regularly saw boys on the bus
carrying Lee Enfield Rifles and Bren guns. This is such palpable
nonsense that it casts doubt on all his other reminiscences. By
this time the reader is wondering how Sissons ever obtained
his reputation as an interrogator of difficult and evasive public
figures because his autobiography is so dull, pedestrian and
unanalytical.

But hang on – here's another insight: the Liverpool
Dockers were all crooks and their strikes were devastating.
They obviously don't come under the salt of the earth
sobriquet he saves for all other Scousers, but at least he
acknowledges that some people hate going to work. Before
finding his own vocation he considered becoming a priest.
Three years later his once obsessive religious faith had
vanished. Worryingly, this suggests that there might be
priests out there who fail to realise soon enough that all
religion is mumbo jumbo and are no less going through the
motions than a disillusioned plastic window salesman.

There's nothing wrong with digressions, they make for
an interesting read, but gratuitous name dropping is boring,
especially when its only function is to rubbish a contemporary
he doesn't even know, such as principled campaigner Tariq
Ali, while providing no context at all. The driven Scouse hero
with humble beginnings persona is tiresome. He's actually

a mainstream, conservative, anti-working class snob who got lucky. The contrast between him and Alan Bennett, for example, who also had humble origins and went to Oxford, is stark. Beside Bennett, Sissons' narcissistic writing is dull and prejudiced, it lacks humanity and empathy.

He touches on the Arab-Israeli six day war, but for someone who calls himself a journalist there's no detail. It is quite remarkable how he reports on the industrial unrest of the 1970s compared to John Pilger. Sissons pretends to be neutral, Pilger doesn't. Pilger's subjects are the downtrodden, Sissons' subject is himself and everyone else is a bit player. His self-promoting account of the period stops short of clichés about the unions holding the country to ransom, but not far short. One chapter of Pilger's *Heroes* is called *A Question of Balance* and opens with a quote from the chair of BBC Radio 4's *Any Questions*; 'Well, we've heard two points of view for and against capital punishment, and probably the truth lies somewhere between the two extremes.' This kind of fake impartiality could have come from Sissons when he chaired the TV equivalent *Question Time*. So keen is the BBC to be neutral that it cannot even stand up for humanity and the law of the land. The death penalty is cited *ad nauseum* as the reason why the fickle and simplistic unwashed can't be asked their opinion on matters of great importance, which should be left to the judgment of our betters.

Peter Sissons spent some time anchoring the newly launched Channel 4 News. He notes positively that one of its presenters was married to a Tory MP and was the daughter-in-law of Lord Hailsham, who went on to head John Major's policy unit, that two of the team had been president of the Oxford University Union and that one went on to become a Tory MP. In fact he makes a virtue out of what most critics see as a fundamental failing of broadcasting in general. To his credit Sissons doesn't deny that Thatcher's plan in 1984 was to break the miners' union, or that in doing so she destroyed their communities. At least when it comes to the Miners' Strike, the Brighton bomb and Lockerbie he gives us an insight into how TV news is made, and between the self-praise he writes quite extensively about the Hillsborough disaster in 1989.

Three quarters of the way through the autobiography we come to his much trumpeted opinions about the BBC. He charges the corporation with capitulating to political spin doctors and adjusting its programs to suit their agenda, in fear of government reprisals. He claims that ITN is immune to such pressure, but surely the privileged backgrounds of its senior staff is enough.

It is on climate change that Sissons shows his true colours, insisting that both sides should get equal airtime. Under the pretence of impartiality he exposes himself as being on the side of climate change deniers. His objections to what he saw as the one-sided debate look rather silly a decade later.

The book is perhaps necessarily egocentric, but Sissons is too staid (i.e. conservative) and self-obsessed to broaden any argument. While obsessing about anti-establishment bias he is dishonest in making no reference to Margaret Thatcher's jingoistic imprecations during the Falklands War or her attempts to shoot the messenger when such as Roger Bolton attempted to report fairly from Northern Ireland.

Sissons spends a lot of time trying to convince himself that he is a journalist and not just an overpaid celebrity newsreader, but he has never discomfited the privileged or privileged the downtrodden as a good journalist should. The status quo is safe in his hands and he's got a brass neck to bracket himself with such as Paul Foot and John Pilger, who quotes Czech writer Zdener Urbanek, 'The censor is no longer at his desk he is in my head,' going on, 'And that applies not just in Czechoslovakia but in countries with a so-called free press. Indeed it seems perverse to argue, as some do, that while our 'free' press may be flawed it is better than that in the eastern bloc. Britain, like the United States, has honourable journalistic traditions... at the same time the very notion of a free press is being undermined by a monopoly which, as general fare, serves up distortion, non-news, violence and soapsuds anti-journalism.' As with the press, broadcasters.

Peter Sissons is right about one thing – that young people have better things to do than listen to the TV news or Radio 4 – and yet over twenty years later the BBC is still chasing the youth audience like it is a panacea for all its problems. The largest section of the book is given to the death of Princess Diana, which as usual, according to himself, Sissons handles impeccably. And then there's 9/11, but there's always Peter Sissons.

To the end he bemoans the easy ride any environmentalist gets on TV news programs and the bias shown in 'controversial environmental concerns,' before having a pop at Jon Snow for having strong views on 'controversial' topics. Jon Snow, in common with Benjamin Zephaniah and Alan Bennett, turned down an OBE – as anyone who refuses to be patronised by our fundamentally corrupt system should. Sissons also castigates BBC producers for being *Guardian* readers.

The bottom line is that he thinks the BBC is too P.C. and too left-wing, as do people like Donald Trump and Tommy Robinson. To not take sides in a war between the oppressed and their oppressors is to take the side of the latter. There is no such thing as neutrality. Under the cloak of impartiality Sissons pretends political liars and crooks will expose themselves through his polite questioning. If this were the case we wouldn't be where we are. Under the present blatantly unequal system the pretence of neutrality is just one more form of bias. And that is the end of my argument with a dead man.

A TABLEAU OF CRIMES

The Assassination of Julius Caesar – Michael Parenti

In the *The Assassination of Julius Caesar*, which is subtitled *A People's History of Ancient Rome,* Michael Parenti seeks to turn two millennia of received wisdom on its head by asserting that Caesar was not stabbed to death on the steps of Pompey's theatre on the Ides of March in 44BC because he sought to be a dictator over the Roman people, but because he was a dangerous political reformer.

It may seem irrelevant to us now how an ancient ruler met his end, but Parenti says; 'History is full of examples of politico-economic elites who equate any challenge to their privileged social order as a challenge to *all* social order, an invitation to chaos and perdition.'

Shakespeare, from whom most people who know anything about Julius Caesar have garnered their information, shares the view of the contemporary Roman elite that the common crowd are a 'mindless aggregation easily led hither and thither' and says that 'The view of the Roman populace as mindless bloodthirsty riffraff remains the anti-people's history purveyed by both the entertainment media and many classical scholars.'

To back up his exposure of this conspiracy Michael Parenti quotes George Bernard Shaw, who in his *Caesar and Cleopatra* says; The Romans 'robbed their own poor until they became great masters of that art, and knew by what laws it could be made to appear seemly and honest.' Parenti says 'After squeezing their own people dry, they stripped the poor throughout the many other lands they conquered.' Shaw, says Parenti, was inviting his audience to make a comparison with the small-minded British colonialists of his day, and we are forced to make a comparison with the supreme small-mindedness of George W Bush at the head of today's imperialists.

WHEN AMERICA SNEEZES

The Dirty War on the NHS - John Pilger

During the long-running 2016 junior doctors' dispute, deliberately engineered by then Tory Health Secretary Jeremy Hunt, I was shocked to discover that two private ambulance companies were operating in and out of our local hospital. I was told by medics on the picket line that they used budget second-hand vehicles and equipment and, never being properly supplied, begged necessary medical supplies from the casualty department.

John Pilger's documentary film *The Dirty War on The NHS* begins with the logical conclusion of this outsourcing race to the bottom: a man dies because an outsourced private ambulance crew's second-hand defibrillator has not been properly tested and doesn't work. They can only contact their unmanned base for a replacement by text and nobody replies.

The next interviewee is a man whose routine operation is seriously and life-threateningly bungled in a private hospital to which NHS operations have been outsourced. Like most of them the hospital had neither the equipment nor the personnel to rectify the situation and an NHS surgeon had to be quickly summoned to save his life.

The calculated destruction of our National Health Service in the interests of private capital has been deliberately obscured by the scurrilous lies told by both Tory and Labour politicians, most famously that they are fully committed to it: 'It runs in my very veins,' said third generation millionaire David Cameron, 'it is safe in our hands.' This is untrue.

DAVID P RAMSDEN

What is euphemistically referred to as health service 'reform' is reported by our famously free press and the impartial BBC at face value, almost as if they were reading from government press releases. Not only should Tony Blair be on trial for war crimes, he should be in the dock, with many others, for the theft of our public services. Surely any journalist worthy of the name would have reported on this scandal, were not their jobs at stake if they did.

The original plan for privatisation, written by Nicolas Ridley under Margaret Thatcher (another war criminal), acknowledged that any open attempt to privatise the NHS would be resisted by the public. It would therefore, and this is openly stated, have to be done *by stealth*. We were knowingly and wilfully deceived, as politicians from all three parties told barefaced lies to camera while they systematically dismantled one of the most progressive and humanitarian institutions in the world. In varying degrees they did so for commercial gain and out of ideological hatred of public services. This calculated and orchestrated, cross-party deception is as worthy as any of Plato's dictum that the *hoi polloi* simply do not need to know what is being done to them.

The conspiracy, for that is what it is, is the product of a global economic consensus that has come to be known as neoliberalism, which is itself the product of a declining rate of profitability the capitalist class has so far been unable to address. In the absence of a sufficient level of profit it will maintain its luxurious lifestyle through the only means it knows possible: us. *We* are paying for *their* crisis with *our* public services and, in some cases, with our lives.

We know what will happen if this continues because Pilger's film contrasts the NHS with the healthcare non-system operating in the US, where hundreds of thousands of people have no access to treatment whatsoever and die in droves of eminently curable conditions, or worse still when they are given a death sentence by mercenary physicians working for multi-million dollar insurance companies who decline to pay for life-saving treatment, knowing full well what will happen. The example given was of a seventeen year old girl who died after being denied a liver transplant. A perfect match had been found and she was already at the hospital.

The only access to healthcare for one featured semi-rural community is the once a year visit by a charity hospital set up in the local cattle market. In American cities 'patient dumping' is rife. This practice sees private hospitals physically taking patients, some of them mentality ill, and dumping them outside the doors of charities to free up beds, that they might be refilled with faceless money-making potential. This is also beginning to happen in the UK.

I might have found it incredible that in the richest country in the world the only access to healthcare for people with untreated diabetes and mouths full of bad teeth is something akin to a field hospital in a war zone; if I hadn't been told years ago that some of the more extreme neoliberals currently running this world care nothing for ordinary people and genuinely believe that every penny spent on the working class is a waste.

There can only be one consequence of the American insurance based system that is the eventual aim: reduced access, destroyed lives and an increase in unnecessary deaths. The British politicians who by design or default go along with this philosophy, and that is practically all of them, are as guilty of a crime against humanity as many who have ended up in The Hague, not that the international court of human rights would consider them to have transgressed; their actions are orthodox and global. They will have to be tried before a people's court at some later date.

There is certainly no wonder the American people voted for Trump. One woman sleeping in her car overnight awaiting a consultation actually says she thought Trump would address this dire situation. He has never made any such suggestion, and with few exceptions, nor has any other politician there or here. The Donald can only have come to her in a dreadful dream because the hope she placed in him was pure fantasy.

Britain used to brag that its infant mortality rates were better than Portugal's. They aren't any longer. And if we carry on like we are we'll soon see the same declining life expectancy they have in parts of America. One senior nurse who worked at the only British hospital so far fully privatised (and later taken back into the NHS having failed by every single criteria) was in tears describing how her hospital had been transformed into a ruthless business by profit-grubbing privateers. The formerly cooperative clinical team had been made into reluctant competitors, their worth measured by how quickly they could vacate beds in an inhuman production line that would have made Henry Ford proud.

There is no doubt that a corporate cancer is destroying our health service. But that's not all. It has already infected every other area of public services from schools, through pathology laboratories, to prisons. The only guarantee we've got from cradle to grave today is that some bastard will be making money from us. The coronavirus pandemic has revealed how deep the dogma is. We are governed by sociopaths who would rather let people die than have it demonstrated that local non-profit public sector agencies could provide a better track and trace system than Serco, Surrealion or Caputica.

At the end of the eighteenth century British politics

were described as 'the old corruption': the sole function of government was to protect wealth and privilege. Great landowners and their allies used the state as a means to pillage and enrich themselves. Place and position were wholly at their disposal. This was all made possible by massive social and economic inequality. There was a relatively short period in British history when corruption was not central to the function of the state, when civil servants were selected on the basis of examinations, not patronage, and the state at least pretended to have the wellbeing of the sovereign's subjects at heart.

All this began to change under Thatcher. It could have been stopped by the Labour government in 1997, but Blair had no intention of changing the direction of his predecessor. It was under him that the privatisation of the NHS really took off. Under this new corruption the state has once more become a vehicle for pillage by the rich. The NHS no longer exists except as a cynical brand logo, they have stolen it. It is an ex-National Health Service.

In a recent *Financial Times* article Martin Sandbu refers to the rise of a kleptocracy, an elite who capture political power for the purpose of theft or embezzlement. Britain is not yet quite a kleptocracy, but the cronyism and corruption at the heart of capitalism are obvious in the distribution of NHS contracts and the appropriation of posts. This is not an aberration requiring minor tweaking. It is the obvious symptom of an entire system in decline, a system running out of ideas.

One could naively imagine that if only the sceptics saw this film they'd believe what we've been trying to tell them for years, but they wouldn't watch it, and if they did they'd dismiss it as left-wing propaganda.

FLOG IT!

The Tories have ambition
You can see it in their eyes
They're on a deadly mission
They want to privatise

There's nothing they won't privatise
No matter how perverse
They want us all to go to hell
In a subcontracted hearse

They've privatised the houses
That people needed most
They've privatised the garden gate
And privatised the post

They've privatised probation
And made the system worse
Now folk who've served their sentence
Have to do another verse

They've privatised adoption
And getting a degree
They've privatised existence
As far as you can see

They're privatising Britain
They're privatising France
They'll privatise humanity

If we give them half a chance

If it's motionless they'll flog it
And if it's moving too
If it's possible to privatise
Then that's what they will do

Their paymasters are greedy
They're like pigs at a trough
And nothing is so sacrosanct
That they can't flog it off

They'll privatise the landscape
And all the trees and plants
If you stand still long enough
They'll privatise your pants

They've privatised being poorly
And getting better too
It's a privatised pandemic
And it's coming soon to you

FLAMMABLE MATERIAL

56: The Story of the Bradford Fire – Martin Fletcher

On 11 May 1985 a raging fire tore through the ancient wooden main stand of Bradford City's Valley Parade ground, killing fifty-six people. The club's chairman, local businessman Stafford Heginbotham, had in the previous eighteen years suffered at least eight fires at other premises with which he was connected, resulting in huge insurance claims. Many of these fires involved not real human beings but cuddly toys and soft furnishings stuffed with highly flammable foam.

A year before the Bradford City fire the West Yorkshire's Fire Service commander told the Bradford *Telegraph & Argus* that he was very concerned about the high number of commercial and industrial fires in the city. His deputy told the same paper that they believed up to 85% of them may have been started deliberately. Eight years earlier, to amuse themselves while on strike, fire-fighters ran a book on which of Bradford's citizens would be the first to have a fire. Such was the level of professional cynicism regarding his activities that Stafford Heginbotham came out on top, and he duly had a fire at one of his premises in December while fire-fighters were otherwise engaged.

On the day of the tragedy, football commentators who heard of the fire at Bradford City while at their own matches, not yet realising that people were being burned to death, joked with each other that the Bradford City chairman had set fire to the stand on the last day of the season for the insurance money, in order that he might build a new one. This suggestion, made in jest or not, should have rung alarm bells for the authorities, as should have Heginbotham's extremely unfortunate past, which stretched credulity and the laws of chance to their very limits. But no one saw fit to properly investigate him or the fire.

In a serious break with tradition Margaret Thatcher, the prime minister at the time, chose to make no parliamentary statement on the disaster. One was prepared for her, but she declined to read it out. She chose instead to entirely wash her hands of the matter. It was suggested in the press that Stafford Heginbotham, who had miraculously escaped investigation and prosecution for all his other accidents, and was deliberately not investigated for a fire which killed fifty-six people in very suspicious circumstances, must have had some very serious hold over the government.

There was certainly something very fishy about the decision to hold an enquiry lasting only five days almost immediately after the fire, when sufficient evidence could not have been gathered, or tests properly carried out. A public enquiry seriously reduces the prospect of prosecutions because it makes it less likely that anyone implicated would get a fair trial, a fact that would have been apparent to those who called the inquiry. When compared to the investigations into other fires, such as that at King's Cross underground station, the inquiry into the Bradford City fire was not even the normal whitewash. It was a charade that rather resembled the absence of an inquiry more than a serious attempt to get at the truth.

Twenty-five years after the Bradford City fire the coroner at the original inquest into the deaths admitted to the *Guardian* that he'd privately considered advising the jury to adopt a verdict of manslaughter, but had decided against it in favour of misadventure. It is very difficult to believe that there wasn't a high level conspiracy. Even three decades later no one in a position of authority or media influence would touch with a bargepole any serious investigation into one of the worst domestic disasters in British history.

THICKER THAN WATER

The Blood Never Dried – John Newsinger

As a way to judge historians of the British Empire John Newsinger looks at how they treat the Bengal Famine of 1943-4. Generally, they don't. This omission by the celebrants of Britain's civilising mission is no accident; its inclusion would demonstrate what utter bastards they were. Chief among them was Winston Churchill, though there isn't room in any of the weighty encomiums to this un-reconstituted racist to mention that five million people starved to death on his watch.

Newsinger demolishes the self-delusion that Britain is the uncrowned master of counterinsurgency due to its judicious use of minimal force. Britain was (and is) an expert in intimidation and collective punishment. As Newsinger was writing four Kenyans were claiming compensation from Britain for their mistreatment in the 1950s. Two of the men had been beaten and castrated, a third was nearly beaten to death and left on a pile of corpses and a women had been raped with a heated bottle a soldier pushed up her vagina with his boot. The burning alive of detainees was mere routine. These are not the myths of some long forgotten era, but from the time when my father was in the forces and less than twenty years before I was.

Having given us a taste of the possible penalties, Newsinger moves on to how the imperial thieves were resisted. Our delight at the 1736 plan by Antiguan slaves to blow up the planters' ball as the precursor to a general uprising is tempered by the revenge the planters exerted. The torture, mutilation and burning alive of black men only stopped when the treasury ran out of money to compensate the owners. Extreme violence was the only way a minority of white planters could maintain control over countless thousands of black slaves in what was effectively a two hundred year war.

Every single slave involved in this disgusting business was personally violated in a way that any reasonable person would consider an outrage. One tires of hearing in justification that Africans enslaved their own people first. They did, but they didn't industrialise the process and work its victims until they died, and they weren't allowed to torture and beat them to death. In the West Indies it was unquestioned convention.

The slave system provided the ideal opportunity for sadists, ruffians and rapists to satisfy their desires. One particularly noble representative of the master race routinely had slaves shit in each other's mouths as a punishment. Another nailed a slave woman's ear to a post. Castration and hobbling by amputation were run of the mill.

There were rebellions from the start, but the slave uprising on St Domingue in 1791 was one of the greatest revolutions in modern history. Along with other revolts it brought about the end of an economic system that regarded human beings as animals. Put simply, had Britain not ended slavery voluntarily it would have been made to end it by the courageous actions of the slaves themselves, perhaps with their tormentors receiving some of their own medicine in the process. The only choice was between a peaceful end and a violent end. All the efforts of anti-slavery parliamentarians would have come to nought had it been possible for the system to continue: the resistance at home and abroad made it economically unviable.

The decisive revolt involved 60,000 Jamaican slaves

on over a hundred estates in 1831. For many of the slaves Christianity had become a revolutionary ideology; so much so that the planters turned their anger onto Christian missionaries as the cause. This fed back into the dangerous cauldron of British working class resistance and the abolitionist movement rooted in the non-conformist church.

When slavery was eventually replaced with something very much like slavery it was enforced with exactly the same brutality, particularly by the governor of Jamaica after a revolt in 1865. His actions got him recalled and dismissed, though working class protesters would have preferred to lynch him.

There are many other equally barbaric episodes in Britain's glorious history, from Ireland through India to Egypt, but Newsinger's excellent exposé is bookended by Blair, one of the most disgusting characters ever to walk across the British political stage. When this lying charlatan assumed the leadership of Britain's famously left-leaning party he stood in a very long tradition of Labour leaders prepared to sanction any injustice for the sake of Empire. He told the British people he would stand shoulder to shoulder with the USA. His Chief of Staff Jonathon Powell actually told the British ambassador to Washington to 'get up the arse of the White House and stay there.' Attlee sent troops to Korea to appease the Americans and Blair sent them to Iraq and Afghanistan to appease George W Bush, arguably the worst, and certainly the most ignorant US president ever. Harold Wilson was the only Labour prime minister not to bolster US adventures with British troops. He didn't commit them to Vietnam for one simple reason; he daren't.

Leaving aside Blair's evangelical continuation of destructive Thatcherite policies, his blatant nepotism, his naked courting of a union-busting megalomaniac media baron, his making of lying into an art form and his worship of the rich, he was convinced that the mantle of benevolent imperialism had passed to the USA. He bought into their fantasy of world domination and was simply unable to see why France and Germany distanced themselves.

Blair was forty years too late to play John Bull so he played poodle to Uncle Sam, saying that when the UK and the US worked together there was little they could not achieve, as if it was some kind of partnership. In practice this meant backing the superpower whether it was right or wrong. When the US bombed a pharmaceutical factory in Sudan it was most certainly wrong, as all Blair's senior circle accepted, but political expediency stood in for morals and Tony Blair was virtually alone in defending it. He lied about the sanctions the US imposed on Iraq, he lied about US bombing of the country and he lied about the war in Kosovo.

The 11th September attacks were an outrage, but there was no justification for the response. It was not the worst atrocity since the Second World War as was claimed: they were perpetrated in Korea and Vietnam. Al Qaida is not the most dangerous terrorist organisation in the world: that dubious honour belongs to the CIA. Declaring a 'war on terror' was stupid and counterproductive, as was attacking Iraq. The country had nothing to do with the attack on the US, but Blair the pocket imperialist produced the lies to justify it. If Iraq had really possessed weapons of mass destruction there would have been no invasion. The truth is that the country was already on its knees and should have provided a quick and easy victory to boost American prestige. Blair was determined that British capitalists should get their share of the loot.

Only six British soldiers were killed by Iraqi forces during the 'war' (the other twenty-seven were either killed by the Americans or in accidents). It was just one more imperialist massacre. The occupation was a different matter.

There had been resistance to imperialism in Jamaica, Kenya, Ireland, India, Malaya and Egypt and there was resistance in Iraq. There was also resistance in Britain, including the biggest demonstration in history. The fact that the Labour government could still go ahead with an illegal war in the face of such opposition demonstrated its complete abandonment of the people it had always pretended to represent. Blair thought the war would be popular after the event, but he was exposed as a hypocritical liar responsible for the deaths of thousands of people.

Britain long ago lost its ability to plunder the globe independently. Its armed forces are now deliberately configured as second fiddle to the US, their very presence sanctioning the actions of a bully. The next time Uncle Sam embarks on murder, rape and pillage our noble politicians will be ready with the lies. If they could justify slavery, Diplock and the Basra road they'll justify anything.

Slavery is not some accidental adjunct to British history, it is the very foundation of British capitalism. It funded the textile industry, it paid for many of our stately homes and city buildings. It made the fortunes of men who became our rulers. Because it was fundamentally inhuman it required the conscious construction of a pseudo-scientific racism, the terrible legacy of which we live with today. Slavery's everyday reality was taken for granted by philosophers, theologians and politicians, it is woven into the very fabric of our society and it cannot be wished away.

Nor can the effect of Tony Blair's decision to back America to the hilt be overstated. It too destroyed the lives of millions of people. It lined Britain up with the bully when it should have spoken up for what was right. America was attacked because of its past actions, not because of some abstract hatred of western non-values. The leader of the

Labour Party made Britain what it is today: a nation divided against itself, distrustful of its own citizens and ripe for the serious rise of the far right. Only the spirit of slave rebellion and Stop the War can save it.

MISSIONARY POSITION
Things Fall Apart - Chinua Achebe

Chinua Achebe was born in 1930 in the British colony of Nigeria, his novel is set in the closing years of the nineteenth century during the scramble for Africa. It is a celebration of his ancestors, the south east Nigerian Igbo, whose culture was trampled on by the invaders and denigrated by western writers. The title comes from Y.B. Yeats' *The Second Coming*; 'Things fall apart: the centre cannot hold/Mere anarchy is loosed upon the world,' and describes perfectly the physical and spiritual dislocation experienced by the characters. But these words also have a contemporary relevance, having been applied to the collapse of traditional political parties of the so-called centre. Our rulers may view this as anarchy, but we might see it as a refreshing challenge to the stifling stranglehold of hypocritical mainstream fraud.

None of us is so clever that we cannot learn from aboriginal wisdom and the text is full of local proverbs. When I read 'The proud heart can survive a general failure because it does not prick his pride. It is more difficult and more bitter when a man fails *alone*' I think of Trump, the self-anointed egotistical superman who has no notion of the collective: a member of nothing except the rich and powerful and only by default of the human race. He oozes baseless superiority: 'Looking at the king's mouth one would think he had never sucked at his mother's breast.' The same superior arrogance is evident in the Christian missionaries who seek to impart upon an 'uncivilised' collective a hierarchical religion that had managed to coexist with slavery and brutal imperial conquest.

There is no need to idealise pre-colonial African societies. People lived as they lived. It was no better and no worse than the way most people lived in Britain, just different. The men are warriors, but they settle disputes in council rather than go to war. They take hostages on fixed terms as punishment and they ostracise troublemakers. The gods occasionally require sacrifices, but then so does mammon. The yam harvests come and go, the annual wrestling festival takes, people dance and drink.

This status quo is not threatened like ours by the failed policies of neoliberalism, not even by swarms of locusts, which are good to eat. It is threatened by those who bring them something they never asked for; the big white capitalist God.

Achebe's protagonist, Okonkwo, is recognisable as a man with orthodox ambitions who is angry and confused inside and doesn't always treat others as he should. Like all young men he is trapped by his duties, his ambitions and his reputation. Completely by accident he is responsible for a boy's death and has to leave the village for seven years. His hopes of becoming a clan leader are dashed and he has to begin again elsewhere. While wallowing in self-pity he is told in no uncertain terms that there are people much worse off than him.

The villagers have heard stories of white men with guns and strong drink who take slaves, but no one believes the stories are true. When the first white man comes he is compared to lonely locusts, who are the harbingers of a welcome relief to the staple diet of yams. The oracle says more will follow to break up the clan and spread destruction among them.

When the missionaries arrive they only recruit the weak and worthless, men who will never make anything of themselves. But their converts gain in confidence and call the villagers heathens who worship false gods and will burn in hell, unless they be saved and live forever. The older men dismiss all this as nonsense, but those with youthful doubts are attracted by the singing.

When the missionaries ask for land on which to build a church the villagers laugh and give them land haunted by evil spirits, expecting them to be dead in no time. They don't die and the power of the white man's god increases. No one has disobeyed the villagers' gods for more than seven markets, it's only a question of waiting. Again they don't die; what have those with troubled lives got to lose? When Okonkwo's son takes the pledge a beating only drives him further away. The Christians teach the converts to read and write.

The villagers hear rumours that the missionaries haven't just brought a religion: they've also brought a government. They've built a place of judgement and hanged a man for killing a missionary. But the Christians in the village cause no real trouble and they are tolerated. The villagers know they can drive them out if they become a problem. The missionaries demonstrate their unshakeable faith by welcoming the local outcasts and their credibility is further enhanced. Their followers are told that the heathens speak nothing but falsehoods; the fact that they are still alive is the proof.

Eventually the villagers decide to ostracise the missionaries and their followers, who are now a community in their own right, and to ban them from the well. When one of the converts dies they change their minds and decide the gods can fight their own battles. The old men fear for the young. They do not speak with one voice and have allowed an alien religion to settle among them, a religion that curses the gods of their ancestors and takes young men away from their fathers and brothers.

Okonkwo returns from his forced absence with great plans for his children. His sons will become clan leaders and his daughters will marry influential men. He finds that even worthy men have taken Holy Communion. The white men have built a court where the district commissioner passes judgement. They have built prisons and filled them with men of title who have offended Christian sensibilities. These men are beaten, forced to work and filled with shame.

Okonkwo thinks they should drive the white men out, but it is already too late, their own sons have joined the new religion and are helping to uphold the white man's government. The white man came quietly with his religion: the people were amused by him and allowed him to stay. Men who once received just punishments for breaking their own rules are now hanged for breaking someone else's.

The white men build a trading store and make friends with influential villagers, telling them that if their children do not learn to read and write others will come and rule them. The influential villagers allow their sons to learn the white man's knowledge in his schools and give them Christian names. Those who study become clerks and even teachers. More churches are built. Membership becomes a mark of prestige.

Trouble starts when zealous converts disrupt ancient rituals and the tribe sees the coming of its own death. The assembled representatives of the village spirits and the warriors tell the white priest he can stay and worship his own god, but the church must be destroyed. The church is burned and the spirits of the clan are pacified.

For two days Okonkwo is happy. It is like the good old days. But the village men now go about armed: they know a neighbouring village was wiped out for resisting. The

District Commissioner asks to see the six leading men. Being honourable they attend, are arrested, beaten, humiliated and told they are subject to the law of the most powerful ruler in the world. If they had killed the priest, as Okonkwo wanted, they would have been hanged.

The villagers can see that the men have been whipped. The white men have insulted them, their religion and their ancestors. They swear vengeance and prepare for war, knowing if they fight the white men they will kill their brothers who have joined them, but there is no other choice.

While they are deciding what to do the white men's lackeys come to break up the village meeting and Okonkwo kills their leader. He knows the villagers won't fight and he hangs himself. The district commissioner refuses to degrade himself by helping to bring down the body. All he can think about is the interesting story he will include in the book he is writing about bringing civilisation to Africa. He already has a title: *The Pacification of the Primitive Tribes of the Lower Niger.*

In October 2020 a desperate twenty year old man killed several people in Vienna. The Austrian Chancellor said it was part of a fight between civilisation and barbarism. The civilisation/barbarism argument is code for white and non-white and it has always been bogus. So-called civilised people were responsible for Hiroshima, Napalm, My Lai and the Holocaust. There are people in America less civilised than nineteenth century Nigerians and one of them is the president.

NATIONAL TREASURE

Time Bites – Doris Lessing

Doris Lessing's judgements are sympathetic and her conclusions human. She is well-read and well-travelled. She knows that prostitution is caused by poverty not loose virtue, but her sensible attitude, sweeping knowledge and erudite exposition obscure the fact that her outlook is narrow.

In a sketch on *Pride and Prejudice* she says 'The French revolution had unleashed in England not only terrors of revolt and guillotine, but of the unfettered females who yelled for more blood as the heads fell, who rampaged about streets in screaming mobs, giving the world a glimpse of just what manic rebellions were being kept in check by chaperones and corsets.'

In examining Virginia Woolf Lessing draws attention to the snobbishness and anti-working class sentiments of her bohemian set. She tells us that in Forster's *Howards End* upper class women, on seeing working people suffer say, 'They don't feel it like us' and compares it with her white friends in South Africa seeing the misery suffered by black people and saying, 'They aren't like us, they have thick skins.' She seems to suggest that prejudice is a trait rather than a one off. Today it is almost taken for granted that those who voted to leave the EU can safely be ascribed other undesirable prejudices, by liberals at least: some of whom would disgrace democracy by overturning a popular vote. But Lessing falls into a trap she has laid for herself when referring to Mrs Tolstoy's loss of her children, 'We are not talking about a peasant woman, a farm woman, with expectations for a hard life, but an educated sensitive woman who could never have dreamed of the kind of life she in fact had to lead.' Are education and sensitivity related? Otherwise the account of uncontrolled motherhood is all the more touching because Lessing knows that what was endured by Russian women in the nineteenth century is still endured by Indian and African women today.

Tolstoy was a thorn in the side of the Tsarist regime, but later in life became a puritanical fanatic. Lessing compares him to ageing politicians who forget they were young and urge teenagers to 'just say no.' She also uses his fanaticism as a means to attack 'extremists,' taking for granted the benign objectivity of the current status quo, when in fact we are under the spell of a fanaticism more corrupting than anything religion can offer: the all-pervading free market.

Lessing shares with Alan Bennett a concern for the current state of education, where 'a development of the whole person is not seen as useful to modern society' and where people ask "What was the French revolution?" Perhaps she is right, or perhaps the decline in class consciousness is to blame for ordinary people's ignorance of their own history. Almost blind Lessing wrote a preface for a new edition of Ecclesiastes, which she sees as being full of contradictions; 'Wisdom is better than strength, nevertheless, the poor man's wisdom is despised and his words not heard.' '…thus do the living springs of knowledge, of wisdom, become captured by institutions, and by churches of various kinds.'

Behind Doris Lessing's attack on communism are the misplaced assumptions that the Soviet Union practiced it and that the timeless natural state of humanity, the pinnacle of our possibility, is an unfair and unjust economic and political system which has not yet endured five hundred years. Lessing has a great deal to say about the Soviet Union, but within her legitimate criticism is the blindness that affects all of those who base their fake liberalism on the hatred of its apparent opposite; their beloved country has been just as bad and worse. The irony is that the regime they so revile had nothing to do with the ideology they ascribe to it. Marxism didn't cause the First World War, the holocaust, the colonisation of Africa, endless wars in the Middle East, the genocide of the Palestinians: capitalism did. Marxism isn't destroying the very planet we live on: capitalism is.

Doris Lessing has many redeeming features, but a willingness to understand Marxism is not one of them. For her, human history is a series of accidents incapable of a coherent explanation. She refuses to consider Marx's premises because they lead ineluctably to his conclusion: there is no solution but that we stop, take stock and start again, to rise again from the ashes of our own self-defeating and self-destructive stupidity.

In the next article she says; 'it is a fact as yet unknown to science that when you tackle a new subject then suddenly it is everywhere, on the television, in the newspapers, on the radio, people start talking about it, an overheard conversation on a bus – there it is again, and a book falls open at just the relevant place.' How true, but when your subject is the world and everything in it you make links the BBC would never dream of and every living day confirms your thesis. Lessing says that if she had written an account of herself aged twenty it would have been a petulant and belligerent account. So what: is that a bad thing? Is there actually something wrong with this world or not?

Writing about writing an autobiography Lessing says it suddenly dawned on her how unreliable memories can be; 'I think that what makes you remember something, important or unimportant, is that you were particularly awake at the time, paying attention.' We also forget things because they are inconvenient, especially when we are old and comfortable. The piece ends with, 'I am sure everyone has had the experience of reading a book and finding it vibrating with aliveness, with colour and immediacy. And then... reading it again and finding it flat and empty. Well, the book hasn't changed: you have.' Maybe: on the first reading I thought Pursig and Turgenev were brilliant, but *Zen* is intellectual masturbation and Bazarov is simply self-destructive. What Robert Tressel says in *The Ragged Trousered Philanthropists* is *now*, sadly, no matter how many times you read it.

Of her native South Africa Lessing says, 'Conformity, even for an ordinary non-political person, wasn't easy either. It was an unpleasant society, for dissident whites, as well as for blacks. If you were not dedicated to sport, and to conversations that nearly always centred on the Native Problem, seen as being the fault of one of your black servants or labourers, if you were not prepared to see the white occupation of the country as "civilisation" you were much on your own. Now I had been brought up with all that, I knew how to dissemble, and the cost if you didn't.' South Africa is an extreme case but all hierarchical societies require dissembling because they are all based on a lie, as Plato recognised, and justified, two thousand years ago.

In the introduction to the new edition of her *Golden Notebook* Lessing says, 'There are some pessimists who think that our strongest need is to have inferiors to despise.' But this 'need' is fostered by our rulers to their own advantage. Our actual strongest need is for community and cooperation, which the current competitive system actively prevents.

She begins her *Trail of Feathers*, a review of an explorer in the Andes, with a sentiment that summarises the jaded state of humanity. 'The complaint goes that this planet, like an overused adventure playground, no longer provides the thrills of the unknown, and that from Kamchatka to Cape Horn there is no more to be said or done.' In the same review a Vietnam veteran encapsulates a glibness for history and suffering that disposes us to forever repeat our mistakes when he says, 'The Tet Offensive, Battle of Hue, Hamburger Hill and all that shit.'

In an obituary for William Philips she says there were always members of the Communist Party in the House of Lords. Were there? She paints herself as a former Stalinist turned reactionary, in contrast to Philips, who was 'a Trot.' In her assertion that Trotsky would have been as bad as Stalin had he 'come to power' she dismally fails to appreciate what each man stood for. Only someone in complete ignorance of Trotsky's history and writings could say this. She hits the nail on the head when she imagines a left that had not slavishly followed the Soviet Union and by it become mortally wounded and corrupted. That possibility was always there: it was why Trotsky got an ice-pick in his head at Stalin's instigation. It is simply nonsense to say that Trotsky would have done the same had the boot been on the other foot. It is all too easy for a Stalinist to become a reactionary. Stalinism *is* reactionary. Paul Foot described Doris Lessing as having, 'thrown out the communist baby with the Stalinist bathwater.'

In the same article the national treasure has a swipe at political correctness without any bolstering argument. Attacking political correctness from the right is easy. Understanding why it came about is much less so.

Doris Lessing reviews Arthur Deikman's *The Wrong Way Home*, a seminal work on the nature of cults, along the way eliding the discussion from cults to terrorism via 9/11 and George Bush's 'with us or against us.' Deikman's central thesis is that key elements of our 'normal' society are cultish. Using *The Wrong Way Home* only to identify the activities of others is to completely miss the point.

THE POETRY OF PROTEST

The Life and Rhymes of Benjamin Zephaniah
– Benjamin Zephaniah

I read Benjamin Zephaniah's autobiography in conjunction with Maya Goodfellow's *Hostile Environment* about the UK's racist asylum system. They make good companions. Like many black people in Britain he experienced racism at school, and while he couldn't tell if individual teachers were racists, he was sure the Anglo-centric text books they were teaching from were.

Zephaniah grew up in the fast deindustrialising West Midlands, where in the 1964 general election Labour lost the formerly safe seat of Smethwick to an openly racist Tory. Instead of arguing for black and white unity against racism Labour decided to play the Tories at their own game and ramp up the racist rhetoric in a disastrous tit-for-tat race to the gutter. One might expect a party of the left to argue class politics against racism, not pander to it, but that would be to seriously underestimate the desire of the Labour hierarchy to attain power at any cost. This is the art of establishment politics.

Benjamin Zephaniah expressed his anger at this and other affronts in verse. In a world where working class people aren't supposed to understand art he speaks the language of the artisan-artist who sticks at it. If politics aren't exactly poetry then all poetry is political, and throughout the book they are intertwined and inseparable. For any artist, black or white, Benjamin Zephaniah is an inspiration. Not only did he write the poetry, he learned how to bind it into physical books he could hold in his hand, the material product of his efforts. This is the instinct of someone who doesn't accept the artificial demarcation between mental and physical activity. He was independently minded and wanted to do as much as he could for himself, he is the living incarnation of the semi-fulfilled Jack of all Trades who has found an individual escape from the alienating grind of production-line living death.

Anyone who has written poetry but never had the courage to read it out, feeling it to be only amateurish ranting can only be encouraged by Zephaniah. His subjects are worthy because they are infused with the spirit of the resistance in which he actively participated: the Anti-Nazi League, Rock Against Racism and Thatcher's privatisations. His unabashed, non-conformist offerings have titles like 'This policeman keeps kicking me to death' and 'I don't like Mrs Thatcher.' When he talks about black liberation it isn't in isolation, but with reference to Catholic emancipation in Ireland and the unfolding slow destruction of the Palestinians as a people.

While taking part in a documentary, Zephaniah equated the struggle of black people in Africa with that of Catholics in Ireland, only to realise how cautious the British media was when talking about Ireland's bloody history at the hands of imperial Britain. Today the media has been cowed into silence on Palestine. People have been systematically hoodwinked into believing some kind of battle of equals is ongoing, with, at best, each side equally to blame. Telling the truth about the apartheid Israeli state is no more acceptable than was telling the truth about the apartheid state of 'Ulster', which was incidentally its model. Self-censorship, objectivity and impartiality by the British media makes state censorship unnecessary and helps to prolong the myth of a free press.

As a class-conscious victim of racism Zephaniah didn't

sit on the fence; he supported the troops out of Ireland movement because he speaks for the oppressed and that was the right thing to do.

When Benjamin Zephaniah says every writer needs an editor he doesn't mean someone to see he or she doesn't overstep the mark. He means someone on his side who will see he oversteps the mark in the right direction. He's on the side of the working class and says so: stating your allegiances is the only true objectivity, the pretence of neutrality is a lie. When he talks about police racism and brutality in the mother of all democracies he points to the hypocrisy of the Fundamental British Values rammed down the throats of immigrants and school children. He has an analysis of the Miners' Strike and the solidarity it engendered, the racism and sexism it cut through. The text is infused with working class politics: never once does he sink into black separatist arguments or regard white people in general as the enemy. He knew instinctively what Malcolm X and Martin Luther King had to learn: an injury to one is an injury to all, the oppressed need to unite against their common enemy.

If there's any criticism it is that a man who hates the capitalist press repeats their trope about the far left 'selling their papers and then going to the pub to talk about Marx', as if a) what Marx says on any subject is irrelevant and b) as if the far left allow black people to fight racism alone. He knows very well that neither of these things are true because he's already mentioned Blair Peach the white 'far left' teacher killed by the police on an anti-racist demo, and the highly successful Anti-Nazi League, in which the far left played a leading role.

Benjamin Zephaniah describes himself as an angry ranter of words keen to take poetry to people who don't read books. He says, 'The poet should always be critical... the poet should criticise the country, criticise the weather: poets should even criticise themselves.'

On turning down the offer of poet laureate he says, 'I find it difficult to respect an institution [the monarchy] that has its roots in class division, robbing people of their lands, subjecting people to slavery and claiming a divine right to rule. Then there's the fact of their privileges, their undemocratic positioning, their arrogance, their love of hunting, their support for evil wars, their ill-gotten fortune and their lack of accountability... hereditary privilege does not a meritocracy make... we are being hypocritical if we criticise countries that don't allow people to vote for their head of state when we can't vote for ours.' He clearly doesn't buy into the argument that a blue-blooded and parasitic aristocracy helps sustain the British economy by selling Chinese made plastic union jacks and model London buses back to Chinese tourists. Perhaps he's more impressed that they act as trade ambassadors to weapons-buying despots prosecuting brutal wars; who knows?

It is suggested that the British people had a limited choice in the 2019 UK general election, but in Boris Johnson and Jeremy Corbyn they actually had a wider choice than at any time in British political history. Certainly a wider choice than in the US in 2016, when the American people had a choice between an egotistical bigot and a dynastic warmonger.

In Jeremy Corbyn Benjamin Zephaniah saw a reincarnation of Tony Benn and the possibility of a non-Blairite Labour Party and he was far from alone in that vision. The problem with placing faith in one man's ability to bring fundamental change is that the free market ideology of Thatcher and Blair pervades all establishment parties and they will ruthlessly destroy any truly progressive individual. We're further from where we ought to be than at any time in the last century. You can't build socialism in one country and it won't happen without a mass movement.

On his veganism Zephaniah says, 'to me, eating meat is eating meat, no matter what the species, so every conversation I hear about 'strange' people eating exotic animals sounds to me like racism, plus ignorance.' Given the prejudices attached to coronavirus the hypocrisy is all the more evident.

By sixty Zephaniah had expected to be more relaxed about politics, but whenever he has an audience he feels he should speak out. He never imagined that the far right would be back on the streets when he'd helped to consign their previous incarnations into the gutter where they belong. He identifies fear and division as drivers of politics and says, 'Capitalism needs wars but it also needs a fear industry. It always has to have a new enemy.' During the 1980s he said; 'We always need an enemy; right now it's the Russians but I can imagine in a couple of decades it being something else like... Islam.' Without this external enemy we might focus on widening inequality, the endless search for profit and economic growth, boom and bust, social care and education, the decline of which he blames on Thatcher and Blair, Palestine or deaths in police custody.

It is a weakness that Zephaniah celebrates Mao, Castro and Ho Chi Minh uncritically while disparaging 'old style socialists' for talking about the rank and file, 'as if people still worked in factories and were going to down tools and walk out' because Amazon, Uber and McDonalds' workers have proved the old style withdrawal of labour to be still effective. He was attracted by the left-wing argument for voting to leave the EU, but when it wasn't being heard he decided to vote Remain.

His assertion that the attachment to material things is at the root of all suffering is a bit facile, but it's a truthful book and he's a good man: a reformed criminal who's done more for the community than any of the unreformed criminals in the commons. After a shaky start in life Benjamin Zephaniah is a citizen success on Thatcher's bus of failure and a credit to the society she believed didn't exist.

For all this he couldn't help being in the *Times* top fifty of post-war writers, but when he was offered an OBE, unlike many easily flattered celebrities, Labour politicians and trade union leaders, he became part of a principled and uncelebrated club: those who've turned down the opportunity to be patronised by our fundamentally corrupt system.

LEST WE FORGET

Fall of Giants – Ken Follett, 2010
The Monocled Mutineer – William Allison
and John Fairley, 1978

Theodore Roosevelt is alleged to have said in the face of industrial unrest at the beginning of the twentieth century, 'What we need is a war, any war.' He eventually got his wish, and even advocated then president Wilson leading an army of volunteers to the front. But as no senator sent his son to Vietnam no president, or prime minister, would willingly expose himself to such danger. Patriotism used as a foil to resistance is only one strand in Ken Follett's tome of a novel *Fall of Giants.*

It is easy to dismiss novels as a means by which we can learn about our past. In this case it would be more than usually wrong to do so. Follett claims he used the services of twelve researchers in writing this book and it shows. He attempts to cover every aspect of European life between 1914 and 1920 through the experiences of a handful of families, privileged and working class.

Throughout the work a position of neutrality is maintained. Naturally this neutrality exposes the ruling class to be superfluous, anachronistic, very rich and petrified of any independent action by those they oppress and exploit, whether in the coal mine or on the battlefield.

Welsh miners find themselves at war under the command of the same men who denied them decent conditions in the pit and those who resisted at work continue to resist in the trenches. The trade unionist's son speaks at anti-war meetings while he is on leave and is hounded for doing so. He is eventually court martialled and jailed for giving to the media details of the illegal British counter-revolutionary intervention in Russia, which was spearheaded by that greatest of British Heroes, Winston Churchill. The reader cannot help but make connections with Bradley Manning, currently incarcerated in the US for similar offences.

Meanwhile in Russia two brothers at a St Petersburg factory go their separate ways: one to the Land of the Free, the other to the Bolsheviks, the latter eventually becoming an aid to Trotsky.

Naturally, this being a novel, the character's paths all cross. But this does not detract at all from the unfolding events of the revolution. The period of dual power, the eventual victory of the Soviet and the actions of the Social Revolutionaries and the Mensheviks are all detailed, as well as the battle to defend the revolution against imperialist intervention.

Ken Follett can be forgiven for occasionally seeming patronising by using clumsy sub-clauses to explain things that don't seem to need explaining, because in hindsight many of them do need explaining. A deliberate mass de-politicisation has taken place over the last few decades. This easy to read novel will help those new to the history of the First World War and the Russian Revolution to get things in perspective. Experienced activists wanting a relaxing read can read it more critically if they wish.

The Monocled Mutineer by William Allison and John Fairley was made into a BBC series in the 1980s. It is ostensibly the tale of the cad and con-man, Percy Toplis, who ran rings round the authorities before, during and after the First World War. I did not see the BBC adaptation, but have no doubt that this is the aspect on which they focussed. The book is actually the story of the greatest mutiny ever to take place in the British army: a mutiny in which Toplis was a leader and which went right to the top, putting the whole prosecution of the war in jeopardy.

The action takes place at a British training camp behind the front line where soldiers; veterans withdrawn to recuperate, as well as new recruits, were subjected to a brutal regime overseen by 'instructors' and military policemen. In the same camp are colonial soldiers; Australians and New Zealanders, who are paid twice as much as their British counterparts and who are not subject to the death penalty for various offences. Hundreds of British soldiers were executed by firing squad during the war for cowardice and desertion. Thousands more were subject to the barbaric Field Punishment No.1. These differences were some of the long term causes of the revolt, but the catalyst was the shooting dead of a soldier by a military policeman. During the revolt British and colonial soldiers, as well as those from different regiments together, sought out police and instructors and paid them back for their brutality over a period of several days. They released prisoners from the camp jails, cut down those tied to wagon wheels and fences as punishment and openly defied the officers. Those organised against them refused to fire on them.

The mutiny was hushed up at the time, and were it not for this book I would not know about it yet. Nor would I be aware that during the First World War hundreds of deserters existed in makeshift camps in and around the battlefields, surviving by stealing from military bases or simply walking in and availing themselves of normal rations. Such was the devastating loss of life that no one knew who was supposed to be there and who wasn't. Percy Toplis was one of these nonpeople and he came to the fore as an orator and leader once the revolt on the base started. No wonder the authorities sought to brand him simply as a 'racketeer, rake and rogue.'

Toplis was eventually shot dead by police in 1920: no questions asked. Other leaders of the mutiny were despatched much more promptly, being shot in France by firing squad without the nicety of a trial. The sensitivity around this brutality is demonstrated in the fact that the exact numbers were subject to secrecy under the hundred year rule.

It would be facile to point to the incompetence of the public school toffs who commanded British troops in the First World War; 'Lions led by donkeys' is the phrase often used. However, socialists who engage in discussions about the competence of military leadership need to be careful not to fall into a trap. After all, military incompetence leads to the deaths of workers, military competence likewise leads to the deaths of workers. The celebrated Christmas Day no-man's-land football match is far from the only example of fraternisation and had this significant mutiny spread to the front perhaps the senseless waste of thousands of lives at Passchendaele and the following battles in the war to end all wars could have been prevented.

DOING THE GOD THING

Chosen by God: Donald Trump, the Christian Right and American Capitalism – John Newsinger

In the early twentieth century US workers were restless and Christian evangelists offered businessmen a choice: support and fund a Christian revival or face socialist revolution. They chose to bankroll a spiritual-industrial complex that mobilised religion in support of unbridled capitalism and imperialism while denouncing trade unions, socialists and public welfare as ungodly.

After WWII President Truman said only a religious revival could save America. He spearheaded a campaign that propagated Christianity as an imperialist Cold War prop. Americans were told it was their patriotic duty to pray and attend church.

General Dwight D. Eisenhower rediscovered God to secure the presidential nomination and made his election campaign a religious crusade. He characterised the Cold War as God versus atheism, took an ostentatious oath, was baptised in office, led prayers at cabinet meetings, added God to the pledge of allegiance and 'In God we trust' to postage stamps. Liberal and progressive clergy were purged by evangelical supporters of Joseph McCarthy, with 7,000 identified as part of a Kremlin conspiracy.

Backed by big business, evangelical preacher Billy Graham denigrated communism and trade unions as the work of the devil and told bosses God could increase their profits. He whipped up fears of nuclear attack, said Americans must return to God or incur His wrath and that the battle against the antichrist required increased military strength. He held religious services at the Pentagon as Korea was carpet bombed and while on tour in Britain said Labour's socialism was doing what Hitler's bombs couldn't. He was lauded by the British establishment, met Churchill and was knighted by the queen. Graham trivialised US atrocities in Vietnam, telling troops they were doing God's work. He described anti-war activity as the work of Satan, urged its suppression and called the police God's agents.

In the 1960s evangelical anti-communist crusaders consolidated into the Christian Right. They have since claimed the liberalisation of abortion law as their motivation. It was actually racial desegregation, behind which they saw both Moscow and the devil. They made ridiculous claims about the teaching in secular schools and orchestrated vile homophobic campaigns. When gay men were murdered as a result they said it was the judgement of God.

In the 1970s the Christian Right mobilised against the Equal Rights Amendment and prevented the mild, bi-partisan gender equality measure being ratified. They swamped women's conferences and passed anti-feminist, pro-life, and anti-homosexual resolutions and forced Republicans to represent them in an array of reactionary causes. Using homophobia as a mobilising tool they turned gay bashing into an art form and, a full six years after Roe v Wade, adopted abortion as a relentless organisational cause and the seizure of the Supreme Court as a goal.

The US Christian Right is a fully developed evangelical subculture driven by fear and hatred. Children study creationism and fear of God in Christian schools and universities and visit Christian theme parks. There are evangelical teacher training colleges, an institute for creationism and libraries of books by purveyors of right-wing politics and vicious homophobia. Central to their theology is The Rapture, when the saved will be taken to heaven and Jesus will descend to lead a genocidal war against all those who are not born again. The Rapture Index website details the factors that hasten or hinder its eventual arrival.

While evangelists established semi-secret bodies that brought together leading republicans, right-wing billionaires and leaders of the Christian right to influence policy, televangelists preached the prosperity gospel to millions of TV viewers and got very rich on public donations.

Ronald Reagan was not a religious man before he ran for president but, in order to secure the support of the Christian Right, he discovered he was against abortion and the Equal Rights Amendment and in favour of compulsory prayer in schools. He also conceded that evolution was only a theory and said the Bible would be central to his administration. In gratitude the Christian Right fully supported his policy of propping up murderous regimes in South America on God's behalf, but apart from making the rich much richer Reagan didn't deliver on their agenda. However, they increasingly infiltrated the Republican Party and set up a cabal of evangelical leaders, sympathetic tycoons and hard-line republicans whose aim was the ending of welfare provision and business regulation and promoting US global superiority, as God intended.

George HW Bush pretended to be born again and promised to pack the Supreme Court with anti-abortion judges. In office he ignored the Christian Right's reactionary causes, but they had to support him against Clinton, who evangelicals regarded as the antichrist.

By the 1990s the Christian right had a virtual veto over mainstream Republicanism. They were able to secure the nomination of born again Bush junior and his theft of the election was regarded as a miracle. Bush appointed a hard-line born again Christian as Attorney General and a Labour Relations Secretary who advocated abandoning the constitution in favour of putting the country under biblical law. The Christian Right were kept onside through the awarding of billions of dollars in contracts to run formerly public social services. This meant more and more organisations refusing to employ Jews and gays, more schools teaching abstinence-only sex education and more prisons attempting to cure homosexuality. In return the Christian Right helped Bush restore US inequality to pre-1929 levels.

Bush's main task was ensuring that the rich got richer and extending the reach of US imperialism, but evangelicals rallied to him after 9/11. While they attributed the attack to God's punishment for abortion, paganism, homosexuality and feminism the administration welcomed an excuse to increase US domination of the Middle East and steal Iraq's oil. Things came together in the military, a bastion of the Christian right. There were numerous miracles on the battlefield and a typical imperialist victory secured through overwhelming technological superiority was ascribed to divine intervention. The occupation was gradually subcontracted to private military companies (mercenaries) who supported the Christian right and were dedicated to a Christian supremacist agenda.

George W Bush's second term was an unmitigated disaster and led to the election of Barack Obama, who was subjected to a barrage of lies and abuse from the Christian Right for being a Muslim. He is in fact a devout Christian: his real crime was being a liberal and black. The biggest lie, that he wasn't American, was promulgated by Donald Trump.

By 2016 the Republican Party was dominated by the

Christian right and over several serious evangelicals they chose Trump, the most un-Christian candidate possible. In return he promised them the vice-presidency, control of the entire judiciary and the relocation of the US embassy in Israel. With the chance of rolling back social progress they agreed to ignore his lamentable record. Some gullible evangelicals believed Trump had been born again. Some knew that God had once spoken through the mouth of an ass and thought he may be doing it again. The rest fell for a complicated biblical contrivance I can't even be bothered to detail. Trump himself certainly didn't understand it. But he was seen as the solution to a satanic conspiracy and his many foibles are proof that God indeed works in mysterious ways. Meanwhile, evangelical preachers continue to spout their reactionary bile while pretending to cure Covid 19 through the power of prayer.

In office Trump's main focus has been on self-promotion and winning again in 2020. Serious politicians have despaired at his ignorance, his refusal to read briefings and the endless hours he spends watching TV. Nevertheless, this egotistical narcissist, pitifully devoid of gubernatorial skill, has delivered for the Christian right by proxy, in the person of Vice President Mike Pence; he represented their power in the White House and he filled the administration with their people.

In some areas the interests of the Christian right and big business coincide and the wealthiest cabinet ever delivered tax cuts, rolled back environmental measures and massively expanded the military budget. The avaricious leaders of the Christian right, whose only true faith is in predatory capitalism, have personally benefited, but the main thing Trump delivered on is support for Israel. Despite an undercurrent of anti-Semitism the Christian right is fully committed to Zionism. Whatever rhetorical somersaults they perform to justify this support, they accept that Israel is the bulwark of American imperialism in the Middle East and that its enemies are America's enemies.

American evangelicals have been utilised in the same way that the German ruling class thought they could utilise Hitler and against the same targets. A monster has been created which Trump's narrow defeat has done nothing to slay. God's true purpose will be revealed. One defector from the Trump camp has said, 'As bad as you think Trump is, you should be worried about Mike Pence. We would be begging for the days of Trump if Pence becomes president.' The very last word in John Newsinger's book is one that should never be used flippantly: that word is fascism.

MAKING A PRESENT
OF THE PAST

Confronting the Classics – Mary Beard

When I became politically active in 1992 I was an uneducated bricklayer who'd had several years to get over the nonsense instilled in him by the British Army. Having come to the realisation that I was a revolutionary I sold my motorcycle and went to get formally educated. At the University of Glasgow I found first year politics so dull – the prescribed text cured my insomnia – that I failed the course. Classics, or 'Classical Civilisation' (the study of Ancient Greece and Rome), which I took up at random and in complete ignorance, I found enthralling. I was in mixed age classes with people from various backgrounds who were studying a subject purely for the joy of it, not because they thought it would advance their career prospects. This was what education should be about. I also felt incredibly privileged, as a tattooed tradesman, to be studying at an ancient university with oak panelled lecture halls and lecturers who loved their subject and floated about the grounds in black gowns.

Why am I telling you this? – because on a recent chance visit to the hallowed halls of Glasgow University with two of my old mates, who'd never seen such things, I discovered that Classics had been relegated from the prestigious place in the east quad it had occupied for a hundred years to an office up a back street, to be replaced in that prominent place by... you guessed it: *Business Studies*. Need I say more? I instantly joined the ranks of those bemoaning the decline of Classics (not to mention the decline of real education).

Mary Beard in her excellent exposé *Confronting the Classics*, which is really a compilation of her book reviews, tackles this phenomenon head on, insisting in her introduction that the decline of classics has been a topic of discussion ever since study of the Ancient World began. She also expresses a much more profound and fundamental truth: that the writing of history says as much about authors and their times as it does about the events and characters depicted. And this is why, while Classics may seem to be currently marginalised within academia, along with other subjects that teach students to think, the ancient world continues to provide, as it has always provided, a wealth of precedent by which just about anything can be justified, from slavery to tyrannicide. The American Founding Fathers, for example, loved ancient Rome and it provided the template for their pseudo-democratic political system.

Beard is essentially an iconoclast, who not only savages long established orthodoxies propounded by long-dead historians, but takes no prisoners in her criticisms of more recent authors who have tried to bend what we do know about events two thousand years ago, either to fit tenuous theories or to rehabilitate ancient figures. She is also not without theories of her own, not least the entirely plausible one that Alexander the Great was largely a Roman construction that served to justify their own imperialist adventures.

Only since my time at university have I discovered that classicists fall into two camps; 'Ciceronians' and 'Caesarians'. Cicero (a nick name, meaning 'chick pea nose') who, for public school poshos was portrayed as the doyen of orators and statesman, is here exposed for the self-promoting, cowardly, conservative reactionary he really was. He is also accused of exaggerating the threat from a radical rebellion and, dare I say, terrorism, to bolster his own position when he was one of Rome's two consuls. He had to do this because he wasn't brave enough to lead a Roman army on an orgy of subjection and pillage, which was how other politicians gained their fame and funded their corrupt electoral campaigns. But Cicero was also a master of the sound bite and his slogans pepper speeches and adorn banners all over. 'How long will you try our patience?' turned up in Spain in 1999, in the Congo in 2001 and in Hungary in 2012. And he's not the only one: when I quoted Marx 'nothing which is human is alien to me,' in a packed lecture theatre the lecturer pointed out to me that Terence, the Roman playwright, had said it first. John Major's hypocritical 'Back to Basics' was first attempted by the Emperor Augustus.

And Caesar himself? He was murdered because he wanted to be king and Rome was a republic, everyone knows that. But what if Caesar was a progressive populist who gave a grain dole to the poor and land to former legionaries? Wouldn't that threaten the rule of the rich enough that they'd conspire to bump him off? They'd done it before to Tiberius and Gaius Gracchus, two other enlightened aristocrats who were intelligent enough to see that if you didn't give ordinary people a share they'd rise up and take the lot.

When I was writing my final dissertation on Roman Slavery my advisor was a half-hearted and lacklustre Roman historian who had studied under the Marxist classicist G.E.M. de Ste Croix, author of the monumental *The Class Struggle in the Ancient Greek World* (he insisted the definite article was important). He (my advisor) told me that he had never been convinced by the great man's Marxism. So much was obvious: he was also a Glasgow Labour councillor and chair of the education committee, then engaged in sacking teachers and the subject of a big demonstration outside City Chambers. As part of that demo I was able to shout at him in Latin. Some more forward Glaswegian kicked him up the arse.

So, 'The Greeks invented democracy.' As Mary Beard says, you can't 'invent' democracy; 'it isn't like a piston engine'. There's never been a time when groups of human beings didn't do what the majority of those present thought they should; that's democracy. Actually the ancient Athenians had a democracy for a while, and consequently a great flowering of culture, many of the other independent city states didn't, but it was destroyed by Alexander the Great, or was it?

I celebrated my degree with another tattoo: a big Roman soldier on my leg that I copied from a text book. Classics – the province of the elite – bollocks! It's ours for the taking, just like opera, public transport, healthy food and all the rest. I guarantee that we'll see an end to the decline of Classics when we bring about the decline of capitalism. In the meantime you'll struggle to find a Classics course, and if you do it will cost a fortune. So read Mary Beard's book instead. You never know, you might get interested in a subject that's got nothing to do with what's happening today.

A SUITABLE DETERRENT

Chernobyl 01:23:40 – Andrew Leatherbarrow

With the discovery of nuclear fission came the possibility of limitless energy and a weapon of unspeakable barbarity. Military preoccupations kept research out of scientific journals and, amid concerns it might ignite the atmosphere and destroy the planet, the US tested the first bomb in 1945. Three weeks later it tested two more on the Japanese people.

A convenient cover for this insanity was the energy producing potential, and the US tested its first power-producing reactor in 1951. The first British power station opened at Windscale, Cumbria in 1954. Three years later, while producing tritium for thermonuclear bombs, 260 workers were exposed to cancer-causing radiation and thirty suffered genetic damage that would affect their descendants. Reports of serious accidents at Soviet nuclear facilities were supressed by western authorities to prevent legitimate safety concerns. The potentially catastrophic meltdown at the Three Mile Island plant in Pennsylvania in 1979 naturally caused some disquiet.

With fifty thousand workers housed nearby, the Chernobyl power plant in the Ukraine was set to become the biggest in the world. By 1986 four reactors had been commissioned and a fifth was under construction.

Power-generating nuclear fission usually takes place inside a metal pressure vessel inside a highly reinforced containment building. The Chernobyl reactors were concrete structures with a metal lid and base. The reactor hall was not capable of containing a major incident. The nuclear power industry generally takes for granted human fallibility and numerous failsafe mechanisms are factored in. The Chernobyl plant incorporated outdated systems and design faults and should never have been built. There had been near-disasters with similar reactors in Leningrad in 1975 and Lithuania in 1983. A serious accident at Chernobyl in 1982 was blamed on staff, rather than poor design, and recommended improvements had not been made. It was a disaster waiting to happen.

On 26 April Chernobyl's engineers set out to test No. 4 reactor's ability to deal with a forced shutdown. The reactor needed 37,000 tons of water an hour to keep it cool and the pumps were powered by its own turbines. In an emergency, power could be obtained from the national grid and then from back-up diesel generators. There was a time lag in the switchover and the system relied on the slowing turbines producing enough electricity to keep the pumps going. The plan's effectiveness was not established prior to commissioning and three belated tests on reactor No. 3 all failed to sustain the voltage the water pumps required.

The test on No. 4 reactor was carried out on almost spent and unstable fuel. It was postponed until the shift trained to carry it out had gone off duty. The backup diesel engines and the Emergency Core Cooling System were disconnected. An inexperienced reactor control engineer reduced the power too far and the test should have been abandoned. The now unstable reactor was returned to full power in order for it to be repeated, requiring the further overriding of safety systems that would have shut it down. Things went immediately wrong and the emergency shutdown was activated. A fundamental design flaw the reactor's designers had 'forgotten to mention' prevented the shutdown and eighteen seconds later the top blew off the reactor, the incoming air caused an explosion that half-demolished the turbine hall and threw 750 tons of nuclear material into the air. The atmospheric radioactivity was equivalent to ten Hiroshima bombs and local levels were sixty times higher than fatal. The reactor's core became a raging inferno.

The control room team refused to believe the reactor was destroyed and took inappropriate action for six hours. Heroic action by the plant's firefighters and other staff prevented the fire spreading to the other reactors and their probable destruction. They had no anti-radiation equipment or respirators. As the eventual 186 firefighters succumbed they were taken to hospital to irradiate doctors, nurses and ambulance drivers. The other reactors were not shut down for a further sixteen hours. Construction workers employed on reactor No. 5 arrived at work at 8am and were not sent home until midday.

When it was finally accepted that reactor No. 4 was destroyed, permission to evacuate the site was denied to avoid panic and the news escaping. No information was provided to the nearby city's residents. Children went to school and adults went to work while being slowly irradiated.

Eventually politicians were convinced that the accident was of lasting global significance and could not be kept secret. They agreed to the dropping of tons of radiation and fire damping materials from helicopters into the burning crater, raising even more radioactive dust. Very little of it reached the burning core. The restricted airflow caused a total meltdown and fears that a further explosion could detonate the other reactors and make half of Ukraine and Belorussia uninhabitable.

A full thirty-six hours after the explosion, in colossal

levels of radiation, the population was calmly evacuated forever. Eventually half a million people were displaced. Kiev's children, their mothers and all pregnant women were evacuated. Along with the city six hundred towns and villages had to be decontaminated. In hospital the bodies of the badly irradiated victims turned black and slowly disintegrated until they choked on their own internal organs. The three thousand medical staff who treated them were all exposed to radiation.

Two days after the catastrophe dangerous radiation levels were detected in Scandinavia: their trajectory was traced and the Soviet authorities had to admit an accident had taken place. Plans to save the situation were based on the number of lives it would cost. Attempts to clear radioactive material around the reactor using robots largely failed. Scientists calculated that military reservists wearing single-use lead covered suits could work for forty seconds at a time and 250,000 workers received their maximum lifetime dose of radioactivity. Wearing inadequate protective clothing 600,000 'liquidators' took part in a four year clean-up of the massive exclusion zone. Handling radioactive material with their bare hands they removed 300,000 cubic metres of contaminated topsoil and built a twelve kilometre, thirty-metre deep, concrete wall to prevent radioactive rainwater entering watercourses.

In one of the biggest engineering tasks ever undertaken the remains of reactor No. 4, containing plutonium sufficient to kill millions of people that would be radioactive for thousands of years, were covered with a massive 'object shelter'. Nicknamed the Sarcophagus it took 206 days to build and contained 400,000 cubic metres of concrete and 7,300 tons of steel. By 1996 rainwater was endangering the still volatile core and the building was in danger of collapse. Forty-seven countries and organisations contributed to a permanent cover. At 30,000 tons it is the largest moveable structure ever built and has to last a hundred years.

In an attempt to prevent a public backlash the inquiry into Chernobyl explosion ignored design faults and did what all governments do: it found scapegoats whose trials were held in secret. The International Atomic Energy Agency (IAEA) initially went along with this, but in 1991 it was admitted that known design faults were to blame. The senior operators were largely exonerated and the IAEA revised its report.

No one knows how many people suffered slow, agonising deaths as a result of the catastrophe, but the bodies of those who died in the initial stages are buried in zinc coffins to prevent their radioactive remains polluting the soil. The contaminated area covers 23% of Belorussia, 7% of Ukraine and large parts of western Russia. Two million people are officially classed as victims. Infant mortality has risen by up to 30%, there are levels of thyroid cancer, leukaemia and genetic mutations previously unheard of. There are also increased risks of other cancers, infant and perinatal mortality, delayed mental development and diseases of the respiratory, cardiovascular, gastrointestinal, urogenital and endocrine systems.

The Chernobyl explosion caused several countries to review or abandon their nuclear energy programs. However the memories of our rulers are short and they hardly ever learn from their mistakes. Insatiable boffins are already working on evermore contrived ways to utilise nuclear power, having accepted the suicidal orthodoxy that there is no alternative to ever-increasing levels of energy consumption.

We might comfort ourselves that the twisted Soviet system was responsible for Chernobyl and that such a thing could never happen in the west, but perhaps we've just been lucky. When leading members of the International Atomic

Energy Agency were asked if western reactors were safer than Soviet ones they avoided answering the question. The Chernobyl disaster has exposed one stark fact: the continued possession and even theoretical use of nuclear weapons is ridiculous.

A LAND OF MAKE BELIEF

Down Under – Bill Bryson

Australia is big: so big that some things about it are still unknown. Other things about it are very well known, such as that Captain Cook discovered it in 1770. Except that he didn't and he wasn't a captain. No one really knows which Europeans first landed in Australia or when it was, but it had been discovered many thousands of years earlier by the aboriginal people. Cook's visit merely confirmed the existence of a big island and he claimed the east coast of it for Britain, mistakenly believing it to be something like an English country estate. The first white Australians were disappointed to discover something less than the paradise Cook had described and were singularly unprepared for the task before them.

The Aboriginal people considered the white explorers a ridiculous joke, even nursing back to health those who got lost in the desert. In typical fashion, and long after it became too late to do anything about the invaders, the peaceable occupants were driven off their lands and murdered. Attitudes to the aboriginal people became entrenched and even in 1999 Bill Bryson has no difficulty finding a complete stranger who says, 'They want hanging, every one of them.'

In the late eighteenth century Britain attempted to rid itself of its excess poor and hungry by transporting them to a remote, unknown and inhospitable place. The only upside of this cruelty was that it was better than being hanged for stealing the means of survival. Some Australians are not keen to admit that their ancestors were low class petty thieves, or that their modern, safe and fair-minded white society is built on the genocidal ill-treatment of the original inhabitants.

The country was transformed by a mid-nineteenth century gold rush: the population doubled and Sydney became the world's richest city. Britain stopped sending convicts, but the racism continued. White Australian prospectors launched a race war against Chinese immigrants, beating and robbing them with impunity. Rather than urging compassion the Australian government took a leaf out of Britain's book, pandered to racists, and introduced the White Australia Policy, which until the 1970s forbade the immigration of non-Europeans.

Much of Australia was once green for much of the year. It is now virtually desert due to the introduction of the rabbit entirely for posh sport. The population soon reached millions, they had no natural predators and they ate everything. The deliberate introduction of myxomatosis from South America in 1950 killed 99.9% of them, but the survivors became immune and their numbers have since recovered.

There were those who would have used similar methods against the Aboriginal people. In 1816 Australian governor Lachclan Macquarie ordered soldiers into the Interior and more remote parts of the colony, for the specific purpose of punishing the natives who dared to resist. He intended to entirely clear the country of them and ordered that any resisters were to be killed and their bodies hung from trees 'in order to strike the greatest terror in the survivors.'

Australia's original inhabitants have the oldest continuously maintained culture on earth. This unparalleled human achievement is hardly recognised by most Australians and the Aboriginal people were only granted any human rights in 1972.

Until 1949 there was no such thing as Australian citizenship. The people who lived in Australia were British, learned British history, fought and died in Britain's wars and called Britain, a country most of them had never seen, 'home.' Britain repaid Australians by leaving them to be invaded by Japan and it was only by good luck that they weren't. The lesson Australia learned was that it had to dramatically increase its population. Millions of Greeks and Italians poured in and were made very welcome, the only condition for immigration was that the applicants were white.

In the 1940s and 50s Australia was very prudish and conservative. There was a long list of proscribed books that was itself secret, but which contained many titles freely available elsewhere. One long serving state premier said he couldn't see the point of universities.

For 99.7% of their history the Aboriginal people had Australia all to themselves. They lived in every extreme of the climate for thousands of years, completely at one with nature. As such they are dismissed by one archaeologist as being of 'a very primitive technical and economic phase.' They were incredibly industrious, but had no government and very little sense of property. They were clearly in great need of civilising.

In his journal Cook wrote of the Aboriginal people, 'All they seemed to want was for us to be gone.' This is possibly one of the most sympathetic comments made about them. Until the 1960s they were regarded as sub-human and weren't included in any census until 1967 because they did not count as people. In the first century after the white man arrived the aboriginal population fell from at least three hundred thousand to at most sixty thousand. Many died from disease to which they had no immunity. They were also butchered for dog food, deliberately poisoned and tortured for sport: men, women and children. When it eventually became illegal to kill and torture Aboriginal people the killing and torturing went underground and lasted for another century. White men still murdered them for fun, they just didn't brag about it in the pub.

The last official mass murder was of seventy people in 1928. It warrants no memorial because it was nothing special. Three months earlier two hundred Aboriginal people were massacred nearby. Bryson is told that if every massacre of Aboriginal people was commemorated you wouldn't be able to move for the monuments. In 1985 the Australian government gave Ayers Rock, 'Uluru', back to those who regarded it as sacred, but they have to share it with thousands of tourists. Generally the Aboriginal people have two choices: they can stay on the grudgingly allocated missions or move into town to live in penury and dereliction.

Between 1910 and 1970 the Australian government carried out a social experiment which resulted in between one tenth and one third of aboriginal children being forcibly removed from their parents. The idea was to denativise them into the civilised white world. Until the 1960s aboriginal parents in most Australian states did not have legal custody over their children, it belonged to the state. Children were told that their parents were dead or didn't want them. This led to widespread grief-related alcoholism and very high suicide rates. No aboriginal family remained untouched by this inhumanity. The policy didn't work and in 1999 every social indicator possible showed the Aboriginal people were at least twice and sometimes twenty times worse off than the general population. Australia is the only advanced nation which has a high rate of trachoma. It causes blindness and only affects Aboriginal people. Aboriginal people don't appear on TV, they don't work in shops or banks and they don't become plumbers or postmen. To all intents and purposes they don't exist.

Australia has more varied and numerous flora and fauna than anywhere else on the planet, much of it in danger of extinction. In the 1960s the country was transformed from a sheep rearing backwater into a global mining colossus. Minerals were discovered in great quantity one after the other and what was once wilderness was destroyed by men with no conscience whatsoever.

This has created a great number of very rich, tasteless and vulgar people and Australia's current Prime Minister, Scott Morrison, having flagrantly disregarded human rights while immigration minister, is their unapologetic representative. He refuses to countenance any curb on the extraction and export of coal, even though it is clearly largely responsible for climate change. Consequently Australia has suffered unprecedented drought and forest fires.

Aboriginal people now make up three percent of the Australian population and occupy 28% of the places in its prisons. They are locked up for the crime of being black and poor. In 2015 John Pilger wrote that the genocide of Australia's original inhabitants had been influenced by the same eugenics movement that inspired the Nazis, and that Queensland's 'protection acts' were a model for South African Apartheid.'

Bill Bryson finishes *Down Under* by saying that once you leave Australia, Australia ceases to be. This is no longer true. The country's devastating wild fires have become global news, along with its climate change denying prime minister in hock to big coal. We are perhaps also more aware of its disgusting history, which is mirrored in imperial conquest and racist oppression around the world.

Studying pictures from the 1950s Bill Bryson says that Australians don't today seem to have the same happiness in their faces, and adds, 'I don't think anybody does.' Indeed. Australians are not alone in believing life is getting worse, but research has shown only a fifth of them have any hope of it getting better. By the turn of the millennium it was becoming obvious that the dream was over.

In the two decades since Bill Bryson wrote *Down Under* Australia has begun to accept the right of the Aboriginal people to exist. However, in the twenty-first century there is still no likelihood of an Aboriginal person becoming prime minister of the country they took care of for thousands of years before the white man came and, given that the USA has had a black president and Asian people have made it to the top of British politics, there's no reason to assume life for the majority would be any better if they did.

THE BALLAD OF THE GENERAL BELGRANO

There are no rules of engagement
When hubristic Tories are drunk
And when principles go the bottom
Miners and seamen and are sunk

What are the lives of some sailors
Adrift in a tin pot fleet
When capital needs an election
To show that labour is beat

Sending a ship to the bottom
Gave Tories and tabloids a treat
There's nothing like killing some conscripts
For impressing the man in the street

They raised the flag of convenience
On the sinking of so many souls
But there's something adrift in the ballot box
When murder goes to the polls

Standing up to the system
Is like a red rag to a bull
And anyone confronting Tina
Got a big hole in their hull

There's more than one way that the army
Can see that the workers are beat
And drowning some enemy sailors

Played proxy for troops on the street

Sinking the General Belgrano
And the enemy that was within
Meant the Tories had taken the gloves off
And the war against all could begin

If only Galtieri had balloted
Before he seized the Maldives
He may have avoided being beaten
By the uniformed thugs of the thieves

People don't matter to capital
It will simply eradicate them
Be they miners or tin pot dictators
In ships or the NUM

A PEDESTRIAN MEMOIR

Gas Masks and Garston – Beatrice Smith

As one approaches maturity, with perhaps idle hours to fill, there is something very tempting about setting down an account of one's life. It can perhaps be compared to researching one's family tree. I say this as one who has succumbed to the former temptation, though thankfully not yet the latter. Psychologists might say that such enterprise is undertaken by people facing their own mortality, who fear that nothing of them will remain.

As it says on the front, this is an account of a childhood in Garston, Liverpool, before, during and after WWII. There is much for social historians contained within – just as there is in hundreds of similar books filling the shelves of every book store in the land. The family are commonplace and their lives are ordinary. The author goes to school and goes on cycling holidays, noting every bird, bee, flower, castle and stately home on the way, in what is often close to an unrelenting stream of consciousness.

It may be wrong to expect a memoir of this kind to provide any kind of political overview. A child's world is necessarily small. But this book wasn't written by a child – it was written by an adult with the benefit of hindsight. When the author tells me that she obsessively kept a scrap book on the royal family I want her to tell me that she was misguided and now recognises them to be an anachronistic bunch of useless parasites, but she doesn't. She doesn't criticise them at all.

Nevertheless there are oblique references to things the reader would like to know more about. For example, the author's father was a pacifist and joined the Auxiliary Fire Service (AFS) just before the war, as did my own grandfather.

Smith remembers seeing on Pathé News the relief of the concentration camps and the aftermath of the atomic bombs dropped on Japan; what does she think about fascism and nuclear weapons? One uncle was a career soldier and remained 'an unrepentant self-opinionated bigot and defender of the British Empire till the end of his life.' What does the author think of the British Empire? We don't find out. Nor do we find out what the she thinks of Churchill, who visited Garston in 1930 and was apparently pelted with rotten fruit. Or women's rights, given that her parent's marriage was loveless and her mother believed that providing sex to a husband was a duty. Or current societal attitudes to child sexual abuse, given that she herself was abused by her sister's boyfriend.

There are hints within the book that the author went on to become a socialist. If I was writing a memoir of my childhood I would write it as the socialist I am now, not as the child I was then. Churchill was a bastard, Victorian attitudes to marriage stink, fascism needs to be actively fought. I hesitate to condemn Beatrice Smith's childhood memoir out of hand, but in all honesty it is rather pedestrian and un-analytical.

But worst of all; the culmination of the work, the very denouement, is a twenty page account of the 'fairy tale' coronation of our present monarch; 'The coach moved so slowly it appeared to float towards us. Now it was level and we were looking straight at the queen.' This really is sycophantic twaddle.

The memoir only takes us to the author's nineteenth year. Perhaps the sequel will be better. After saying virtually nothing political for 286 pages the very last sentence of the book is a completely random reference to the poll tax riots in 1990; thirty seven years after the narrative closes. I didn't hate it and it wasn't hard to read, but I can't go any further than the back page blurb; '*Gas Masks and Garston* is a heart-warming memoir.' If you want a cosy fireside read perhaps it's for you. If you want to change the world, perhaps not.

CRIMINAL TYPES

The Body – Bill Bryson

Hardly anyone today disputes that throughout history people have been despised, vilified, enslaved, deprived of their rights and murdered due to the colour of their skin. Irrespective of the actions of contemporary racists, who take their lead from above, this *prima facie* assertion serves only to short-circuit a much more fundamental process. In the modern era rampaging imperialists have either subjected non-white peoples to hyper-exploitation in their never-ending search for profit or to oppression for political purposes, which in the end amounts to the same thing. For obvious reasons between the seventeenth and nineteenth centuries the European powers needed to prove other races inferior; their skin colour has only provided a convenient excuse and they have relied on eminent philosophers and spurious science to bolster their disingenuous intentions.

There is no such thing as race: the different peoples of the earth cannot be defined by their skin colour, which exists only in the top one millimetre of our epidermis. Hairy proto-humans did not need dark skin and it is believed to have developed between 1.2 and 1.7 million years ago. The skin colour of human societies can change in as little as two millennia and, mainly as a means of synthesising extra vitamin D, light coloured 'de-pigmented' humans have evolved on at least three occasions. It goes without saying then that skin colour is utterly useless as a determinant of individual, let alone national character; it is simply a reaction to sunlight, and that racism is nothing but an economic and political weapon in the armoury of our collective exploiters.

Dissatisfied with 'race' as the singular instrument by which our masters divide us, the better to rule us, elitists, eugenicists and quack scientists have sought other means by which to demonstrate that the right people are in charge. Cesare Lombroso asserted that a tendency toward criminality was evident in the shape of some human skulls. Lombroso's crack-pot science became known as phrenology, and it attempted to correlate the lumps and bumps on the human skull with character and intelligence. In opposition stood craniometry, simply the measuring of the size, shape and volume of the skull to provide equally spurious results. In the 1840s the Midlands doctor Barnard Davis was prolific in racially-based books on craniology, which also considers the shape of the skull, along the way amassing the biggest collection of skulls in the world, many of them obtained by theft and deception. Davis set out not only to prove that dark-skinned people were different, i.e. inferior, but to justify class hierarchy by showing that, irrespective of their skin colour, an individual's morality and intelligence were intrinsic in the dimensions of their skull. Those with skull shapes he considered peculiar he regarded as potential criminals or dangerous idiots. The motives driving privileged scientists subject to the realities of their era are evident also in John Langdon Haydon Down, who first described the syndrome named after him as 'Mongolism'. He called sufferers of the condition 'Mongoloid idiots' and believed 'Malay' and 'Negroid' to be equally regressive human types.

Lombroso, without a scintilla of scientific validity, fathered 'criminal anthropology', seeing criminals as evolutionary throwbacks whose tendencies could be established by anatomical scrutiny. Despite the crude and unscientific nature of his extremely convenient observations Lombroso is even yet referred to as the father of criminology and posthumously called as an expert witness. Craniology was enthusiastically taken up by the Frenchman Pierre Paul Broca, who insisted against all evidence that female, criminal and non-white brains were inferior to white male ones.

In *The Discovery of France* Graham Robb tells us that by measuring people's skulls Broca was able to determine that those of the modern bourgeois were larger than their proletarian counterparts and that the bourgeoisie of Paris 'was the very apex of the socio-anthropological pyramid.' Robb also describes how notions about the (non-existent) 'pure' Frenchman were utilised to divide the French citizenry from lazy dark-skinned Mediterranean people and the over-regimented barbarians across the Rhine. This kind of pseudo-science has been used by fascists and lesser nationalists throughout France's modern history. It was especially necessary to demonstrate that the people who lived in areas of France subject to German invasion were intrinsically French.

Charles Darwin showed that all humans have a common ancestry, but pseudo-scientific racism had played its part in justifying imperial conquest and lingers yet in any stereotypical racist generalisation, as it does in partisan definitions of criminality. It is often overlooked that those who decide who is committing crime also have the privilege of deciding what it entails, thereby excluding their own outrageous transgressions. It should not surprise us that Caucasian pseudo-scientists, in establishing a spurious hierarchy of 'races', placed themselves at the top, or that those who seek to maintain a criminal system based on exploitation, enslavement, robbery and war continue to grasp at whatever straws are available.

LAGOS TO LEEDS

The Hounding of David Oluwale – Kester Aspden

At a community meeting in January 2020 I reiterated that I had been made into a racist by the British army. Perhaps it wasn't just the army. Opening Kester Aspden's book at home I am confronted with a joke told by Bernard Manning on national television in 1972, the year I joined up; 'Heard about the Pakistani who wanted converting?... They took him to Leeds rugby ground and kicked him over the goalposts.' Thankfully the unrepentant opportunist oaf whose act consisted entirely in such tasteless bigotry was eventually dropped by TV stations, but, like all comedy, Manning's refusal to compromise both reflected and encouraged the racism in wider society.

In May 1969 a lifeless black man was pulled from the equally lifeless River Aire in West Yorkshire. The forensic examination was shoddy, the coroner found death by drowning and the body was committed to a pauper's grave. In 1970 a police cadet raised concerns, a criminal investigation began and the body was exhumed. The undertakers had taken the opportunity to bury their rubbish and the coffin was stuffed with old telephone directories.

It is impossible now not to make comparisons with another famous case in which black people were treated with contempt, but Stephen Lawrence was a promising and conscientious student, whereas David Oluwale had been stigmatised as a mentally deranged, half civilised and dangerous public nuisance, in which no reference to monkeys and jungles was spared.

The Nigerian attended a mission school in Lagos, where pupils discovered the mother country to be a place of decency, liberty and law. Denied their own heritage the students learned the history of Britain, its empire, literature and manners. In 1940s Nigeria even one so lucky was not guaranteed a good job and, after working as a tailor's apprentice, David Oluwale stowed away on a ship bound for Britain. After twenty eight days in Armley Jail as punishment for his illegal passage, he was free to remain as one of Britain's privileged colonial subjects.

With its long tradition of tailoring Leeds seemed ideal, but things didn't work out and after spells in engineering, on building sites and in the city abattoir he received a blow on the head in a street scuffle and was never the same again. Reliant on drugs and in and out jail David Oluwale was eventually committed to the notorious High Royds Asylum, where he received not a single visitor. He was in all likelihood subjected to Electroconvulsive Therapy, which is known to cause severe headaches, confusion, restlessness and memory loss.

Unsurprisingly, he could be violent: in fact he fitted the psychiatric stereotype of a black man. The same psychologist who judged patients in High Royds, judged the Mau Mau uprising in Kenya as being carried out by sub-humans, to whom the rule of law was irrelevant, and against whom any force was justifiable. Unable to access mental health services on release David Oluwale resorted to hostels, some of which didn't take black men, semi-derelict squats, and shop doorways. He only assumed any importance again when he was dead.

In the late sixties there was much anti-immigrant feeling in Britain, which the Labour government had helped to fuel by passing blatantly racist anti-migrant legislation. Enoch

Powell became the most admired man in the country after his *Rivers of Blood* speech and some members of Leeds City Police relished putting the political rhetoric into practice.

Early one morning in April Police Sergeant Ken Kitching, with a record of mindless violence against detainees, and inspector Geoff Ellerker, under suspicion for shielding a colleague who had killed an old woman in a road accident while drunk, went to beat 'a coon' in the entrance to a city centre shop. As the culmination of a nine-month vendetta the two officers chased David Oluwale through Leeds to the river in which he was later discovered dead.

Detective Chief Superintendent John Perkins led the Scotland Yard investigation. In making a case he had to pierce the police code of silence. The immediate reaction of the Chief Constable was to protect the good name of the force. A racially motivated murder could finish it. There were proposals for its incorporation and other officers were under investigation for serious crimes.

Ex-Inspector Ellerker was already in jail and refused to cooperate. He claimed to have lost his duty book, an individual officer's record, which were in any case routinely falsified. Relevant duty sheets and radio transcripts also went missing. Sergeant Kitching admitted using violence on David Oluwale, saying it was the only way to deal with him. He denied assaulting him on the morning in question or chasing him towards the river. Perkins, under intense pressure to supress the truth, had previously described the ideal officer as a 'protector of the weak, shield against the oppressor.' He saw the accused officers as despicable individuals with no regard for another human being. Almost certainly due to the Oluwale case he suffered a complete nervous breakdown, from which he never recovered.

Kitching was a long-serving police officer with a chip

on his shoulder, described by investigators as a crude and unintelligent man. One colleague said he would have made a good traffic warden, another that he told a member of the public who asked him the time to 'fuck off'. Ellerker was a rising star who had learned how to treat black people with the RAF police in Kenya during the Mau Mau rebellion, one of most shameful episodes in Britain's long and shameful history. The two officers were inseparable. Ellerker was a poor manager and relied on Kitching the thug, who believed he had the inspector under his thumb. Both men drank regularly on duty. Drink made Kitching volatile. The rest of their shift had no respect for either of them.

Kitching saw it as his duty to give vagrants a kicking and he bragged openly about beating David Oluwale. There were stories that he had rolled him in a barrel, set fire to the newspaper he slept under and pissed on him while he slept, with Ellerker holding the torch. During one frenzied attack in a police van Oluwale bit both men. Other officers thought it served them right, but Oluwale went to prison for it, and Kitching promised revenge. Three days after his release he was rearrested. A WPC witnessed the police station doors flying open and David Oluwale going sprawling across the floor. Ellerker kicked him in the groin with such force that he was lifted off the ground. Both men punched and kicked him, including in his private parts, as other officers looked on.

Several times the two officers kidnapped him in the middle of the night and dumped him outside the city, often in a dark wood. They joked in the station about sending him back to the jungle. During the investigation two charge sheets pertaining to David Oluwale came to light. On one, under nationality, 'BRIT' had been scored out, to be replaced with 'WOG'. On the other 'WOG' was simply typed in the relevant space.

In the early hours of Friday 19th April 1969 another officer heard Ellerker say to Kitching that Oluwale would not assault him again. When they heard his body had been found in the river Kitching was heard to say to Ellerker that they'd 'have to find another playmate.'

The prosecution's problem was that David Oluwale was the kind of victim a *Daily Mail* reader might consider had got what he deserved. He was someone society has absolved itself of responsibility for. In attempting to chase him out of town the officers were effectively on official business. Leeds City Council was intent on cleansing the city of the homeless, as they had cleansed it of gypsies by towing their caravans beyond the city boundary. A year earlier another black man had been chased into the river. Officers 'failed' to save him and his body was found miles away at Allerton Bywater.

Throughout the manslaughter trial the judge expressed his distaste for the victim and his belief that the judiciary should be firmly behind the police. He directed the jury to find the accused not guilty, which they did. In the subsequent assault cases the same judge, in his summing up, declared the police to be a splendid profession, but the jury found the officers guilty and both men served derisory jail sentences.

The *Yorkshire Evening Post* praised the trial as a manifestation of the British sense of fair play and said no one could claim there'd been a cover up when a 'faceless nobody' had been given justice 'that no VIP could expect'. Correspondents complained that the paper was bowing to the city's do-gooders in arousing undue sympathy for a useless vagrant who should have been deported. The vicar of Meanwood declared the trial a travesty of the truth, but said the good name of the police had been maintained. In publishing the public's opinions the paper reminded its readers that the British bobby, only an average man, is expected to clear up society's mess while they sleep.

The truth was that the investigation led numerous police officers to divulge that they had actively colluded in the violence, racism and lawlessness of their superiors. All feared breaking the most insidious of the gang member's maxims; 'my brother right or wrong.' Without the conscience of one uncorrupted initiate the story of David Oluwale's persecution would never have come to light. How many other crimes have been obscured by the silence of this mafia?

Too often the police seem not only to consider themselves above the law, but to *be* the law. The above shows them to be no better than the worst of us. It would be wrong to say that *nothing* has changed, but a class divided society needs racism and thuggery, or the Black Lives Matter movement that grew up in America would never have been so easily transferable to the streets of London and Leeds. The names of the victims are legend – Christopher Alder, Mark Duggan, John Charles de Menezes, Yassar Yaqub, Sean Rigg, Azelle Rodney and Stephen Lawrence. As Kester Aspden says; 'It's possible to see in Oluwale's life the shadows of a long and violent colonial history in which the bodies of native people were worthless and expendable.'

After such a devastating indictment the Home Secretary did all he could to bolster the good reputation of the police. Kester Aspden points out that when Leeds City Council, who were more bothered about motorways than the mentally ill, had the Town Hall and former assizes power washed it took 100,000 gallons of water to wash away the muck of ages.

The abiding sentiment is from one who knew David Oluwale, 'Has anything really changed. At least thirty odd years ago something did happen. But now nobody gets convicted of anything.' Yesterday the police shot dead a Muslim man in London. Whether he was actually a terrorist or not is irrelevant. He had been failed by the system; and so were we.

A NATIVE AT LARGE

The Lost Continent: Travels in Small Town America – Bill Bryson (1989)

In setting the scene for his grand tour across America by modest family car Bill Bryson refers to Ronald Reagan, the then leader of the Free World, as 'a personable old fart' and 'a nice, friendly kind of dopey guy'. As Reagan was actually a red-baiting zealot in cahoots with Thatcher in rehabilitating the twisted, sociopathic economics of Hayek and Freidman we might expect a superficial exploration of his native country, but Bryson goes on to describe an America blighted by obesity, greed, ignorance, violence and institutional racism, where every place of historical interest is ruined by hordes of bovine tourists and countless shops selling rubbish.

He recalls the first time he drove through Georgia only five years after three freedom riders were arrested for speeding and never seen again. The police had released them to a waiting mob and three weeks later their bodies were found in a swamp. That was just the south, and Bryson almost expects to see chain gangs of black men and crosses burning in front gardens. He generally regards southerners as ignorant rednecks, but he's pleased with Elvis's birthplace.

Heading through states that only twenty-five years earlier had denied blacks the vote he is confronted by the poverty in which they still live, side by side with the opulence of whites. In 1989 segregation was very much alive. He also likes FDR's country ranch, though it reminds us only of how rich anyone who runs for US president needs to be. When

Bryson sees a nice place it only reminds him how much cars and indiscriminate wealth have spoiled American life.

America has gone much further than Britain in caricaturing and commodifying its history, turning much of it into overpriced Disney parody. The numerous 'historic markers' usually detail something really shit, but occasionally they describe the destruction of native peoples who got in the way of white men making money.

When Bryson was a child in Washington it was hot and black people didn't sit at luncheon counters. In 1989 everywhere is air-conditioned and black people can sit where they like, but the pace of change has slowed and an urban black American has a one in nineteen chance of being murdered. Right opposite the White House there are people begging. Lunchtime joggers in the park could well be involved in destabilising some Central American government.

Philadelphia, the largest city in the US, is very poor. It spends more on public art than any other US city, but 40% of its population can't read and write, which may account for its high levels of violence.

Bryson says Americans get what they want, right now, whether it's good for them or not, and there is something deeply worrying about this endless gratification, but despite the restaurants where people are actively encouraged to eat grotesque amounts of food, it's clear some Americans don't get what they want, or very badly need. The only Americans who travel by long distance bus are sad individuals who can't afford a car, which is the next thing to living on the streets.

In Gettysburg he discovers the famous address was only ten sentences long, took two minutes to deliver and was made months after the battle. The battlefield itself is surrounded by crap. He finds the Amish areas thronged with outlets selling every kind of tacky shit imaginable to tourists who have swamped their culture.

New York frightens Bryson as the most exciting city it is possible to visit full of solitary and friendless people. It has 36,000 vagrants who live alongside one of the greatest concentrations of neon incitements to excessive consumption in the world. Some guy called Donald Trump is gradually taking over the city by building tasteless skyscrapers.

In Connecticut the shabbiness, dog shit and litter reminds him of London. It's also got its moneyed quarter full of obscene and tasteless mansions. Cape Cod has only a few hundred inhabitants, but it gets as many as 50,000 visitors a day. He has never seen a place so singularly devoted to sucking money out of tourists and finds it to have no redeeming features whatsoever.

New Hampshire has the same endless retail park ugliness. It also has Bretton Woods, where in 1944 economists and politicians from twenty-eight countries set up the World Bank and the International Monetary Fund, which have done so much since to create a world in America's image: a world of obscene contrasts.

In the 1960s Lake Erie was declared dead, having been turned into a massive toilet. Bryson avoids staying in Detroit, much of which today is also dead, though he can only wonder what it will be like when the motor industry goes tits up. Henry Ford's expansive museum is one of the more tasteful places on his itinerary, but he is reminded that Ford was a bully and an anti-Semite.

By 1989 American hospitals were already advertising on the radio; 'At North Wisconsin General Hospital we'll help you achieve your birthing goals.' Fake social workers advise patients how to stay alive based on what they can pay.

Bryson is hard on his fellow Americans: most bars are full of moody characters drinking alone and staring straight ahead. Young people don't know who the president is and have never heard of Nicaragua. 'They can barely read and you can't teach them anything. There's no spark of enthusiasm there. It's as if years of watching TV have hypnotised them. Some of them can hardly speak a coherent sentence.'

We're told that John Wayne was born in Winterset, Iowa, but not that while he was glorifying genocide on celluloid this American hero enthusiastically supported McCarthy's witch-hunts that actively ruined the lives of thousands of American progressives.

Tourism hasn't yet ruined all the ex-gold mining towns high in the Rockies, but if there's money in it there'll soon be a massive car park and air conditioning. Bryson rants about having his world stolen piece by piece, but still expects the Grand Canyon to be a seminal moment comparable to the death of his grandfather.

Nevada has the biggest Indian reserve in the US. It is so bare and harsh no one else wants to live there. It also has the highest crime rate in the US, the second highest violent crime rate, the highest highway fatality rate, the highest rate for gonorrhoea, the highest proportion of transient people, more prostitutes than any other state, high levels of corruption, long links with organised crime and Las Vegas. At Caesar's Palace Bryson joins the ranks of people mechanically losing money. Then he hates the place and is angry with himself for being taken in by the flashing lights.

He bypasses Los Angeles, dismissing it as full of smog and mad people. Yosemite National Park he finds beautiful, but Yosemite village is full of fat people in Bermuda shorts.

Nevada is a desperate and sparsely populated state full of desolate towns where people live on the edge of existence. Idaho boasts the houses of Clint Eastwood and Barbara Streisand and the place where Ernest Hemingway killed himself. It also has the biggest nuclear dump in the country, from which plutonium, with a shelf life of 250,000 years, is slowly seeping into the local water source.

Wyoming is fiercely western and a man's gotta do what a man's gotta do, which is ride about in a pickup truck and appear kinda slow. The Wild West was really just about squabbling farmers and the gunfights are exaggerated out of all proportion, but the place has to survive on something and the traveller passes alternately through rotting dead holes and towns full of tat shops.

The essence of the trip is encapsulated in South Dakota in the famous Wall Drug Store, an overgrown emporium and cathedral to crap. One of the biggest tourist attractions in the world, it receives up to 20,000 visitors a day. Otherwise these states have a population density of two people per square kilometre (Britain has 236 people per square kilometre) and there are still hobos riding the freight trains.

Bryson sees Custer's Last Stand as an arrogant bully getting what he deserved, while vainly sacrificing American lives. It is impossible not to think of Vietnam, Iraq and Afghanistan, though in these wars expendable American youth managed to take many more of the natives with them.

The Yellowstone Park Geyser Basin is one of the most unstable natural landscapes on a planet full of unstable political landscapes, many of them caused by one single fact; 'When you grow up in America you are inculcated with... the understanding that America is the richest and most powerful nation on earth because God likes us best. It has the most perfect form of government, the most exciting sporting events, the tastiest food and amplest portions, the largest cars, the cheapest gasoline, the most abundant natural resources, the most productive farms, the most devastating nuclear arsenal and the friendliest, most decent and most patriotic folks on earth. Countries just don't come any better.' How did a country with such a small town mentality ever come to dominate the earth?

ON READING BEEVOR'S STALINGRAD

It was just a book, I wasn't there
But in its folds like faded flowers
The horrible truths were pressed
Men, already dead, discussing homes
They'd clearly never see
Speaking of death like a forthcoming meal
But not daring to speak of breakfast
Padres' pockets heavy with dead men's discs
And regiments of lice

It was just a book, I wasn't there
But crammed between its cardboard covers
Carnage, cruelty and cannibalism
It was just a book, a very open book
Of open skulls and open bellies
And regiments of lice
Marching from the dead
Toward the soon to die

It was just a book
One of a stack of books I could have read
But from a stack of books
I read of stacks of frozen dead
The smell of smoke and blood and rotting wounds
Crows pecking out the eyes of corpses
And mice feasting on the frost-bitten feet

Of men too weak to stop them
And regiments of lice
Using straggly beards for barracks

It was just a book, I wasn't there
And after three score years and ten
Why should I care?
And yet the vivid vision meant for days
I saw the frozen dead of Stalingrad
Twisted, from the corner of my eye

WASTED YOUTH

We need to talk about Kevin – Lionel Shriver

In *We Need To Talk About Kevin* Lionel Shriver tacitly critiques sterile, fully fitted, material domesticity for its inability to produce automatic and boundless joy. This is not entirely unconnected with the enquiry into the purpose of existence. Anyone who has suggested to someone with children that existence is futile will know what it feels like to be beaten with the crutch of parenthood. To consciously have children is to invent a purpose. The parent's reason for existence is to see that their offspring are well cared for.

The husband in Shriver's novel is blind to the faults of his progeny and it is asserted that having children is the answer to this Big Question;

'Yet if there's no reason to live without a child, how could there be with one? To answer one life with a successive life is simply to transfer the onus of purpose to the next generation; the displacement amounts to a cowardly and potentially infinite delay. Your children's answer, presumably, will be to procreate as well, and in doing so to distract themselves, to foist their own aimlessness onto their offspring.'

For many people the Big Question has a different answer and the discussion of purpose is cleverly woven into a chapter on religious belief. It is suggested that by being overtly non-religious parents don't do their offspring any favours, because resisting the religion of one's parents is a kind of belief, a starting point on which to build a personal philosophy;

'The fact that you and I were brought up with something to walk away from may have advantaged us, for we knew what lay behind us, and what we were not.' Knowing what you are not has a lot to do with knowing what you are.

I well remember a boy I tried to teach. He had a record of dangerous behaviour and had to be handled with kid gloves, being extremely volatile. Between periods of confrontational and aggressive behaviour he spent the rest of the time in class drawing tattoos, quite often of cannabis leaves.

In the novel Kevin carries out a mass shooting. The boy I tried to teach was set on going into the army so he could kill people legitimately. He already had a lot to live with and didn't need to be told that even the army didn't want him.

AXE GRINDING AS ART

A People's Tragedy – Orlando Figes

The reputation of Orlando Figes' *A People's Tragedy* as contemptible revisionism is such that one obituary writer finds it necessary to tell us that the scrupulously principled campaigning journalist, author and historian Paul Foot refused to read it. No doubt there are other books he refused to read, for far less justifiable reasons. *A People's Tragedy* isn't an academic book and it comes complete with horrifying pictures, precisely because its main purpose is to convince ordinary people that communism is a very, very bad idea and, therefore, that the Russian Revolution was a terrible mistake, along with all other revolutions and, by implication, any serious socialist party misguided enough to believe in real and lasting social progress by any other means.

Early on Figes quotes Ernest Gellner; 'Having a nation is not an inherent attribute of humanity.' Nor, it might be said, is nationalism the mark of a communist. As nation building and defence of the Motherland were central to Stalin's distorted vision, we might begin to doubt that he really stood in the tradition he is reputed to have represented. But doubt has no place here. It is essential we believe Stalin's brutal dictatorship was the inevitable consequence of a misguided revolution, or, to continue the distortion: a cynical elitist coup. If we do not believe this the whole house of cards collapses. If there is even the slightest whiff of discontinuity between the worlds' only popular mass working-class revolution and the coronation of a tyrant who purged, incarcerated and tormented it's most active participants something must have intervened in the process.

It is this degeneration of the revolution into its antithesis that revisionists would rather not have us visit, because for them *ipso facto*, revolution leads to dictators. This is a fact so important for us to imbibe that we have to have it drilled into us from infancy, until we repeat it like stuck records in public houses and works canteens like so many dribbling fools. It is second in the top ten of crass clichés only to the facile and ahistorical assertion that religion causes wars.

For Figes, revolution in Russia was almost inevitable because the Church had failed to establish itself in the growing cities, priests were acting as spies, orthodox Christianity was only superficial in the peasantry and the church hierarchy and the government were deeply reactionary. This tacitly acknowledges the use to which ruling classes put religion, but it might be added that numerous and sizable revolutionary parties had existed in Russia for half a century. There are two conditions for revolution: the first is that the ruling class is unable to rule in the old way, the second is that the working class aren't prepared to let them.

Without the second condition revolutionaries are pissing in the wind. In 1917, amid the worst imperialist slaughter the world has ever seen, their demands chimed with popular feeling, and it becomes essential for Figes' to discredit them. According to this historian-cum-psychologist the leading Russian revolutionaries, to a man, lived an empty existence and merely sought purpose, as well as absolution from the guilt of being wellborn. They did not, as they regularly and passionately asserted, seek the liberation of the common people from a ruthless autocracy, in pursuit of fairness, justice and control over their own lives. Here

Figes stands in a long tradition of right-wing historians who disregard copious evidence of what radical progressives said and did, in favour of looking into their disturbed minds for the signs of the guilt and self-reproach that drove them to live in poverty and insecurity, while sacrificing their lives to a cause, when they could have enjoyed a comfortable and peaceful existence as politicians and lickspittle state bureaucrats.

In order to sully the reputation of leading revolutionaries further Figes introduces, *ex machina,* Bazarov, the anti-hero of Turgenev's *Fathers and Sons.* Bazarov is a nihilist bent on self-destruction by bringing the temple down about his ears. He has no vision of a better world and no agent in mind that could bring it about. It matters not that this puts him in complete contradistinction to those who vocally rejected all that he singularly failed to stand for, so long as they are branded mindless destroyers.

Next it is the nihilist Nechaev who is enlisted as a means to cast the revolutionaries, Lenin in particular, as monsters unconscious of human feeling. According to Nechayev;

'The revolutionary is a dedicated man. He has no personal feelings, no private affairs, no emotions, no attachments, no property and no name. Everything in him is subordinated towards a single exclusive attachment, a single thought and a single passion: the revolution.'

These are the words of an obsessive: irrespective of Lenin's lifelong commitment to the revolution he did not model himself on Nechayev. He had also specifically rejected the anarchist methods of Narodnya Volya as elitist and counterproductive, in favour of a properly organised and *participatory* workers party. If Lenin was the misanthrope Figes pretends he would hardly have needed to seek recuperation in his regular sojourns to the mountains with

Inessa Armand. Similar single-mindedness and eccentricity can be found in many a politician, scientist, businessman and explorer, and the allegation that Lenin had no personal courage and little regard for others is slander. Lenin addressed crowds of thousands any modern politician would disdain, and was once shot for his trouble. It is a travesty that Lenin, who repudiated imperialist war with relentless passion, could be considered inhuman, while those who prosecute it are considered statesmen.

In any case the calculated character assassinations are in vain. There was a fundamental necessity of revolutionary change in Russia because the autocratic Tsarist regime was holding back history and had repeatedly demonstrated that it was not going to surrender power without being made to, and someone had to lead the overthrow. Would a jealous general have been better?

There were those hungry for power in Russia in 1917 whose mantra was 'this far and no further' and it is for those people our eminent historian speaks when he pretends interim leader Kerensky somehow fulfilled the aims of the revolution. He even pretends a parliamentary democracy had been established in order to disingenuously ask, as Lenin's Bolsheviks become ever more popular, 'How many communist takeovers have been based on the apathy of the voters in a democracy? This only reminds us of the duties of the modern western liberal intellectual: preach moderation, pretend the status quo is neutral and do not bite the hand that feeds you.

Figes' *coup de grâce* is his insistence that Russian workers (despite their apathy) didn't want what the Bolsheviks were offering but something else, even though the slogan of 'Bread, Peace and Land' encapsulated in three simple words their central demands. And then he gives the game away; 'To the urban propertied classes...' the actions of the workers, i.e. demands for bread, factory occupations and strikes, '...appeared like a descent into anarchy.' It was not anarchy, it was its very negation: the attempt to impose order on a disordered world, where a tiny minority make all the decisions about war and peace and the rich enjoy caviar while the hungry starve. To reinforce the terrible image of anarchy Figes misuses the word *pogrom* to refer to the expropriation of the landed aristocracy by peasants who had, until only recently, been regarded as chattel.

What does shine through Figes' account is the cowardice and elitism of the Mensheviks, which has come to define left of centre reformist parties everywhere, who even in their heyday only wanted to do things *for* the workers. This mistrust of the working class makes them the bosses' best friend. When they win apparent power they turn to the bourgeoisie and say, 'What is it you want us to do?' Consequently no imperialist adventure, no belt-tightening and no scapegoating is too much for them.

Naturally Figes has plenty to say about the Red Terror, but it was matched and exceeded by the terror of the reactionary Whites, backed up by the invading forces of various imperialist countries. It is perhaps significant that the first British army commander to enter Russia against the revolution was a serving Labour MP.

A People's Tragedy does exactly what it sets out to do. It makes the reader ask whether revolution is ever worth the human cost. Orlando Figes is a professional historian who wrote a century after the Russian Revolution, with all the necessary sources at his disposal. He chose to marshal the 'facts' in such a way as to bolster the prejudices of an already rabidly anti-communist ruling class, and frighten to death any worker-intellectual who happened to come across his book in the absence of anything more honest, such as the writings of

DAVID P RAMSDEN

Arthur Ransome.

FROM OUR OWN CORRESPONDENT

The Truth about Russia – Arthur Ransome in *Six Weeks in Russia*

Arthur Ransome is best known for *Swallows and Amazons*, but he only began writing children's books in his late middle age. In 1917 he was a working journalist in Russia who taught himself the language, wrote copiously on the country, knew Lenin and Trotsky and eventually married Trotsky's secretary. He was an ideologically uncommitted man who nonetheless recognised the democratic spirit of the Russian Revolution. He knew journalistic impartiality was a myth and his dispassionate account is worth a hundred anti-revolution rants from sycophantic hacks. He is the only writer to allow Lenin a total lack of personal ambition, a cheeky sense of humour and an enjoyment of the ridiculous that would have spoiled the distorted persona others writers helped to create. Naturally the British government responded to Ransome's reports with anger and contempt. He was accused of bias, censored by MI5, and threatened with prosecution under the draconian Defence of the Realm Act.

During the First World War, as the culmination of decades of struggle, the Russian opposition was united in its hatred of the brutal and autocratic Tsarist regime. The authorities lost control and the tsar politely walked off the stage of history. The great powers applauded the moderation of this bloodless departure, thinking they could carry on their devastating war, 'having forgotten that they were fighting for democracy.'

Ransome saw selfless people throw themselves into the revolution, knowing that they risked losing everything, while the possessors of a fool's wisdom stood back. He is scathing of Britain's lack of support, sure that they are on the wrong side of democracy and history. He knows the British ruling class act entirely out of self-interest, that through relentless propaganda they poison the minds of ordinary people and he predicts that the toll will be paid in British blood.

Actually there was a great deal of support for the Bolsheviks in Britain and the political class knew they must snuff it out, along with the revolution that inspired it. Ransome wanted people to know what the revolution was and, if it failed, who it was that failed it. He sought to record the development of Russian workers' power, knowing that if workers ceased to be in charge the revolution was finished.

With the Tsar gone attempts were made to establish in a constituent assembly the kind of pseudo-democratic charade our exploiters enjoy the world over, but by the time it met it was already overshadowed by the really democratic Workers' and Soldiers' Soviets. A contest ensued between those who wanted to take the revolution forward and those who wanted to hold it back. Arthur Ransome, a man with no previous political interest, knew he would never be as happy as when he saw Russian workers and peasant soldiers sending to the soviets representatives of their class and not his.

The official interim body was led by Kerensky, a man more imperialistic than the monarch he had replaced. He wanted to continue the war at all cost, while the soviets called for peace. All depended upon the army, which 'took the share in politics it had every right to take.' The generals wanted to continue the war; the people and the soldiers decided otherwise. The anti-war Bolsheviks gradually won a majority in the soviet and Russia eventually withdrew.

Ransome's writing drips with the recognition that history is being made. For a century it has been claimed that the Bolsheviks usurped the revolution and that it was actually a coup. A reading of Ransome puts that notion to bed for ever. He makes it clear that the provisional government gradually lost all credibility through its failure to represent the people. He explains that the soviet system was so feared by the capitalist West precisely because it entailed a level of democracy hitherto unimagined in modern human societies. 'Thus the country is free from the danger of finding itself governed by the ghosts of its dead opinions.'

He credited fake democrats in other countries with failing to understand what was happening when they squealed about the unfairness of excluding the rich from power. They had forgotten that the very object of the social revolution is to put an end to the exploiting class and their lives of parasitic privilege in order that class division can be done away with forever.

Not having the space to cover the whole program of the new soviet government Ransome takes two examples that have exercised the democratic minds of its foreign critics, viz. the dissolution of the constituent assembly and the signing of a separate peace with the central powers that took Russia out of the war.

The dissolution of the constituent assembly is the event that best serves those rulers and their history-writing lackeys who wish to convince their respective masses, despite the evidence of world shattering democracy above, that the Russian revolution was a coup led by men who sought power for its own sake. The truth is that the constituent assembly was never intended as an end in itself, it was a political instrument, not a political aim, a tool not a task. It was thrown away when further use of it would have damaged the purpose for which it was intended. In other words the continuation of the constituent assembly only had the potential to undo the democratic progress that had been made and hand back power to those from whom it had been so insultingly removed. It was made up of men the revolution had overthrown who simply bided their time hoping the public would tire of the soviet and normal relations could resume. The Bolsheviks were confident the population was behind them and the Constituent Assembly was swept aside in the interests of the majority. Not anywhere in Russia did ordinary people protest. The assembly died, like the previous short lived coalition and tsarism itself. Not any one of the three 'showed in the manner of its dying that it retained any right to live'. The only people who protested, and continue to protest, the end of the constituent assembly are fake western democrats and their tame historians.

The day after the October revolution, Lenin proposed a declaration of peace and a promise to do away with secret diplomacy and it was carried by the assembly. For the first time the people would be involved in decisions about war and peace. The next step was the stopping of military operations in the Black Sea and the Baltic. The allies ignored Russia's call for peace and Trotsky appealed to workers in Germany and Austria to force their own governments to stop the war. Eventually, rather than sign up to an unjust peace the Russians said, 'we will not sign peace, but the war is ended.' The Germans replied with, 'we agree to peace, but the war shall continue.'

Whereas the Bolsheviks worked tirelessly until they could achieve a majority by the force of their arguments, their enemies sought outside military assistance to overturn the will of the masses who were expressing themselves through their own organisations. The protectors of democracy sought to overturn real democracy through the force of arms. The western allies supported the anti-Bolshevik factions in Ukraine and Finland, thereby handing land and resources to their German enemies, and proving that even warring imperialists will unite against any progressive force that threatens their combined rule.

In laying the blame for the possible failure of the most progressive revolution in history firmly at the feet of the capitalist allies Ransome asserts that every true man in his youth is the potential builder of a New Jerusalem and that every old man owes it to the youth he once was to recognise the liberating spirit of what is taking place. He is trying to cut through a 'fog of libel' which exists to this day. He says that if the men of the soviet government fail, they fail with clean shields and clean hearts. They have written a page of history 'amid mudslinging from all the mean spirits in their country, yours and my own.'

Ransome was not a party man, but having witnessed first-hand the liberating revolution he was all the more angry that the capitalist powers did their best to destroy it. His writings prove beyond doubt that Lenin did not lead inexorably to Stalin and that to establish his tyranny Stalin had to smash every vestige of the revolution's democratic potential. Today the pseudo-democratic West gloats at the destruction of its ideological enemy, but what they destroyed, largely at the expense of its people, was a caricature.

It is in the interests of all working people to recognise that the Russian revolution did not fail, it was actively destroyed by the kind of people we still allow to rule us. Retrospective ideological support for the Russian revolution does not in any way entail support for the Stalinist counter-revolution or the subsequent horrible and oppressive dictatorship. The revolutionary spirit is encapsulated in a Victor Serge character who is down, but not out. He says to his tormentors, 'Write them that I shit on the bureaucratic counter revolution.' Write them that *I* shit on the system that makes revolution ever more necessary.

IF ONLY THEY KNEW

Prison Diary (Vol. 1) – Jeffrey Archer

Such is the perception of Lord Jeffrey Archer that David McKie, former deputy editor of the *Guardian* and author of *The Rise and Fall of a Victorian Rogue*, says he's the only detrimental thing he knows about Lichfield. In July 2001 Archer, an ex-British sprinter and former Conservative Party Deputy Chairman, was convicted of perjury and sent to Belmarsh high security prison. It is tempting to celebrate his symbolic incarceration, but the diary he keeps to fill the time and preserve his mental health suggests that within the caddish Tory millionaire is a decent man trying to escape.

Archer is at first placed in a dark, dirty cell on the hospital wing, where the days are measured by the banality of bureaucracy and the night is punctuated by hourly floods of fluorescent light and a warder checking if he's in the process of doing away with himself. A walk to the shower block becomes a luxury and the opening of his cell door a kind of freedom.

On transfer to the lifer's wing Archer is advised to be guarded as the tabloids are ready to pay handsomely for stories about him. The *Sun* reports falsely that he has shaken hands with Ronnie Biggs. He can't face the prison food and can't sleep for other prisoners shouting. His autograph becomes a currency and his door card is repeatedly stolen as a souvenir. He is soon condemning right-wingers for their stupidity in locking up seventeen year-old shoplifters with murderers and rapists.

At first the lifers regard him with suspicion, but he soon

earns their confidence and trust, as inmates ask him to help them write letters, read manuscripts and for legal and writing advice. He receives a TV script for his consideration that has been smuggled out of Holloway and into Belmarsh.

His cellmate went through a care home, borstal and a remand home. Sniffing solvents as a child led to drug use and crime to pay for his habit. He has nightmares about being beaten by his stepfather and protecting his mother. Archer acknowledges that people like himself cannot begin to understand what such young men have been through. Selecting provisions from the canteen he realises he now knows the price and value of things. At sixty-one years old he is told he has an attitude problem when he complains about not being allowed to shower before meeting a visitor. When an open prison turns him down because they can't handle the publicity Archer refrains from telling the governor that under the Human Rights Act this is not reasonable grounds for refusal.

For £1 an hour he teaches other prisoners to read and write. For £2 he delivers a lecture to the creative writing class he was last flown first class to Las Vegas and paid $50,000 for. He is annoyed that prisoners get £12 a week in the workshops and only £6.50 for signing up for education. His survey of twenty lifers reveals a split between those who deny the offence and those who admit it happened in a fit of temper they will forever regret. He worries some of the first group might be innocent.

In the exercise yard he's offered any drugs he wants by dealers he considers despicable, though he lacks the courage to say so. A charming black man asks how he can stop being a burglar. Another man hopes he finds Christ. Two young men seek legal advice and become abusive when he can't provide it. He refuses to name them because he doesn't want to read in the paper that he is a grass or requires extra protection at the taxpayer's expense. The *News of the World* reports that he is 'lording it' over other prisoners. The men on his wing know it's untrue: the rest of the prison don't and he's advised to avoid the exercise yard.

While he is away from his cell a convicted murderer makes his bed with clean sheets in return for help writing a letter to his mother. A prisoner asks him to read a self-assessment piece he has written as part of a drug rehabilitation course. In it the man describes being beaten by his stepfather and sexually abused by his uncle, who is on a different block in the same prison for assaulting a minor. Another convicted murderer wants to discuss a paper he is writing on globalisation, another a piece about his life as a football hooligan. He feels for those who have to fill endless hours, but cannot read and write.

In the prison workshop Archer meets a twenty-three year old builder who has been sent to a top security prison full of murderers for stupidly driving his brother's van without a licence. His cellmate is on remand for murder and is pressing him to beat up a witness. Archer hopes those responsible will read his diary and stop doing irreparable damage to decent people's lives.

Another prisoner tells him that previous soft drug users resort to heroin in jail because it can't be detected by mandatory drug tests. They become addicts and are dead within weeks of release because the stuff outside is stronger. He is told that drug rehabilitation provision on the outside is so woefully inadequate that people deliberately get themselves locked up to be put on detox the next day.

Invited to another prisoner's cell Archer finds his shelf full of books on quantum mechanics, and copies of the *Financial Times*. The occupant has had a successful butcher's shop, a successful car dealership and a chain of fourteen pubs. He received a twelve year sentence after taking on the marijuana business of a new partner rather than see it run badly. He absconded on weekend leave from an open prison and did sixteen months in a Spanish jail before being extradited to finish his sentence in Belmarsh. When he gets out he's going to sell agricultural equipment to Senegal.

When the unlucky builder is due for release his cellmate offers him £40,000 to kill one of the witnesses in his trial. Another prisoner on a short sentence for a driving offence tells Archer he's learned a lot about crime and drugs, the third resident of his cell has become hooked on heroin while in jail.

Prison 'Listeners' came into being after a fifteen year old boy hanged himself in his cell. One evening one of the devoted Listeners reads Archer an account of his life so appalling he cannot doubt its veracity. It keeps him awake because he knows people like him on the outside are blind to such hardships, though he is told half the inmates could tell a similar story. Having decided it must be made public to shake politicians out of their denial he is given permission to include it in his diary.

From the age of nine the man was repeatedly gang raped in a children's home by staff, a social worker and a probation officer. At twelve he knew all there was to know about perverted sex and at thirteen he ran away. While sleeping rough he was raped by a man who befriend him and who then rented him out to others for six months. His customers were judges, schoolmasters, police officers and politicians. When he was caught he spent two weeks in a home run by a magistrate, who raped him repeatedly before issuing a court order returning him to the same home. He was transferred to a hospital for disturbed children where he was also abused. He ran away again and the same man who had rented him out installed him in a flat where he was raped up to eight times a day, sometimes with extreme violence. By fifteen he was sniffing glue, getting drunk and having sex with numerous men. This continued for four years, during which he was photographed for porn books and filmed for porn movies. At eighteen he was of no more use and was thrown onto the street.

Eventually he got married and had two children, but after many years of living a lie and going through the motions of sex he decided to tell his wife the truth. She left him in revulsion and he decided to kill his five main abusers. He kidnapped one of them, but he was murdered by other victims in his absence. A man who had been wronged all his life got twenty-two years for a crime he didn't commit. He didn't tell his story in court through shame. As a prison Listener he feels useful for the first time in his life. He has no one on the outside and has decided he will die in prison by his own hand.

Archer is kept awake wondering how normal decent people will react to the story. He doubts the man should be in jail, and he's sure we ought to make sure no one else's life is ruined at nine years old.

As Archer is preparing for his move to another prison he receives a heartfelt letter from a convicted murderer thanking him for bringing life to the prison, for his friendliness, his advice on prisoners' writing and his willingness to help others. He finishes the letter by calling him *Primus inter Pares*. On his last day in Belmarsh he leads a last creative writing class and is subjected for the first time to an unannounced cell and strip search.

Having unburdened himself the badly abused prisoner wrongly imprisoned for murder decides to appeal his conviction and to name his establishment abusers if asked to do so. Archer kept in touch with him and three years later he attempted suicide.

On the twenty-second day of his sentence Jeffrey Archer is taken by secure van to his next home. Among his endnotes are some statistics. In 2000 1,500 prisoners in UK jails attempted suicide, a rise of 50% on 1999. In 2001 seventy-three inmates succeeded in killing themselves, twenty-two of them first time offenders. In June 1990 there were 1,735 British prisoners serving life sentences. By June 2003 this number had risen by 163% to 4,540. Half of all murderers have never committed any other offence and don't commit further crime on release.

Several reviewers have called Jeffrey Archer's *Prison Diary* the best thing he's ever written. The *Daily Mail* called it 'A chilling insight into the stark reality of life in British jails.'

MY FAVOURITE THINGS

Bent politicians and murdering cops
Depressing high streets with dark empty shops
Congested roads and suburban sprawl
A buoyant right-wing and a dog-whistle call
A supplicant press and a witch hunted left
A backscratching mafia and corporate theft
An old school tie pulling the strings
These are a few of my favourite things
Not having access to most of the land
Seeing our future built upon sand
Walking past mansions with too many rooms
Waiting to cross while breathing in fumes
Parcels delivered in six different vans
A dystopian future without any plans
Free market fetish and the chaos it brings
These are a few of my favourite things
Talking to robots and being put on hold
Not asking questions and doing as I'm told
Essential services being sold off
Suited dissemblers their snouts in the trough
Bureaucrats promising targets they miss
Pensioners languishing in their own piss
Kites that don't fly and pigs that have wings
These are a few of my favourite things
Overpaid toffs with massive great motors
Pseudo-democracy hoodwinking voters
Distressed adolescents performing like seals

Crap special offers and two for one deals
Never quite knowing for who the bell rings
These are a few of my favourite things
Mindless air travel and electronic gates
Self-harm, bulimia and suicide rates
Sailing by, self-delusion and stiff upper lips
Pompous pretensions and going down with
                                                    ships
How we sit back and wait till the fat lady sings
These are a few of my favourite things
But how we live in the past and endlessly boast
That's what I like about Britain the most.

ONE BAD APPLE

The Stalker Affair – John Stalker

In common with many European states Northern Ireland has had a paramilitary police force since its foundation in 1922. Since then the Royal Ulster Constabulary (RUC) has faced a sporadic republican insurgency. By 1982 some officers clearly saw themselves as judge and jury. In November a covert police squad killed three unarmed men; Eugene Toman, Sean Burns and Gervaise McKerr. A fortnight later they killed seventeen year old Michael Justin Tighe and seriously wounded nineteen year old Martin McCauley. In December members of the same squad shot and killed two more unarmed men, Seamus Grew and Roddy Carroll. The ensuing media furore forced the RUC to allow an investigation, the aim of which was to show that the force *did not* have a secret, officially sanctioned, Shoot to Kill policy.

The enquiry was led by the Deputy Chief Constable of Greater Manchester, John Stalker. His brief was to reinvestigate the deaths, the conduct of the officers involved, the misleading evidence they had given in the original investigation, the handling of informers and police incursions into the Irish Republic. He was then to determine whether there was sufficient evidence to bring charges. The RUC Chief Constable, Sir John Hermon, saw things differently. He believed Stalker would review the cases and make a few operational recommendations he could ignore. However, the authorities had inadvertently chosen someone unwilling to deliver the traditional whitewash.

At their first meeting Hermon gave Stalker a detailed copy of his (Stalker's) Irish family tree and told him he was now in a jungle. Senior RUC officers were hostile and obstructive and Stalker's team soon realised they could trust no one. Their office was bugged, they were denied files and regarded as traitors. This gang mentality was at odds with Stalker's romantic notion that the police were meant to serve the public. He saw the RUC as policing a democracy, with officers subject to the law. His open-minded attitude received a blow when three officers accused of murder were acquitted by a Diplock judge who congratulated them for bringing the deceased 'to the final court of justice.'

The incomplete files on the six dead men were full of lies: officers had not been properly interviewed, vital evidence had been removed from the scenes and withheld from the CID and no witnesses or family members had been interviewed. Senior RUC officers regarded any involvement of victims' relatives as a coup for republicans. Even junior RUC officers felt free to upbraid Stalker for giving respectability to republicans and their solicitors by speaking to them.

At considerable risk to themselves, unarmed and without security, Stalker and his team painstakingly interviewed relatives and witnesses. Many had never encountered police officers in a passive setting and the team earned some respect, though relatives had no faith that police officers would be brought to justice. Stalker was told several times that he would not be allowed to complete his inquiry.

It became clear that the dead men were the victims of revenge killings by RUC officers. Two died in their car when an officer emptied the magazine of his pistol into them, before reloading and firing again. Three others died when officers riddled their car with bullets. Both vehicles had been followed and were not stopped in road blocks as was claimed. The RUC then deliberately disregarded all basic forensic procedures in order not to discover that they were dealing with targeted assassinations.

Stalker and his team interviewed over three hundred RUC officers and discovered that Special Branch had orchestrated the shootings, fabricated the cover stories and decided what evidence CID officers would have access to. Junior officers had been threatened with the Official Secrets Act and were glad to unburden themselves. One told Stalker's team that a CID officer had said they could interview whoever they wanted, they wouldn't get anywhere because the government wouldn't allow it.

Seventeen year old Michael Justin Tighe had no criminal record and no political affiliations. His parents were bewildered that he had been shot dead by the police. Three years later Stalker's officers were the first to ask them to discuss it. Stalker could not in conscience cover up what he regarded as state murder befitting a Central American assassination squad, carried out by an out of control police force.

After twelve months in Ireland, his investigation nearing completion, Stalker sought an audio tape made when the two youths were shot and discovered that MI5 were involved. The spy agency authorised release of the tape, but Chief Constable Hermon refused. All RUC cooperation ceased and Stalker considered resigning from the investigation. He decided instead to keep making requests and logging the refusals, believing he had the support of MI5 and the Inspector of Constabulary. He also asked Chief Constable Hermon to suspend two officers involved. Hermon flatly refused: there would be no tape, no access to the records of informers and no suspension of officers. Hermon forcefully declined to submit his officers to the type of investigation Stalker was now conducting.

In the absence of the tape and other evidence Stalker had no choice but to submit an interim report, stating that he had been wilfully denied access to evidence he saw as crucial. His final letter to Sir John Hermon said he believed five men had been unlawfully killed, as probably had Tighe.

The interim report of the fourteen month investigation contained six hundred police and witness statements and ran to sixteen volumes. Stalker made an appointment to deliver it to Sir John Hermon, but the Chief Constable didn't turn up and it was received by his deputy. It was Hermon's job to pass it to the Director of Public Prosecutions (DPP) and Stalker was sure Hermon would be told to hand over the tape he needed to complete his investigation. Hermon held onto the report for five months.

On eventually receiving the report the DPP immediately instructed Hermon to grant Stalker full access to all the evidence he needed to bring his investigation to a conclusion. Hermon stalled for a further six weeks before making an appointment to see Stalker in Belfast, again failing to turn up. Stalker and his team demanded the evidence they required, but still left Ireland without the tape they had been requesting for eighteen months.

Stalker was now prepared to tell the Northern Ireland Police Authority he believed very senior RUC officers, including the Chief Constable, had committed offences in respect of the six killings and he intended to formerly interview them. He also told his own Chief Constable, James Anderton, of his intentions. He was immediately told by the Inspector of Constabulary not to return to Northern Ireland to carry out these interviews. He was subsequently telephoned at home and told he was being investigated for a disciplinary offence by the Chief Constable of West Yorkshire,

Colin Sampson, though no specific complaint or allegation had been made. Stalker called Anderton to say he was concerned about his Northern Ireland investigation. Anderton told him to worry only about himself. The next morning Stalker was ordered by Colin Sampson to leave his office and go home. In the absence of an official statement the media made up their own stories.

The informal accusations made against Stalker by Sampson and his small army of investigating officers were contemptible in the extreme. After a three month media shit storm, during which all the authorities rode roughshod over Stalker's life and all protocols, he was reinstated and attempted to resume his job as Deputy Chief Constable of Greater Manchester. His position was then systematically rendered untenable by Anderton and other senior officers and he was eventually forced to resign. *This is conjecture*, but there are substantial hints he was subject to a concerted blackballing campaign by freemasons and that they were instrumental in his removal from the Northern Ireland investigation.

Whatever the mechanism, John Stalker's personal life and career was unceremoniously torpedoed on the basis of spurious suggestions of impropriety concocted entirely to prevent him revealing officially sanctioned murder by British police officers. The authorities simply did not want to hear what he had to say. This caused widespread loss of faith in the fairness of British justice and the belief that police officers were operating under cover without proper oversight.

The Stalker investigation was one of the most serious ever into the conduct of the police. Stalker regarded it as a unique episode in the history of modern policing. His self-acknowledged failure meant the British police had failed a fundamental test. He set out to show that officers are not above the law, but four decades later the evidence suggests otherwise and the arbitrary execution of suspects has spread to the mainland. The police didn't kill Jean Charles de Menezes, Mark Duggan, Yassar Yaqub and Usman Khan because they needed to, they killed them because they could.

The incredible thing is that John Stalker ends up justifying his own destruction on the grounds that it was for the greater good. One thing is certain: no other police officer will ever be so silly as to come to the conclusion that his senior colleagues are guilty of serious crime, unless he is prepared to have his own life destroyed as a consequence. One honest and conscientious policeman is no match for an organised and politically sanctioned state mafia.

THE DEVIL'S MADNESS

War and Peace – Leo Tolstoy

There are without doubt those who love *War and Peace,* for one reason or another, just as there are those who love the *Iliad* and war itself. Others may have embarked on the archetypal literary doorstop because they felt they ought to. Rather more by accident than design I studied Russian writers in translation at university and was compelled, after Pushkin, Gogol, Turgenev and Dostoevsky, to read *Anna Karenina,* a love story, and progressed to hate. In *War and Peace* Tolstoy quotes Sterne, 'We don't love people for the good they do us, but for the good we have done them.' This cannot be true of books: we surely love them for the good they do us, even if they only take us to different places, reinforce our world view or fill the chasm of our inner emptiness.

The superfluous man is a constant in pre-revolutionary Russian literature, but Tolstoy's choice of an engineering metaphor to describe Pierre suggests a familiarity with the practical. 'It was as if the thread of the chief screw which held together his whole life had stripped, so that the screw could not get in or out, but went on turning uselessly in the same place.' Having too much time on his hands leads Pierre to ask the big questions of life, only to be told, 'You'll die and know all or cease asking.' Rather than seek gainful employment Pierre's solution is to find God and join the freemasons, which are certainly options. Another surplus bourgeois might opt for the church, the army or the civil service.

Meanwhile Prince Andrew Bolkonski has social

questions on his mind. It is not always fair to attribute the words of the characters in novels to their creators, but Tolstoy was a member of the nobility and may well have agreed with the prince about the futility, the danger even, of attempting to help the less well-off. He's not just concerned about dispiriting welfare dependency or encouraging the feckless and undeserving poor: he makes a powerful argument that if the less well-off are to have their lives improved, they must want that improvement and fight for it themselves. We are left wondering whether this desire should be expressed individually or collectively and what the latter might mean for princes who make contrived excuses for inequality. Prince Andrew might indeed be better employed in considering matters closer to home, because all is clearly not well between him and Natasha Rostova.

War obscures many a social question and in discussing its causes Tolstoy is text book perfect: numerous incidents that amount to nothing in themselves eventually make war inevitable. His analysis applies as much to the First World War or the wars with Iraq and Afghanistan as it does to the war with Napoleon. All he is short of is the spark of Sarajevo, the Gulf of Tonkin or the excuse of 9/11.

However, our literary giant wanders blindly onto the field of social psychology when he suggests an irrationality that makes millions of men travel vast distances to murder their brothers, as if they just one day got up and decided to do so. Like many of those who fall to facile assertions about testosterone and masculinity, he conveniently forgets that some kind of compulsion is usually involved, be it formal conscription, poverty or general dissatisfaction with life. When men seem to go to war voluntarily they have invariably been fed lies and intrigue on top of lies and intrigue, propaganda and deception. Or they may be bored and believe it will be over by Christmas.

The resort to theories about herd mentality is crass: we are not wildebeest or lemmings, we are self-conscious beings capable of making rational decisions, having been availed of the relevant facts. No worker wants to go abroad to murder other workers unless he has been successfully convinced that his rulers' enemy is guilty of some affront that requires the temporary or permanent sacrifice of his own existence, and *never* is everyone convinced. Regular soldiers simply do as they are told, having signed away their right to an opinion on proceedings.

As I read *War and Peace* the British public were being pumped for their compassionate reserves as the sad remains of gullible young Britons were being uselessly paraded through the streets of Wooton Bassett and across our TV screens. Rather than clapping the dead corpses of our sons and brothers we might consider what Prince Andrew says in *War and peace*, 'The aim of war is murder... and in spite of this the military class is the highest class, respected by everyone. All kings wear military uniforms, and he who kills the most people receives the highest awards. And then they have thanksgiving services for having killed so many people.' The medals are mere trinkets to the ordinary ranks; they are what they always were; cannon fodder, usually in a cause that is not theirs. A lower-class man who might never have been anything is elevated to high office only in death, his name carved on cold stone.

The ruling class warmonger's trump card is Love of Country, what Tolstoy refers to as 'latent patriotism.' This unquestioned orthodoxy is an intellectual absurdity; you can't be born with a natural attachment to a temporal contrivance like a country, any more than you can be born with a religion, such things have to be carefully instilled.

Much work has been done to dispel the great man theory of history, in favour of materialist explanations of individual events and sequences of events, but Tolstoy gives the red card to the great man only to replace him with the will of God, which on the one hand gets us nowhere and on the other sanctions every conquest. If our side wins, God must have wanted our victory. God never disappoints, like governments.

I took *War and Peace* to northern France and read it among the cemeteries. While my partner improved her French with a teenage magazine that asked if a boy and a girl could be just good friends I read about Hélène, the wife of Pierre, and her desire to be rid of him and his endless ruminations on the purpose of existence. 'For fuck's sake Pierre,' She might have said, 'Look for some charity work, patronise some poor people or something.'

War throws up rogues as well as heroes; See Flashman in Afghanistan for that. Tolstoy's major allows a mob to murder a man to get himself off the hook. He then convinces himself he did it for the public good. The public good is a slippery character, at times so very vague and at others so very certain. Blair and Brown backed an illegal war for the public good, but which public? Likewise the attack on civil liberties that accompanies all wars, an early casualty like truth, thereby proving every conflict's questionable character.

National tragedy has a habit of bringing people to their senses. 9/11 made previously perfectly happy people downsize and reassess what was important. Tolstoy has Pierre realise that man is made for happiness and that happiness is within him. He conveniently comes to the conclusion that unhappiness arises not from privation, but from superfluity. Like the rest of us all he needs is some invented purpose, like children, church, charity or career.

In his epilogue Tolstoy expresses his personal opinions on war and the writing of its history. Those accounts that drip with glory and good intent only exist because historians have chosen to set down the beautiful words and sentiments of various generals and politicians and not the brutal reality of events. And so Iraq and Afghanistan, where fake humanitarianism, smart bombs and talk of heroism has only one purpose: to obscure the mindless slaughter of innocents and the wasted lives of young men in the interests of capital.

I think we can safely assume that Tolstoy was not militarism's biggest fan. One wonders if he would agree with Sylvia Pankhurst; 'I could not give my name to aid the slaughter in this war, fought on both sides for grossly material ends, which did not justify the sacrifice of a single mother's son. Clearly I must continue to oppose it, and expose it, to all whom I could reach with voice or pen.'

There are far more graphic descriptions of conflict than Tolstoy's, particularly in semi-fictional accounts of that war to end all wars, written by men who were there. If only we could all be appraised of its destruction, of its debasement, of its gory reality, we might not be so willing to spout macho tabloid jingoism in public houses.

Fearless and 'controversial' war correspondent Robert Fisk, who made it his life's work to scrupulously report on the true consequences of war, rather than parroting the press release and the propaganda fed to the embedded reporter, had some advice for budding journalists; '...you've got to feel passion and, second, you've got to read: Read *War and Peace*. It's an extraordinary book about the reality of war. I remember in Sarajevo being with a Russian soldier who was in the UN force, under fire with him, shells are falling around us, and we're discussing Tolstoy's description of the Battle of Borodino and how it was exactly the same as what we were in now.

You've got to read *Anna Karenina* about lost love and betrayal. You've got to read novels about the First World War, you've got to read World War One poetry. Be fascinated and always carry history books in your pocket.'

LET THOSE WITHOUT SIN

The First Stone – Carsten Jensen

Carsten Jensen dedicates his novel to a twelve year old assassin with a dozen victims under his belt and opens it with a quote; 'Manuel began to realise that to make war successfully you must riddle the living flesh with fragments of steel.' This is Afghanistan, where the bulk of the population endure crippling poverty and endless war, a country through which the US wants to run an oil pipeline.

Our heroes are a platoon of Danish soldiers, some gung-ho and some self-preserving. They drive their armoured personnel carriers (APCs) down the middle of the road like arrogant invaders and work with local death squads. The first kill goes to a bearded naturalist who pisses himself and spews up. His fair-haired victim has a Danish made backpack: previous demeaning epithets no longer fit.

It's an open secret that the Danish commander bribes the local warlord not to fire mortars at their base. Over a meal he tells him they're in his country to bring democracy. The warlord doesn't give a shit about democracy, and he isn't going to give up his private army. The Danish commander's hero is a general who replaced the hatred of war with good business sense. He suggests the warlord's militia is re-categorised as a security firm with the warlord as director. He outsources the war like he outsourced care homes as a city councillor back home. It's as easy as awarding a cladding contract or outsourcing hospital cleaning.

The platoon member who killed the fair-haired Talban

can still see his face and he's given him a name. He can't seek help because that would show weakness, when he joined the army to prove his own worth. Instead he sees the chaplain, whose altar is covered with a Danish flag. Another soldier discusses her dysfunctional family. Another really believes in the stated mission and films everything for posterity. They know nothing about the people they dehumanise with puerile nicknames, though at least one of them has realised he's on the wrong side.

On patrol the minesweeper's footprints are sprayed blue so the rest of them can put their feet in them. Then the man with the spray can is blown half to pieces and his dead finger releases an arc of blue in the air and another on the ground. If the Taliban had decent weapons they knew how to use they'd have killed the lot of them. Instead one is dead, one has had his legs blown off and several others have shit their pants.

At the APC the legless man counts down to his own death. The others pretend they haven't heard him, but they've seen his shattered jaw and spilled out entrails. The commander reports the dead men wounded and a helicopter takes them away. Already dead soldiers have to be carried back to base between their feet on the floor of the APC. It's all been recorded on their body cameras and by the resident obsessive. They call in air support and flatten several compounds. That's how they win hearts and minds.

Maimed Afghans turn up at the clinic on their base with missing limbs and open abdomens. An officer says it means they trust them. But the clinic can't cope and the relatives protest at the inhumanity, to be dispersed with warning shots.

Honest Afghans have no power, so the foreign armies work with thugs and warlords who do. When reporters tell the truth the military swamps it with lies. They don't want to hear they are the best recruiting tool the Taliban ever had, and they don't want people at home to hear it either.

The Danish Commander further corrupts the already corrupt police force by stuffing it full of thugs from the warlord's militia. An Afghan advisor who tells him he's sewing dragon's teeth is mysteriously murdered. The foreign commanders don't want to hear the truth, they want to win an impossible war they should never have started. There is no law but the law of the gun, as foreign forces work with the powerful criminals they have helped to create. A nod or a wink can get someone killed and the Danish commander is complicit.

The chaplain has seen the devil, it is terrorism and it is in Denmark. They're fighting for their country and for their loved ones by killing innocent Afghans. They are killing out of love and love is the best motive for killing. By some topsy-turvy logic terrorism isn't the product of western foreign policy, western foreign policy is a response to terrorism. Lies are truth, truth is lies. To the soldiers this means 'kill them before they kill us; fuck the hearts and minds.'

The soldiers think they are there to win, though they don't know what winning would look like. The Danish Commander knows victory is impossible and has things on his conscience. The Afghan warlord tells him; 'Conscience is just a tenant in your house. If he makes too much noise kick him out.'

When relations break down mortars start falling on the camp, children stop being friendly when they're on patrol. It's slowly falling apart. Then they get trigger happy and start killing anyone. The soldiers think they're at war when they are supposed to be peacekeepers. To ease their frustration they are given the green light to go on the offensive. On a flimsy excuse the Danish commander calls in airstrikes and kills everyone in the warlord's compound, men, women and children. When they enter the compound arms and legs are all around and a pile of dead children are huddled together. The police chief tells the Danish commander his soldiers will pay the price. The Danish commander thinks he's taught them a lesson for turning their backs on him.

The clever soldiers know they've helped to make Afghanistan into the place it is. The people back home fool themselves their sons and brothers are child-friendly peacekeepers, not trained killers who call up massive airstrikes that destroy innocent people. If the ordinary soldier thinks too much he's in trouble. The young ones don't know the difference between real life and computer games. They don't know their own history. They don't know what democracy is and they know nothing about the country they are fighting in.

Only a fifth of the dead are Taliban and civilian casualties rarely appear in official statistics. Many of the airstrikes rained down from drones piloted by spotty youths in Nevada are the result of warlords denouncing their rivals. American mercenaries, euphemistically referred to as contractors, also work with thugs and warlords. They are an extension of the lack of conscience at the heart of the whole enterprise. As part of a perfectly logical continuum they are respectable international companies whose shares are traded on the stock exchange. They do things that are illegal even under the dubious rules of a very dirty war. They are a private army in a privatised war, many of them psychopaths answerable to no one. They are no less ruthless than the Taliban and the warlords, but their brutality is sanctioned by a superpower keen to keep unpalatable truths from its citizens. They have different rules of engagement. They do what the fuck they want. They don't give a toss for the liberal bullshit about Afghan girls going to school. They think they are doing what Washington would do if it had the guts. Their casualties don't show up in statistics and neither do their victims.

The US drone pilots see poor people with no shoes and they leave them with no legs. The foreign armies supply plundering militias with arms and money if they promise to kill Taliban. Young Americans revel in killing, as limbs are torn off and flung in the air and abdomens spill entrails on the ground. US Special Forces cut their bullets out of women and children and blame the deaths on the Taliban, who they say have a tradition of mutilating their victims.

The words good and evil have no meaning. The invaders are fighting for pipelines and markets dressed up as democracy. The Afghans are fighting for community, land and peace. The official foreign forces curse inconvenient rules of engagement that prohibit firing on women and children. Afghans are accused of using human shields, but mixed groups are simply safer. The foreigners call it human shields, the Afghans call it family.

Tens of thousands of contract mercenaries have the same equipment as the army, including helicopters. Torture is routine. Drones are piloted by contract drone operators, who attack invisibly from three kilometres up. The victims don't know what's hit them. It's a high tech war, but only one side has the tech. Like all imperialist wars one side has overwhelming military superiority. The foreigners don't play fair. If the other side looks equal the foot soldiers call in airstrikes and blow the opposition to scattered limbs, men women and children. They use white phosphorous shells that set everything and everybody on fire.

The Afghans are in the wrong tribe, they live in the wrong place and the follow the wrong god. The invaders fucked up Afghanistan and they demeaned and fucked up themselves. There's only one consolation, the west's faith in its supremacy turned out to be a fantasy. This book is a novel. It couldn't possibly be true. If it was true the good folk of the democratic west would never re-elect the people who made it happen.

FROM RUSSIA WITH LOVE

Lady Death: The Memoirs of Stalin's Sniper
– Lyudmila Pavlichenko

I bought *Lady Death: Memoirs of Stalin's Sniper* in a publisher's remainder shop. The Greenhill imprint is one of a series on snipers. One has to ask what kind of a world it is in which such a genre even exits, though the forward celebrates 'sniper literature' as an endeavour worthy of recognition. During WWII Lyudmila Pavlichenko achieved 309 'official' kills and probably 500 in total, and is credited in the introduction with a natural hunting instinct that is allegedly rare in women.

She was wounded four times and toured the US and the UK raising money for the Russian war effort only weeks after her soldier husband had been killed. Pegler says in his introduction that no one has looked at combat stress in women, so we don't know how she felt. After the war she never remarried, became a military historian, suffered long term-effects of head wounds and fought a lifelong battle with alcohol. She died aged 58 in 1974.

Pavlichenko was the daughter of a multi-lingual teacher and a Ukrainian factory worker who fought with the Red Army in the post-revolutionary civil war and. She was encouraged to read the Russian literary classics, but was more interested in military history. While at school she had an illegitimate child and at sixteen began work in the local arms factory, qualifying in 1933 as a metal turner, describing the work she did with passion. After a short flirtation with gliding she joined the factory's shooting club and the civil defence unit, becoming a markswoman. After training as an engineering draughtswoman she was helped by the Young Communist League to secure a place at Kiev University to study history, Latin and English. She was interested in world affairs, particularly the resistance to fascism in Spain. While there she attended a school for snipers, which was really full military training.

As the German army advanced across Europe in 1940-41 Lyudmila Pavlichenko was combining study with work as a researcher. On the day the German army invaded the Soviet Union she was in Odessa and left a performance of Verdi's *La Traviata* after the first act to look at the Soviet fleet in the harbour. The Soviet republic had treated her well. She considered it a workers' state worth defending and enlisted in what became the Great War for the Fatherland, seeing the German advance as an attempt to wipe out her people. There was a shortage of weapons and she had to take a rifle from a fallen comrade to obtain her first kills.

The Russians were driven back for miles before making a stand at Odessa. After being wounded and hospitalised, Pavlichenko was promoted to corporal as her tally continued to mount. She details how a sniper operates, the aim being to give the enemy no peace, deprive him of the opportunity to move safely in his own lines and to demoralise him. She refers to all her victims as 'fascists', describes the ranks of men incinerated by Russian Katyuska rockets and comes across women who have been treated as the spoils of war. One rape victim urges her to 'kill them all' and it is these words that give her comfort when after the war she is described as a coldblooded killer.

Pavlinchenko was wounded twice more at Odessa, promoted to sergeant and awarded an inscribed sniper's rifle. In October 1941 the city was abandoned: 50,000 Russian personnel were withdrawn and taken by sea to Sevastopol in the Crimea. When she returned to her regiment after recovering from a head wound, casualties had reduced it from 3,000 to 700 men and she was the victim of unwanted advances by officers abusing their power.

After adjusting to the forests of Crimea Pavlichenko led sniping patrols against the German invaders and vowed to avenge the deaths of whole families. Like all soldiers she speaks of the bond between those who have endured combat. As part of an entrenched army she endured filth and lice. While in snipers' hides in no-man's land she was subject to wasps, ants and mosquitoes. Sometimes she went into the forest alone and shot a passing enemy motorcyclist. In August 1941 she told her sister she intended to personally kill 1,000 Nazis and made a rule; 'No day without a dead enemy.'

In a German assault that was only repelled at the cost of 23,000 Russian casualties Pavlichenko was badly wounded and nursed back to health by Lieutenant Alexei Kitzenko. She prided herself on being an unsentimental person but was touched by Kitzenko's attention and they were married at the front in December 1941.

In early 1942 she was detailed to take out a dangerous German sniper with 215 kills and shot him between the eyes. Afterward, in direct opposition to the low profile code of snipers, she was interviewed and photographed for a morale-boosting front-line newspaper. This was followed by the attentions of numerous other journalists and filmmakers, who forced her to pose as if she was about to fire at the enemy. They then fabricated stories about her 'duel' with the German sniper.

Having become a celebrity Lyudmila Pavlichenko was withdrawn from the front line and sent on a propaganda tour. In February 1942, along with a female machine gunner, she took part in a conference with other Russian heroines, military and civilian, steadfast in the faith that they would eventually repel the Nazi invaders.

Back in the Crimea Pavlichenko was chosen for special operations. When her husband was killed in an artillery barrage she swore revenge and ordered her snipers to aim for the stomachs of enemy soldiers, that they might die slow agonising deaths that would demoralise their comrades. In June 1942 she was badly wounded in a shell blast and evacuated. It was her last day of war. As Sevastopol fell she was promoted to junior lieutenant, given the order of Lenin, sent to a sniper training battalion in Moscow and began speaking at morale boosting meetings. She rebuffed the advances of her mentor, preferring to spend spare time on her own rereading *War and Peace*; she wrote leaflets for the troops and was fictionalised in newspapers and propaganda pamphlets.

In August 1942, at President Roosevelt's invitation, Pavlichenko was chosen with two others to speak in Washington and met Stalin beforehand, referring to him as 'The leader of the world proletariat.' She had great faith in the Soviet system and speaks of the aim of creating socialism in one country. They arrived in Washington to the waiting press and were taken by limousine to the White House to be welcomed by Eleanor Roosevelt. The first lady doubted that another woman could see the face of a man in her telescopic sight and kill him. She was reminded that the US had not seen its territory invaded and its people butchered. Many of the press questions were directed at Pavlichenko as the only woman in the delegation, most of them about her appearance. Press reports ranged from doubts that she was actually a soldier to accusations that she was a cold-blooded killer. There was further humiliation in the collections that were taken wherever they spoke, as if Russia was reliant on the charity of rich Americans. The president asked about the fighting, but did not promise active assistance or the opening of a second front to draw the Germans away from Russia.

In Britain the press were more respectful and the delegates spoke at Birkbeck College and Cambridge University, visited various military facilities and met the 'Red Dean' of Canterbury Cathedral, who had supported the Russian Revolution, but still patronised her with talk of motherhood and the proper role of women. Churchill left Pavlichenko to his wife and spoke to the male delegates. They went on to visit Cardiff, Brighton, Newcastle, Liverpool and Coventry. It was while in the UK that the delegation heard that General Paulus's army had been surrounded at Stalingrad, a defeat from which the Germans would not recover.

In her comprehensive report Pavlichenko made particular reference to the racism and destitution in the US, being surprised in particular at segregation. Her request to return to the front was denied and she was sent to train snipers at a new school, a job she retained until May 1944. When Kiev University was reopened she resumed her history degree. Afterward she was a navy research assistant until her war wounds forced her to retire in 1953. She then worked for the organisation of Soviet War Veterans, visiting schools colleges and military bases, and helped in the development of a new Soviet sniper's rifle. She always held that being a sniper was more than a profession, it was a way of life. What was important was a hatred of the enemy. Like most soldiers she lived the two years she spent on the front line for the rest of her life. The book closes with her laying a wreath at the Fraternal Cemetery in Sevastopol for those who fell in its defence. Including her husband of only a few months. She never exhibits the slightest regret or sympathy for the 309 officers and men she killed in cold blood.

COWBOYS AND INDIANS

A Cloud Over Bhopal – Alfred de Grazia

In 1984 Bhopal in India was home to a million people with one of the lowest per capita incomes in the country. At around midnight on the third of December a cloud of highly poisonous methyl-isocyanate gas began to escape from the sixty acre Union Carbide chemical plant to the north of the city. An unusually cool night kept the cloud low and a breeze blew it directly over the congested slums. People emerged from their homes gasping for breath. The 'uncontrolled emission' lasted for two hours until the tank was exhausted. Those who were able to ran five kilometres in three quarters of an hour, leaving those who couldn't to die in agony. The plant's operators were unprepared and did nothing. The advice to stay indoors meant nothing to people who lived in simple huts.

Initial estimates were of 3,000 dead, 30,000 seriously disabled and 180,000 suffering the long-term effects of a virulent mutagen, teratogen and carcinogen. Union Carbide's Connecticut HQ went into damage limitation mode, suggesting that methyl-isocyanate wasn't much worse than riot gas. Two years earlier a local journalist had warned of a potential disaster, drawing particular attention to the corrosive symbiosis between Union Carbide officials, ministers and civil servants. Indian Union Carbide officials were arrested, the plant was seized, the company's license to operate was revoked and it was promised the plant would never reopen. People began to demonstrate for financial assistance. The protests were condemned as premature.

As hospitals struggled to cope 853 doctors and a thousand volunteer orderlies improvised treatment for eyes that seemed to have been rubbed with hot chillies and people choking to death. Respirators, oxygen and lung suction machines were scarce. There was no antidote for methyl-isocyanate poisoning and Union Carbide were unprepared for a single case, let alone a quarter of a million. Patients suffered decomposing, fluid filled lungs, inflamed bronchial tubes, glazed eyes, and gastrointestinal upheaval. Damage to the central nervous system led to eventual coma. People were still dying months later. Medicines were dispensed but no one said; 'See here, you have a mass [mental] trauma as bad as those of the Nazi camps and Hiroshima. This requires as many doctors and clinicians as the physical trauma.' This was India after all, not New York.

An American specialist invited by the people's movement noted breathlessness, conjunctivitis, and general weakness, loss of taste and smell, abdominal swelling, lack of physical coordination, the disruption of menstruation, spontaneous abortion, liver damage and internal bleeding. He thought birth defects might last for ten years. The Indian authorities failed to properly test people, record their symptoms or count the dead. A newspaper wondered if Union Carbide might escape its responsibility for poisoning only Indians, noting that US servicemen had been compensated for exposure to Agent Orange, whereas the far more numerous Vietnamese on whom it had been liberally dropped had not.

While the US media assured Americans that such a thing could never happen at its plant in West Virginia, Union Carbide and government secrecy meant it was left to campaigning journalists to push for medical help and compensation. There were attempts to find scapegoats, among them illegal squatters near the plant. Most of the dead were poor and illiterate. Alfred de Grazia says;

'The very poor, already inured to insult and injury, grieve more sincerely than many of the rich for the loss of their loved ones. They have little in life besides their loved ones – a few clothes, several pots, a goat, and sticks of furniture in a room that they can hopefully regard as their very own. They have no job guarantee, no welfare system to speak of save family and friends; ... The ill must now live on, partially blinded, with coughs and weakness of the limbs, musing upon the dead. Even the workers of Union Carbide... will become the instant poor, living on next to nothing and flooding into the crowded slums.'

Such people could not afford to petition the Indian courts and American lawyers descended on the city, some asking for 30% of any pay-out. The legal precedent was set in the British House of Lords in 1868; '...a person who, for his own purposes brings onto his own land and collects and keeps there anything likely to do mischief if it escapes, ...is *prima facie* answerable for all the damage which is the material consequence of its escape.' Only the source of the poison needed to be proved; the American company's major shareholding in the Indian operation meant it was responsible.

Union Carbide's initial report focussed on technical negligence and hinted at sabotage, though its investigators had not visited the site. Water had entered the tank of Methyl-Isocyanate, causing what was effectively a prolonged explosion. No one in India or the US admitted being aware of the chemical's lethal potential and there were suggestions that the company had double standards regarding safety. Indian law did not prohibit the siting of chemical plants near populated areas, but the tanks concerned were too big and too full and there was no empty tank available in case of an emergency. There was no culture of ongoing training and maintenance schedules were lax. Union Carbide USA said 'compliance with safety features is a local issue, the plant should not have been operating without procedures being followed.'

Alfred de Grazia praises Union Carbide for not resorting to colonial and racist distinctions when considering compensation. It was not Americans who objected to possibly generous payments, they were used to such things. Wealthy Indians said the poor had never really had anything and wouldn't know what to do with a windfall. The author refers to what he calls a 'holocaust syndrome', in which the details are belittled: 'It can't have been that bad.' 'We are dealing with the poor, aren't we really? ...after all there are so many of them.' The lost breadwinners included old men who rolled cigars in their own huts, young girls who minded animals and mothers who laboured on building sites. They were all part of a community no less worthy than those in any other country.

De Grazia calculated that $1.3 billion would be necessary to adequately compensate the victims. This would almost certainly have bankrupted the global multinational, who paid its workers at Bhopal about a tenth of their US counterparts for handling very dangerous chemicals.

'Chemistry... is inextricably bound up with every major problem pressing upon mankind, except the problem of justice and human rights, that is, the proper governance of the world.' It is certainly bound up with war: think only of Agent Orange. 'The viper that both rich and poor states nourish at their very bosoms is the armaments industry. This too is a creature of chemistry... The armaments industry is extremely hazardous, largely multinational, riddled with corruption, enveloped in secrecy through most of its operations from conception to use, [its] public relations managers are the governments

191

themselves, causing in fact an infinity of fatal accidents, capable of blowing mankind and his works and life itself off the face of the earth.'

'It is well for all who are concerned about the peaceful uses of chemistry to bear this in mind. Armaments are the king of hazards, the breaker of poor backs, the exploiter of human recklessness, the pamperer of degraded officialdom, the privileged dealer in hazardous chemicals down to the last bullet.'

'With this clarification of issues and priorities, our attention can return to the problems of the multinational corporation. Every corporation entering from a rich country into a poor country smacks of imperialism and colonialism...'

In 2004 Amnesty International estimated that 7,000 Bhopal residents were killed immediately and that 15,000 more died in the following year. Twenty years later thirty people a month were dying from attributable causes. Hundreds of thousands were chronically damaged. Adequate compensation has never been paid. The derelict Bhopal plant leaked its lethal chemicals into the groundwater and produced a new generation of victims, with highly dangerous substances finding their way even into mothers' milk. When Dow Chemicals took over Union Carbide in 2001 it brought an end to further claims. In 2012 WikiLeaks revealed the company had employed an intelligence organisation to spy on activists and campaigners.

The main question after the Bhopal tragedy was of how much a life is worth. The calculations spoke volumes about global disparity. Here are some examples from history

Korean War 1950-53; 33,686 US deaths and five million Korean deaths

Vietnam War 1956-75; 58,316 US deaths and two million Vietnamese deaths

Afghanistan since the 2001 US invasion; 2,372 US deaths and 157,000, Afghan deaths

Iraq War 2004-2009, 4,424 US deaths and 109,032 Iraqi deaths

These ratios reveal an American life to be worth those of seventy-three foreigners. If the victims of Bhopal had been compensated even on this basis they would have done much better than many of the other victims of American misadventure.

A QUESTION OF PRIORITIES

Diaries - Alan Clark

A selective reading of Alan Clark's diaries might give the impression that the incredibly wealthy right-wing Tory was not without humanity. We can all smile at the self-confessed eccentric who describes climbing a Scottish hill in a suit because it was there, all the while keeping pace with a more suitably dressed and serious walker. Clark is an avid walker and hill climber, who sometimes walks for ten hours and covers twenty-five miles, something that is well beyond most of us. He might have written a walking book and kept his dubious politics to himself, like Alfred Wainwright. But unlike the modest Wainwright, Clark is vain and this is a diary, to which all is revealed.

Our subject says he lives a measured life that allows for spontaneity. This image of an existence to which many can only aspire makes us slightly less sympathetic to his complaints about the inconvenience caused to his personal life by the late night meetings involved in being a member of parliament and Secretary of State for Trade. If they consider an inconvenience what should be considered a privilege we might ask why they do it. Is it a power trip, a means to feel important, the desire to have a purpose? A government minister has a far better life than an international truck driver, receives far greater remuneration and benefits and doesn't have to piss in laybys and eat heart attack inducing food. He usually only does it for a few years and is almost guaranteed, if he wants to, to walk into the boardroom of some weapons or pharmaceutical company from whom he has earned favours at the expense of the public.

Nor would Alan Clark be the first MP to use his employment at the public expense as a stepping stone to lucrative work on the after-dinner speaking circuit, especially if he has more stories like the one he got from another MP. The representative in question took part in a debate at a posh girl's school with Second World War flying ace Douglas Bader. Bader says;

'...And my engine was on fire, I had two of the fuckers on my tail, one fucker was coming up from the left, and there were two more fuckers about a hundred feet above me waiting for...' (At this point the headmistress panicked and interrupted), 'Girls, as of course you all know, there was a type of German aeroplane called the FOKKER.' Bader says; 'I don't know about that. All I can tell you is that these chaps were flying Messerschmitts.'

Some of the biggest bastards in this fucked-up world happen also to be animal lovers and Alan Clark is among them. Being able to show a sympathy for dumb creatures his very existence denies to human beings he was convinced by campaigners to oppose the worst excesses of the fur trade. I am not aware that badger pelts are particularly popular among those with less affinity for the other beings with which we share our spinning globe, but it is difficult not to be touched by Clark's reference to a dying badger, which, while trying to extricate itself from a mediaeval leg-hold trap, excavated a sixteen foot circle in the ground.

Like all of them Clark is, when it suits him, the guardian of all things British. In 1988 he made a prediction about our precious, but essentailly mongrel language, which in retrospect serves to show just how wrong you can be.

'In thirty years' time, although English will be the

lingua franca, Japan's dominance will mean that English will be no more than the language of the global peasantry. The tongue – *and the calligraphy* - of the Elite will be Japanese.' Given the dominance of the Japanese economy today [i.e. *then*], and the fact that the Americans deliberately made Japan into an industrialised country as a bulwark against Communist China, there may be some irony attached to this prediction. If the Japanese are responsible for the decline of British industry, which many of my older motorcycling friends regularly assert that they are, then it was our best friends the Americans, with whom we have a special relationship, who lit the fire. Others might say that the crap management of British industry was responsible for its demise, but that would be tantamount to saying they should have worked their employees harder. Some might point out that if Japanese products flooded the British market then some greedy, selfish and short-sighted British capitalist must have been importing them, perhaps one of those who considers himself a country dweller or landowner and has a 'Keep Britain Farming' sticker in the back window of his Japanese four by four.

It doesn't actually matter where stuff is made: managed global production makes infinite sense, though this has got nothing to do with the get-rich-quick schemes of unscrupulous 'entrepreneurs' prepared to exploit global disparities in trade union membership, employment law and rates of pay, quite often while waving the union jack.

Having had a go at foreigners, Clark is perceptively disparaging of the Liberals and their opportunist attempts to win elections;

'Their trick is to degrade the whole standard of political debate. The nation, wide policy issues, the sweep of history – forget it. They can't even manage to discuss broad economic questions, as they don't understand the problems – never mind the answers.

The Liberal technique is to force people to lower their sights, teeny little provincial problems about bus timetables, and street lighting, and the grant for the new community hall. They compensate by giving the electorate uplift with constant plugging of an identity concept – no matter how minuscule – to which they can attach a confrontational flavour: "Newton Ferrers Mums outface Whitehall."'

Funnily enough this is exactly how the Liberals operate where I live: the bread and butter of council and parliamentary candidates and their ever-loyal underlings is bus shelters, bins, unsightly derelict sites and 'bobbies on the beat'.

Lest the wit and political analysis of Clark should tempt anyone lower down the social scale to become an admirer, there are plenty of entries that identify him as a committed representative of his class and an inveterate enemy of those who work for a living. In a passage about Thatcher's fundamentally unfair Poll Tax he says no one will pay, and;

'By "no one" I mean all the slobs, yobs, drifters, junkies, free-loaders, claimants and criminals on day-release, who make their living by exploitation of the benefit system and overload local authority expenditure.'

Typical in his arrogant upper class failure to recognise and acknowledge spontaneous collective expressions of working class discontent, Clark instead caricatures ordinary people as unthinking drones occasionally tempted into misguided action by demagogues and rabble-rousers;

'Last night there were riots in Central London - just like in 1981. All the anarchist scum, class-war, random dropouts and trouble-seekers had infiltrated the march and started beating up the police.'

Anarchists *were* central in their opposition to the poll tax precisely because they don't believe in government and the poll tax confirmed just how patently unfair and cruel government could be. Otherwise the massive grass roots movement against the poll tax, which signalled the beginning of the end for the most divisive and class prejudiced prime minister ever, involved thousands of well-organised socialists who, far from being drop outs and claimants, tended to be lecturers, teachers and social workers. In any case, the biggest anti-Poll Tax protest on 31st March 1990, turned into a riot because peaceful demonstrators were attacked *by* the police.

Fascism is the ultimate destroyer of working class solidarity and Clark, by his own admission, is an admirer of the fascist National Front. Reading between the lines one suspects he was also an unofficial fan of that famous animal lover Adolf Hitler. After Clark has killed a heron for doing what comes naturally and taking fish from the moat of his stately home he says;

'I cursed and blubbed in my bedroom...I was near a nervous breakdown. Yet if it had been a burglar or a vandal I wouldn't have given a toss. It's human beings that are vermin'. Enough said.

BEING BOSWELL
Boswell's *London Journal*

I bought my reassuringly fake-leather bound copy of James Boswell's *London Journal 1762-1763* in a charity shop. As it is explicit to the point of being incriminating, I can only imagine it was edited and complied after his passing by another, who sought to expose to the greedy public the whole man, rather than preserve what was left of his dignity. It is difficult to imagine the following being read out in the writer's presence during a popular tea-time show on the BBC Light Program;

'I picked up a girl in the Strand; went into a court with the intention to enjoy her in armour. [That is making use of a prophylactic sheath] But she had none. I toyed with her. She wondered at my size, and said if I ever took a girl's maidenhead, I would make her squeak. I gave her a shilling, and had command of myself enough to go without touching her. I afterwards trembled at the danger I had escaped. I resolved to wait cheerfully till I got some safe girl or was liked by some woman of fashion.'

This excerpt is typical of Boswell's candidness, but between visits to prostitutes he and his associates speculate on the relative happiness of rich and poor, perhaps betraying the comforting prejudices of the privileged in a hierarchical society ordained by the almighty, where cultural pursuits are distributed accordingly.

'Lord Eglington said that a savage had as much pleasure in eating his rude meals and hearing the rough notes of the bagpipe as a man in polished society had in the most elegant entertainment and in hearing fine music. Mr. Milne very justly observed that to judge of their happiness we must have the decision of a being superior to them both, who should feel the pleasure of each; and in that case it would be found that although each had his taste full gratified, yet the civilised man, having his taste more refined and susceptible of higher enjoyment, must be acknowledged to have the superior happiness.'

There is a hint here that the bagpipes were not always held in such high regard as the essential accompaniment to a noble highland tradition, but more importantly Boswell's friend seems to reject the opinion that money does not equal happiness, the axiom being so obviously aimed at those who have little of it, that they be satisfied with their allocation. Mr Milne may also regard those who seek social amelioration as engaging in the politics of envy, inspired only by base motives. But Boswell is young and idealistic. He speaks for the enjoyment of things in common and upbraids Lady Betty for harbouring a sentiment which the affluent would love to believe were true;

'...it must be very cutting to find so many people higher than one's self and to see so many splendid equipages, none of which belong to one.'

This is the distilled essence of a rampant and unsustainable consumer society Boswell could not imagine, but he tells the noble lady that her taste is too gross, and that 'a person of small fortune who has only the common views of life... can have the most lively enjoyment from the sight of external objects without regard to property at all.'

The privileged, relative or otherwise, need us to be jealous of their grandiose and pretentious possessions: if we are not jealous there is no point in their ostentatious accumulation. The Philip Greens of this world so much want us to be jealous that they have convinced themselves that we are. Though in November 2020 he told a reporter, in his own vulgar way, that it was the media who made us all jealous of his shallow, sad and alienated existence.

Two and a half centuries after Boswell wrote, an obscene and dehumanising philosophy has taken such a hold that we are hoodwinked into believing our consumer choices constitute a kind of democracy. In fact endless acquisitionism is a debilitating straightjacket that prevents us ever being personally satisfied. A decent society would encourage mutual and collective satisfaction, with property and facilities held in common ownership for all to enjoy, but our current masters have no concept of things *but* that they are jealously held in their own grasping hands. We are not envious of the gated prisons they have created for themselves, but they are envious of us for the natural human solidarity they have so far failed to knock out of us.

Despite the tacit expressions of proto-socialism Boswell is full of the arrogant self-importance of a member of the social elite and his entries represent the sometimes unprincipled priorities of a young man. Nevertheless he considers himself perfectly moral. Any doubts he has about his own conduct he discusses with his diary. In doing so he reveals a conceit common to all diarists and consciously writes for posterity, noting as he proceeds the merits of what he has written.

In due course Boswell is confirmed to have contracted gonorrhoea and expects to be laid up for between four weeks and four months. Once over his dose he tells us that since recovering he has been with three prostitutes. He sets down in his journal every detail of his nocturnal pursuits: two prostitutes in one night, two at once. And he lies about his name and profession. The next day he goes solemnly to church or talks with his friends about philosophy.

Boswell's is an entertaining and enlightening diary, and I spent an hour investigating his other literary offerings, of which there are many. I also learned that Boswell contracted gonorrhoea seventeen times and liked to copulate after watching public hangings. Ideal material for a judge or conservative politician, neither of which he became. The London diary ends as Boswell sets off for a tour of the Hebrides with his benefactor, to whom he becomes increasingly sycophantic. Among other things Dr Johnson convinces him that the truth of Christianity is irrefutable.

The historian Macauley said that without Boswell we would not have Dr Johnson. He also said that Boswell was a weak and conceited fop and a bore who talked too much, could not reason and had no wit, no humour and no eloquence, and yet would be read as long as English exists, either as a living or dead language.

A WORM IN THE BODY POLITIC

The 100% Patriot – Upton Sinclair

In February 2021 the *New Statesman* said Sir Keir Starmer, having rescued the Labour Party from the clutches of progressives, needed a big idea to campaign on. It was already obvious, though the working class had clearly suffered unduly from the pandemic, that he had chosen Dr Johnson's last bastion.

A century ago Upton Sinclair wrote, '... who but a pervert would listen to sob stories... now here was the religion Peter wanted... he would no longer do [things] in the name of Peter Gudge... he would do them in the sacred name of patriotism... And... the big businessmen... would go right on paying him fifty dollars a week... while he served the holy cause... As for the Reds... he would... put them in a ship of stone with sails of lead, and send them forth with hell for their destruction.' A concurrent report on the military governments of Myanmar says, 'The arrangement suited the liberal professional class well... These better off types saw no contradiction in an apparently democratic system that kept the majority in poverty.'

The man whose bust Sir Keir might have on his desk, as well as enthusiastically continuing Thatcher's destructive policies, took us into an illegal and unwinnable war, made the world a considerably more dangerous place, cost the lives of numerous young Britons and set in reverse decades of multicultural understanding. 'If I tell you we'd made it understood that every congressman who voted this country into war would be sent to the front trenches, our country would still be at peace,' says one of Sinclair's characters, 'but it ain't the congressmen, it's people higher up than them.'

Naturally people resisted imperialist war, in 1914 as in 2003. So the state and its agents deliberately made out that trade unionists, socialists, anarchists, pacifists and terrorists were all the same thing. Not only is everyone on the left a potential terrorist, they are all in the pay of foreign powers, and the press are only too willing to incite the public against them.

Unlike today half the cops are crooked and the other half are too stupid to be crooked (Ex-Metropolitan Police Commissioner Sir Ian Blair famously said the split went three ways). They can get away with handing over those who demand peace and fairness to upstanding young members of the local Chamber of Trade, who take them to a wood and whip them unconscious, lynching a man who fights back. It is observed that workers and bosses have the whip in common, they are just at opposite ends of it; 'And thus to all eternity was symbolised the truth about the relationship of the classes.' The papers report that the Reds had got no more than they deserved, being, as they obviously were, on the side of the enemy.

Sinclair's protagonist, a snivelling little police spy called Peter Gudge, is paid to infiltrate left organisations and entrap them and their benefactors. One rich sponsor says she can't see how anyone who considered the injustices of the day could fail to be a Red; 'It's because of this hideous war', she said. 'We've gone to war to make the world safe for democracy, and meantime we have to sacrifice every bit of democracy at home. They tell you that you must hold your peace while they murder one another, but they may try all they please, they'll never be able to silence me. I know the allies are just as much to blame as the Germans. I know that this is a war of profiteers and bankers, they may take my sons and force them into the army, but they cannot take my convictions and force them into the army. I am a pacifist and an internationalist – I want to see the workers arise and turn out of office these capitalist governments, and put an end to this hideous slaughter of human beings. I intend to go on saying that so long as I live.'

The infiltrator turns *agent provocateur* and encourages the radicals to risk a ten year jail sentence for urging young men to resist military service. He also endures some of their indignities and considers changing sides. Only the handsome rewards he receives for his treachery make him see sense.

Meanwhile in Russia the people overthrow the government and spoil the imperialists' war. 'Bolshevik' becomes a term of fear and abuse. But radicals take the insult as a compliment and adopt the name for themselves. Theorists demolish the notion that Britain is engaged in a war for democracy, citing imperialist bloodlust in Ireland, Egypt and India as examples.

In the Land of the Free the cops intercept the mail, force the post office to refuse to deliver radical newspapers and tamper with the vehicles of activists. They farm the worst brutality out to paid agents of the employers, the war having given them the opportunity to destroy militants they have hated for years. All they have to do is raise the spectre of pro-Germans and a lynch mob will gather to smash up radical presses and beat up socialists and trade unionists. They are aided by the mainstream press, who spread stories that the socialist program means terrorism and murder.

Even saying the bosses are profiteering from the war is proscribed. The courts are filled with people charged with espionage, clergymen who preach peace, labour leaders who try to organise strikes, members of the anti-conscription league, draft dodgers, slackers, anarchists, communists, Quakers, Wobblies, socialists and anyone else who speaks against war and the mindless patriotic fervour that accompanies it.

From the pulpit patriotic priests denounce Bolshevism and demand its suppression. There are even among the thugs patriotic servants of the Prince of Peace. Conscientious objectors are simply locked up.

In court the *agent provocateur* slanders good men for money, accusing them of doing things they never did or ever thought of doing, things that are against their very principles, justifying it all on the grounds that his country's internal enemies must be silenced while there's a war to be fought.

The papers put side by side the heroic deeds of the brave boys abroad and the entirely fabricated bomb plots of the traitors at home. The public can't be trusted so juries are rigged. The district attorney schools the *agent provocateur's* handlers in how to make his story more convincing. Sixteen completely innocent advocates for peace and fairness get sixteen years apiece. As reward Peter Gudge is promoted and allowed to take part in the raids on activists' premises and the burning of their books.

When the war ends the repression continues. But returning soldiers can't fail to notice that while they've been away making the world safe for democracy America has been made safe for profiteers. To draw attention to this and other injustices is Bolshevism; it is especially dangerous when said by people who learned how to use guns while fighting for their country. The paranoid authorities become afraid of the people they'd only recently called heroes; the ones they can't enlist into smashing strikes and acting as scabs are persecuted and ruined.

Peter Gudge is a simple man who has been tricked several times, but eventually he finds a wife who despises the poor, especially for their failure to know their place and their presumption to criticise their betters. Whereas Peter is just a stupid redbaiter she is clever, able to spy on rich men who sponsor radical causes and get society ladies to fund anti-red activities.

Ex-soldiers are urged to attack IWW meeting halls and the papers report that the Wobblies have fired on a peaceful veteran's parade. They raid every radical meeting place, every progressive bookstore, they threaten newsagents selling progressive magazines; they break up Russian clubs and even Ruskin clubs. After the veterans maul women protesting against the blockade of Russia and a man wearing a red tie they are given deputies' badges and made official.

Peter discovers he isn't a snivelling coward after all. He begins to enjoy the sport of smashing up communist meetings, and anything that might be a communist meeting, as part of a much stronger gang. He takes part in torturing confessions out of people. Hundreds are deported, irrespective of whether they have families, and the papers ignore the trauma. It is safe to do anything to these radicals in the knowledge that the papers will back up the bullies. They refer to them as cattle and treat them worse than cattle while stealing their money.

When Peter hears a man say it is the right of the people to abolish a government that turns to tyranny he arrests him, unaware that he is quoting from the Declaration of Independence. Some of the sentiments the Reds express are also in the Bible. Peter is made to understand that you have to keep the public on side and make propaganda to back up your case. This was the nature of the Red Scare; endless propaganda stories about bomb plots, newspaper pictures of unshaven desperadoes, radicals who ran for office having their reputations trashed by the press.

Peter's wife organises him to speak in churches because the American god of peace and humility never did like reds. Being a reactionary ignoramus he doesn't know America was founded on a revolution. By this means Peter Gudge and his wife make a good life, while the people whose lives the radicals sought to improve continue to live in the shit they deserve, as they do to this day. We leave them celebrating what a great country America is in which to do your patriotic duty.

DON'T LOOK BACK

Redemption Song: Muhammad Ali and the
Spirit of the Sixties – Mike Marqusee

When Mohammad Ali was chosen to light the Olympic flame at the Atlanta games it was a massive coup for corporate sponsors, the former slave state and the American establishment. They had finally incorporated a man they'd previously despised. Parkinson's-ridden Ali was robbed of his radicalism and made into a harmless peacemaker. As Cassius Clay Ali had thrown his Olympic gold medal into a river in disgust at racism and war. In Atlanta he received a replacement from Olympic boss and former fascist Samaranch. A subsequent flood of revisionist writing entirely obscured his militant past. Early in his career Clay refused to comment on the status of black Americans and refused to represent the aspirations of others. This made him the next best thing to a white man, but after his victory over Sonny Liston he spent the evening with Malcolm X and other black activists.

The next day he denounced America, Christianity and the white race, said he was a member of the Nation of Islam and wasn't going to be what the press wanted him to be. In response attempts were made to take away his title, the record company withdrew his album, chat show invitations were cancelled and corporate deals disappeared. Clay was portrayed as ungrateful and full of hate. Black leaders said he was doing white supremacists' job for them, white boxers said they'd fight him for free to recover the title from its unworthy holder.

None of this was without precedent; when black men started winning boxing matches some saw it as a violation of nature. They were hounded, persecuted, fitted up for crimes and driven into exile. To save face white boxers simply refused to fight them.

The Nation of Islam was a typical cult, with a catholic philosophy and a charismatic and hypocritical leader. Its difference was in its Black Nationalism; it expected nothing from white America, knowing it would never live up to its rhetorical ideals. Clay pretended he'd found religion, but he'd actually experienced a social awakening. Malcolm X taught him that self-pride is part of collective pride and that the struggle of his people was integral to his self-creation.

When Clay was renamed Mohammad Ali it was seen as a direct challenge to mainstream America. The authorities wanted him in the army, but he failed the entrance exam. Connections between the demand for black civil rights and American foreign policy were obvious; activists were being murdered and black churches burned as the US actively undermined African democracy. The authorities tried to control who spoke for America abroad. Ali ignored them and on an African tour addressed big crowds and met leaders America reviled. Floyd Patterson said it was his Catholic duty to reclaim the heavyweight title for America. Ali's victory was a victory for black autonomy, but he was denounced as an unfit role model.

When the army intelligence test was reviewed Ali was again eligible. His statement that he had no quarrel with the Vietcong is one of the most potent in history. He was dismissed as stupid, but he knew what kind of war the US was fighting. He knew that black Korean War veterans had been racially abused even in uniform and that there were similarities between the oppression in Vietnam and that in

Mississippi. The idea that military service led to increased rights was gone, and black Americans were more anti-war than whites. As part of a derided minority, condemned by patriots, congressmen, black leaders and fellow boxers, Ali became symbolic of the anti-war movement and accepted his global responsibilities. In revenge a proposed bout with Ernie Terrell was declared illegal, theatres refused to screen a fight staged abroad and his own promoter disowned him. His claim for conscientious exemption was refused. Lodging an appeal he reiterated that he had no argument with his country's enemy.

When Black Power emerged Ali was simultaneously a hero and a criminal, unjustifiably associated in the white mind with its 'violence'. Black Power's internationalism made oppressed blacks part of a global community. Its anti-imperialism made it a target for the authorities; dozens of members were murdered by the police and hundreds incarcerated. Ali was constantly made to justify himself. In the two years before his incendiary statement he defended his title twice, in the following year he was made to defend it seven times. Being forced to fight abroad made him a global symbol of resistance. In London he toured schools and community groups, meeting Jewish, Irish and Cockney boxers. He was honoured with a parade through Tyneside and helped unite the immigrant community. British Muslims went to see him fight as a symbol of black political defiance. His refusal to be party to an atrocity made him a legend.

A judge upheld Ali's conscientious objection, but politicians overruled it. His enlistment was postponed so he could secure another victory in the ring. Boxing's leading magazine declined to name a fighter of the year because it would have been Ali. He made his most powerful speech against the war as Martin Luther King urged resisting the draft and the civil rights movement disowned him. Ali refused to enlist in the same week as the biggest anti-war demonstration in US history. The boxing authorities revoked his licence and stripped him of his title. His refusal to take part in a war he did not support reverberated around the world and he overshadowed other black leaders in influence. As he toured widely, addressed large crowds and moved among people freely the only leader fully on his side was Martin Luther King. An all-white jury found Ali guilty of evading the draft and he received a five year sentence and a $10,000 dollar fine. While at liberty pending appeal he attended his only anti-war demo, witnessing first-hand the violence of the police. He spoke against the war and the FBI said he was promoting a foreign ideology opposed to equality, justice, love of God and country.

No draft resister was more famous or consistent than Muhammad Ali. Without organised support he put his conscience first and considered himself accountable. He toured colleges comparing the civil rights struggle to South Vietnamese resistance. When the American Civil Liberties Union challenged the all-white draft boards it found Ali's file full of prejudiced letters and cuttings, among them one saying 'send that nigger away.' His conviction for refusing to enlist was upheld, but the public was shocked at the FBI's clandestine operations against civil rights activists. Ali's exclusion from the ring represented a wider exclusion. Athletes threatened to boycott the Olympic Games if his title was not restored. Tommie Smith and John Carlos made their famous Black Power salute at the Olympic awards ceremony. As the US army fell apart in Vietnam students revolted wholesale and public opinion turned against the war. In 1970 Ali's boxing licence was restored, but he was threatened and abused before his victory over Jerry Quarry, the first white American he'd fought for eight years.

Unfortunately, a flowering of black pride and confidence coincided with political disengagement and the decline of Black Power. When Ali signed up to fight Joe Frazier, the 'official' heavyweight champion, he said again that he represented the hopes of millions. Frazier resented being cast as a stupid Uncle Tom; Ali lost the bout and the threat of imprisonment hung over him. The Supreme Court overturned his conviction, he was rehabilitated by the Nation of Islam and travelled the world, fighting fifteen times before signing to meet George Foreman in The Rumble in the Jungle. Only Ali thought he had a chance and he cast himself as the underdog of underdogs, fighting for black people with no future. Millions were squandered on the spectacle and Africa was caricatured for a mass white audience, but Ali's victory was shared by black and white people around the world. He was incorporated and flattered by those who had done so much to ruin his life, becoming sportsman of the year and visiting the White House as a symbol of post-Vietnam reconciliation. His decline coincided with the retreat of the movement: black wages fell, black unemployment rose and the race gap widened. The Nation of Islam urged respect for the country and the flag and then effectively liquidated itself.

Defending his title eleven times in three and a half years Ali never recovered from his last bout with Frazier and fell to womanising, hypocrisy and the sexism the black resistance had never challenged. Towards the end of his reign as world champion he became a self-parody, with much money being made from his decontextualized image. His last fights were sad affairs. He retired in 1979 and allowed himself to be used on an official cold war tour of Africa designed to bolster support for a boycott of the Moscow Olympics. Already suffering nervous symptoms he was encouraged by greedy people to make a comeback and his opponent almost nursed his hero through the gruelling fight.

Mohammad Ali did not want to be made to represent black people and today's stars cannot represent them. He was fallible because he was human. His ideas frightened America and he was repackaged and marketed as the rugged individual overcoming adversity. His context was Vietnam, a disgusting war America has yet to fully acknowledge. The theft of Ali's past is a disgrace. His heroism consisted in placing human solidarity above loyalty to national government, in setting conscience before personal convenience. His example requires that we reclaim the historical reality behind the sanitised icon.

A NATION UNDER
ONE BANNER

*Alt-America: The rise of the Radical Right in
the Age of Trump* – David Neiwert

Donald Trump is by any measure the worst US president ever. His arrogance, ignorance and stupidity are a gift to satirists and comedians, but his support comes direct from America's political sewer.

When he announced he was standing for president one of his supporters told the *New York Times*, 'Hopefully, he's going to... say, "When I become elected president, what we're going to do is we're going to make the border a vacation spot, it's going to cost you twenty-five dollars for a permit, and then you get fifty dollars for every confirmed kill." That'd be one nice thing.' Trump has done nothing to discourage such sentiments, held by people who subscribe to a catalogue of bizarre ideas. They've been around a long time, but the media ignored them and his election came as a shock.

In her 2015 book, *Adios America: the left's plan to turn our country into a Third World Hellhole,* Trump supporter Ann Coulter says immigrants worse than ISIS are engaged in a proxy war against the US, Latinos have a culture of misogyny and Americans should get used to having their little girls raped. To her critics she says Hispanics are not black and they should 'drop the racism crap'. Donald Trump congratulated Coulter and said the book was a great read.

White supremacist hate-group member and Trump

admirer Kyle Rogers produces fake black crime statistics and sells the flag of racist Rhodesia; the mass murderer Dylann Roof was directly influenced by his lies. In the years preceding his attack far right attacks rose and activists opted for the anonymity of the internet. Roof inhabited a world of far right fantasy and his actions led southern states to take down the confederate flag. During the backlash the KKK gave out cards saying 'Racial Purity is America's Security', the far right signed up hundreds and politically correct zealots were charged with besmirching the Righteous Southern Cause.

Organised racists went on to intimidate black people and attack movies 'promoting' political correctness and liberalism. Their twisted morality means keeping women in their place and the right to express bigotry. They oppose affirmative action, feminism and homosexuality. They say liberals are ruining America by destroying the white man. One deranged subscriber to this pitiful philosophy shot dead two cinemagoers for being liberals and women of questionable moral values. Fox News tried to blame Muslims rather than admit the US harbours Hitler worshippers in its hinterland.

Behind the Alt-right's fantasies lie a serious belief in white supremacism. They don't hear 'Black Lives Matter', they hear '*only* black lives matter'. Any attempt to address inequality is a threat to their unquestionable superiority. They believe a New World Order is plotting to take over and their dangerous paranoia pollutes the mainstream through right-wing radio hosts and internet heroes; conspiracies are everywhere. Paradoxically many of those who detest all authority crave a strong man who will uphold their beliefs; to them Trump is The Glorious Leader.

Less inhibited members of the alt-right openly call for the 'elimination' of their opponents and inferiors. They are engaged in a civil war and the Waco siege confirmed that the New World Order had it in for good, white Christian patriots, many of whom believe that the county sheriff is the supreme law and the federal government has no legal or fiscal jurisdiction. The Oklahoma bombing was carried out by a man marinated in this philosophy. His fellows said it was a state setup designed to discredit a harmless movement and the beginning of the satanic preparations for the grand climax.

In the 1990s threatening to kill liberals was passed off as comedy. Ross Limbaugh said on air, 'Don't kill all the liberals, leave enough so we can have two on every campus; living fossils, so we'll never forget what these people stood for.' But Fox news said critics of the wars in Iraq and Afghanistan were traitors who hated the country. Some far right supporters thought they should be killed, or at least locked up. Books were written blaming liberals for 9/11 and equating them with terrorists.

The far right's attention turned to Latinos; citizen militias full of white supremacists, thugs, thieves and the odd murderer were reported favourably on right-wing TV. People who advocated shooting migrants were given airtime. One hyped-up liberal hater killed two people in a church and wounded seven. A manifesto in his car synthesising Ross Limbaugh and Fox News said all liberals should be killed. In his home were books such as *Liberalism is a mental disorder*. Eliminationism had become a component of both mainstream and far right rhetoric. It gives permission for 'patriots' to kill people.

When Barack Obama said he was running for president the Grand Dragon of the KKK said someone ought to kill him. Aided by the Republicans the far right threw so much mud at Obama that some of it was bound to stick; he was a Muslim who hated white people, he associated with terrorists. Following his election there was graffiti calling for his murder, crosses were burned in gardens, racial attacks increased. The conservative media broadcast outrageous falsehoods, the most pervasive of which was that Obama was not American, while elements of the mainstream media played along. One Fox front man repeatedly insisted that Obama sought totalitarian government and concentration camps for conservatives, freely mixing the terms fascist, communist and socialist. When the same front man said Obama was planning gun control it hit a nerve. The story had no basis in truth but it spread like wildfire and gun sales soared.

The right had previously set out to delegitimise Bill Clinton, who they simply did not see as a fit person to be president. They went for Clinton because he was a philanderer; they went for Obama because he was black. For the right the election of Obama meant the ruination of America and their ranting led to the foundation of the Tea Party. Fox News's blanket uncritical coverage made the Tea Party a mechanism for mainstreaming the far right, thereby encouraging its white supremacist adherents in their cause.

When a Department of Homeland Security (DHS) report pointed out that potentially violent right-wing extremists were on the rise mainstream conservatives were outraged, taking umbrage at a connection the report hadn't even made, and making it themselves by defending the cranks. The DHS pointed out that military veterans, though they make up only a minority of far right groups, tend to have elevated positions, and was accused of demonising veterans and mainstream conservatives. There were calls for the resignation of the head of the DHS and suggestions that some maverick in her organisation was a committed leftist or a person of questionable sexual orientation. She had to make a grovelling apology at the same time as white supremacist influenced 'loners' were busy murdering people like abortion providers and the curators of Holocaust museums.

Fox News built the Tea Party's protests; placards accused Obama of being everything from a Marxist to a fascist and of stealing their country. The Tea Party objected to the 'socialism' of decent healthcare and their members attended local health care reform meetings *en masse* and shouted down the speakers. As the Tea Party grew right-wingers ran ads calling Obama a socialist and comparing him to Hitler. On a much exaggerated march on Washington placards were openly racist, depicting Obama as a witchdoctor with a bone through his nose, as well as the now normal ignorant Marxist-fascist conflation. Obama was declared a bigger threat to America that al Qaida and as 'The Enemy Within'. Proponents of health care reform were depicted as targets in the crosshairs of gun sights.

When you know all this it ceases to be a surprise that Trump was elected: the country had been brought by the right-wing media to a state of frenzy against progress itself. People were as angry as shit when they had every right to be angry; they just picked the wrong target.

When a twenty-two year old man shot a senator at point-blank range outside a supermarket, along with eighteen other people, the patriots portrayed it as a false flag, saying liberal media messages had inspired the killer to commit an offence so it could be blamed on them, even suggesting that the federal government was controlling the mind of the assassin.

And so it went on...

Trump's presidency has given people permission to reject 'political correctness' and express bigotry and his victory was a product of the success of the alt-right. The rest of the blame for what many Americans hope is an aberration lies with the neoliberal free market that has consistently shafted ordinary Americans while protecting and enriching those at the top. As David Neiwert says, 'The dumpster Donald Trump's campaign set on fire in the 2016 election had been slowly filling for many years.' Trump said of the far right thugs demonstrating for the end of the anti-coronavirus lockdown, 'They've got cabin fever. They want their lives back. These people love our country.'

A MILLION DEATHS
IS A STATISTIC

*We Wish to Inform You That Tomorrow We Will Be
Killed With Our Families* – Philip Gourevitch

The majority of those on our flight to Kigali were white, but some of the older Rwandans had a look in their eyes that made me wonder what baggage they must be carrying. In a poorly lit bar my companion indelicately asked our contact if he was Hutu or Tutsi. He said there were those who would continue the sectarianism, despite noble attempts to suppress it.

Philip Gourevitch says all uprisings, however criminal or stupid, must be seen as ways to establish a new order. They must also be 'compellingly simple and at the same time absolute.' Nothing could be more compelling, simple or absolute than the Rwandan government's order, openly broadcast by radio and press, that every Hutu kill as many Tutsis as possible.

Historically Hutus were cultivators and Tutsis herdsmen. It was a social division perfect for exploitation by Bible-bashing imperialists and racial pseudo-scientists. The Belgians did not need to bring order to Rwanda; it was already one of the most ordered places on earth. Instead they brought measuring tapes and callipers to measure people's noses and skulls. They decided the Tutsis had biblical ancestors, looked more European, and were therefore superior. They also brought Catholicism. The Bishop of Rwanda called for the total disenfranchisement of Hutus and said Tutsi rule must be reinforced or communism would ensue. Whether Rwandans knew it or not, their subjugation *and their Genocide* were part of the west's anti-Soviet paranoia. A generation later every Rwandan schoolchild had been contaminated by the imperialist logic of racial superiority. A perfect example of a sectarian state had been consciously created in the hills of east Africa and a Hutu may as well have applied for a job at Harland and Wolfe.

As independence approached, some Hutus wanted revenge and moderate opinions were drowned out. When carnage ensued the Belgians turned on the Tutsi overlords they had created and the British philosopher Bertrand Russell, described the situation as 'the most horrible and systematic massacre... since the extermination of the Jews by the Nazis.'

In 1973 General Habyarimana seized power and ordered an end to the pogroms: the violence had served its purpose, and he was its fulfilment. It returned, not as the product of some age-old tribal quarrel, but as a deliberate and conscious policy designed to stymie attempts to circumscribe ethnic division in favour of addressing economic inequality. As in Nazi Germany the killing was promoted as being of benefit to the chosen; an internal menace requiring eradication tied together the leader and the people and the individual ceased to exist. The proponents of Hutu Power even referred to their plans as 'the final solution.' The victims weren't Rwanda's external enemies they were its citizens.

After the Second World War the victorious powers vowed to prevent further genocides, though they knew perfectly well they hadn't fought the war to stop the Holocaust. As Rwanda descended into hell they simply stood by. The UN commander in Rwanda said he could have stopped the genocide, and he has never been contradicted. Instead he was withdrawn with 90% of his men. Even the seizure of the radio station could have saved lives, but the US led calls for withdrawal and American UN representative Madeline Albright, whose family escaped the Nazis, even opposed leaving a skeleton force. The UN Convention obliged the US to act in cases of genocide, so they pretended it wasn't a genocide and obstructed all attempts at intervention on behalf of the victims.

France played an even dirtier role, siding throughout with the murderous Habyarimana regime against the liberating forces of the Rwandan Patriotic Front (RPF). The French 'humanitarian' force was welcomed by hyped-up Hutus as an adjunct of their genocidal army. Eventually French forces occupied a quarter of the country, stopped the advance of the RPF and protected the murderers, allowing them to carry on killing Tutsis. The RPF was a progressive force of well-disciplined fighters, motivated by coherent ideas of political improvement. Their leader Paul Kagame said, 'People are not inherently bad. But they can be made bad and they can be taught to be good.' As the RPF swept through Rwanda the retreating *genocidaires* looted and burned everything in their path. Cholera struck and the aid industry went into overdrive. Refugee camps replicated Hutu Power and aid agencies became accessories in guerrilla strikes across the border. 'Rwanda presented the world with the most unambiguous case of genocide since Hitler's war against the Jews, and the world sent blankets, beans and bandages to the camps controlled by the killers, apparently hoping that everybody would behave nicely in the future.'

After the genocide depression was epidemic, latrines and wells were stuffed full of bodies and the infrastructure had collapsed, but Rwandans returned in their tens of thousands, from surrounding countries, as well as from Europe and the USA, from South America and Canada. They wanted to defy the genocide and the country quickly began to recover. But the people who returned didn't trust the people who'd stayed, and the people who'd stayed were overwhelmed by the returnees, who didn't understand what they'd been through. And all the time there was the threat of a new invasion by Hutu Power in exile.

By the end of 1997 a hundred and twenty-five thousand Hutus were held in Rwanda's jails for their part in the genocide. Among them were even nuns, but the guilty outside the prisons far outweighed those inside. Most perpetrators never appeared before a court. Rwanda retains the death penalty, but if the guilty had been punished according to the law another million would have died. Instead reconciliation took place around symbolic re-burials of the dead.

The UN refugee camps on Rwanda's borders constituted a rump genocidal state. Global sympathy was misdirected in the service of Hutu Power's lies. International humanitarian organisations became caterers to the largest society of fugitive criminals humanity has ever assembled. They employed people put forward by Hutu Power patronage and they rented trucks and buses from Hutu Power. The camps were not the solution to a refugee crisis but a means of sustaining it. Their existence increased the inevitability of war and they were a base for cross-border raids. The aid agencies became agents in the conflict, providing a better standard of living for those who had carried out the genocide than most people left in Rwanda. The profits from Hutu Power's cross-border raids and trade in charity provided goods were used to buy arms. As the aid dried up Hutu Power began to ethnically cleanse Tutsis from Zaire, aided by President Mobutu, who had been put in place by the CIA as a bulwark against communist forces in Africa. The genocide in Rwanda was a godsend for the ailing dictator. He became a feted power broker and France, ever the willing aid to Hutu Power, unilaterally restored 'humanitarian' aid to refill his bank accounts. Tutsis were eradicated in North Kivu. The UN lacked any coherent policy and it fed the ongoing genocide.

The West still saw Mobutu as a solution to the problem. France sent him arms and he sent them straight across the border for use by Hutu Power in the genocide. Conflict engulfed the whole region and continues to this day. France's President Mitterrand said, 'In such countries genocide is not too important.' Paul Kagame said he'd learned a lot about the hypocrisy and double standards of the people who said they wanted to make the world a better place. The Rwandan genocide happened because for decades imperialists set Tutsis up as superior to Hutus. When the Hutus eventually fought back in the worst way possible the west backed the murderers.

Eventually the majority of the former refugees began returning to Rwanda. Never before had a people subjected to genocide been expected to receive among them those who had carried out the carnage. They recognised among the returnees people who had killed their entire families. Rwanda had no choice but to hope they could get along somehow.

Rwandans want to make themselves one people to prevent further atrocities, but they can't be one people while corrupt millionaires build palaces around Lake Kivu and ordinary people go barefoot, drink polluted water and bring up children so malnourished they can't walk to school. The division is not between Hutu and Tutsi and it never was, that was a diversion. The real division in Rwanda, as in the Land of the Free and under the Mother of all Parliaments is between rich and poor, between exploiters and exploited. The leaders of African nations know this just as well as the leaders of the ailing old world democracies. The Archbishop of Rwanda's fears about communism entail the possibility of unity, his nightmare was of the disparate groups making common cause. That is what really frightens our rulers. Philip Gourevitch's book closes in 1998 with a story which gives him hope. At a school, girls confronted by Hutu Power killers refuse to be separated into Hutus and Tutsis, saying 'We are all Rwandans.' A popular slogan in Rwanda after the genocide was 'bury the dead, not the truth.'

SEEING AND NOT SEEING

The Art of Travel – Alain de Botton

While celebrity philosopher Alain de Botton is dolefully watching it rain a holiday brochure comes through his door and he decides to go to Barbados. So begins *The Art of Travel*. We are told that the comforts of home are false, that it is not at home where we are our true selves and that only by becoming wanderers can we rediscover human fellowship.

De Botton's first witness is Flaubert, who considered himself ridiculous, doubted humanity's claim to qualities beyond those of other animals and was driven by the prudery and self-righteousness of his age to remind others of mankind's impurities. He was a critic of mindless optimism and went abroad hoping to escape what he saw as the extraordinary stupidity of the modern European bourgeoisie, but 'in Alexandria a certain Thompson from Sunderland has inscribed his name in letters six feet high on Pompey's pillar. You can read it a quarter of a mile away. You can't see the pillar without seeing the name of Thompson, and consequently without thinking of Thompson. This cretin has become part of the monument and perpetuates himself along with it... he overwhelms it by the splendour of his gigantic lettering... All imbeciles are more of less Thompsons from Sunderland. How many one comes across in life in the most beautiful places and in front of the finest views. When travelling one meets many... but as they go by quickly one can laugh. It's not like in ordinary life, where they end up making you fierce.'

Flaubert was no patriot and proposed a new way of

ascribing nationality; not according to one's country of birth or to that which one's family belonged, but according to the places to which one was attracted. 'I'm disgusted,' he said, 'to be back in this damned country where you see the sun in the sky about as often as a diamond in a pig's arse. I don't give a shit for Normandy and la belle France... I don't rejoice in our victories over the Arabs because I am saddened by their defeats... I'm no more modern than ancient, no more French than Chinese, and the idea of a native country, that is to say, the imperative to live on one bit of ground marked red or blue on the map and to hate the other bits in green or black, has always seemed to me to be narrow-minded, blinkered and profoundly stupid.'

The proto-fascist philosopher Friedrich Nietzsche proposed an alternative kind of tourism; one through which we learn how our societies and identities were formed by the past and so acquire a sense of community and belonging. We could do this leaning on a farm gate at dusk looking over former strip-fields and imagining smocked peasants at their tilling, or at the back of a church imagining plain folk being read selected passages from the Bible in a language they didn't understand, or looking at a railway bridge or a canal and making common cause with the migrant labourers who built them, or by standing at a dockside where ships would have moored between bouts of pillage and kidnap. None of this would cost us anything but a spirit of humanity. Because it doesn't cost anything it is valueless. Instead we prostitute our heritage for personal gain and package it like so much shit.

The poet Wordsworth didn't like cities, believing them to foster life-destroying emotions, anxiety about social position, envy of the success of others and the desire to look good in the eyes of strangers. He said 'city dwellers had no perspective, were prone to tittle-tattle and a relentless desire for new things on which happiness does not depend.' The 'mad, bad and dangerous to know' Byron, who suggested a passing traveller might want to piss on the political thug Castlereagh's grave on behalf of the victims of Peterloo, thought Wordsworth's poetry was soppy nonsense, but the privileged appreciated his distracting otherworldliness as the industrial revolution crammed people into the damp cellars of Manchester.

Pursuing Wordsworth in the Lake District de Botton gets all starry eyed about sheep, simultaneously regarding them as part of nature and imposing upon them human attributes. Sheep are not the free creatures he supposes; they are the product of centuries of selective breeding, imprisoned between stone walls built by human beings. They are not the antithesis of civilisation but an essential part of it, as is most of what we regard as nature. Worshipping nature as something separate from human beings is profoundly conservative. We might individually fool ourselves we are in tune with nature but collectively we are destroying it.

Revelling in his own romanticism de Botton says, 'These trees gave off an impression of astonishing health and exuberance. They seemed not to care that the world was old and often sad. I was tempted to bury my face in them so as to be restored by their smell. It seemed extraordinary that nature could on its own, without any concern for the happiness of two people eating chocolate on a bench, have come up with a scene so utterly suited to a human sense of beauty and proportion.'

Even the recollection of such a scene provides de Botton with a reason to be alive. While chained to his computer in London, he can forget the four hundred mile round trip in his Range Rover and lose himself in the memory of a distant wood. Likewise, Wordsworth's daffodils constitute 'a spot in time', to be mentally revisited when times are less than perfect. The image is so powerful that it acts as a natural anti-depressant. This leads to a discussion of the sublime; meaning grand, noble or awe-inspiring, which we are told entails landscape more powerful than humans. Such places teach us that we are frail and temporary and must bow to a power greater than ourselves.

The conservative character of this viewpoint is reinforced with a citation from the reactionary Edmund Burke on the tribulations of Job. Job is not invited to understand the purpose of his discomforts, only to bear them. The implications are obvious; we too must live with 'the natural order' because we can't alter it: monarchy, motorways, the free market and the mother of all parliaments; all these are beyond our ability to comprehend, just like the towering mountains and the raging seas. Our rulers know what they are doing and we must leave things in their capable hands.

To invite human beings to prostrate themselves before natural phenomena, and by extension before social phenomena, is to deny them their collective potential. Humanity cannot entirely conquer nature, but it can reduce its consequences. A mud slide in Bolivia that kills hundreds and a flood in Bangladesh that drowns thousands are not 'natural' disasters. They are natural *events*, the disastrous consequences of which are almost entirely avoidable.

De Botton is wrong to suggest that travellers only want to see natural beauty. In any case his definition is too narrow; the beauty of some attractions is in their man-made utility. No tourist visited the National Mining Museum in Wakefield, a decommissioned trawler in Hull, Beamish in Northumberland or the Bayeux Tapestry because they are beautiful, but then the book is about travel, not tourism.

Having decided that beauty is what the traveller seeks,

de Botton enlists Ruskin, who devoted a great deal of time to questions about beauty and its possession, discovering that; 1. Beauty is the product of various visual and psychological factors. 2. Humans respond to and desire to possess beauty. 3. There are lower expressions of this desire such as buying souvenirs, taking photographs, and carving one's name in pillars. 4. Only by understanding beauty can we really possess it. 5. The only way to understand beauty is by writing about or drawing it, regardless of whether we have any talent for doing so.

Ruskin was critical of the haste of modern tourists, saying they never really looked at anything; 'The Alps themselves you look upon as soaped poles in a bear garden, which you set yourselves to climb, and slide down again with shrieks of delight.' 'The really precious things are thought and sight not pace... not in going but in being.' Ruskin decried the turning of beautiful places into tourist shit-holes and the replacement of appreciation with cheap thrills. But most of all he was critical of people photographing things rather than properly looking at them. Pascal could have been commenting on the 'done that, done this' mentality of the modern traveller when he said, 'The sole cause of man's unhappiness is that he does not know how to stay quietly in his room.'

De Botton summarises thus, '...the pleasure we derive from journeys is perhaps dependent more on the mind-set with which we travel than on the destination we travel to. If only we could apply a travelling mind-set to our own locales, we might find these places becoming no less interesting than high mountain passes and... the jungles of South America.' The best way to appreciate your own surroundings is to show someone else around.

Via Vincent van Gogh *The Art of Travel* becomes the arty-farty guide to travel. Beauty is in the eye of the beholder; looking at things properly also entails looking into their history and meaning. The best way to treat travel is as a metaphor for life. It might even be as empty as being catapulted across the sky in glorified cigar tube, all fulfilment postponed for the inevitably greener fields beyond.

THE JEWEL IN THE CROWN

Burmese Days – George Orwell

Burmese Days would be a satire on the ostentatious racism and arrogant stupidity of the imperial Englishman abroad as the sun sets on the empire of endless daylight robbery if it weren't all entirely believable. The empire's insular administrators, convinced of their own racial superiority, believe that only brutal repression can 'save' India. The worst of them even defend Dyer, the butcher of Amritsar. There's only one thing lower than a native, and that's a white man who treats them as equals.

They live an endless lie in which the twisted morality of the imperial overlord is cemented together with strong drink and false friendship. The singular redeeming character cannot even convince the sycophantic native who has done alright out of the British presence that the empire is organised theft and that the imperialists have systematically ruined the industries, education system, character and self-respect of their subjects.

Rather than creating a desert and calling it peace like their Roman progenitors they enshrined violence and legalised chauvinism by building prisons and police stations and calling it progress.

The best of British officials in India are dull, lazy and drunk, the real work being done by native subordinates while they shelter behind the might of the army. Every one of them is a vital cog in the wheels of despotism; friendship is entirely false and free speech unthinkable. They can be idlers, cowards, backbiters, fornicators, but they are not free to think for themselves. Every opinion is dictated by the distorted code of white supremacy. The overseers live a life of lies, spending their evenings in poxy little clubs with other white men listening to racist rants and their days watching young men hardly out of school abusing people old enough to be their parents and grandparents.

They come to hate their countrymen and long for the natives to rise up and destroy the whole stinking empire. They are dishonoured and insincere, caring nothing for the people they oppress, only for the way it degrades themselves. Many of them become thin yellow alcoholics who cannot even hold their heads up in Britain. They hate themselves and come to love and hate India in equal measure. The only future, especially for a man who remains single, is a boarding house in England full of prematurely aged racists and self-haters living on lies. They rot in dishonour and futility knowing all the while that but for the empire they could have been decent human beings.

One of the ten rules of the minor imperialist is to be deliberately ignorant of native concerns and disagreements on pain of loss of prestige. Inter-racial loyalty and friendship is forbidden, along with any kind of alliance or partnership. Even to defend a slighted native is to invite dishonour; a cavalier betrayal of one's loyal underlings in their hour of need is far more acceptable. The testimony of a white man is worth that of a thousand natives.

The only alternative to lonely self-loathing in the outposts of empire is to find and export a scandalmongering wife who doesn't learn a word of the language and considers it a shame that attractive girls have to work for a living. Properly educated English girls looking for a worthy husband have been inculcated with the opinion that the natives are inferior and that any kind of social interaction is below their dignity. They are automatically suspicious of any white man who treats them with humanitarian tolerance.

For the white women elevated by the tide of oppression the natives are automatically ugly and their women are like animals. The pernicious and calculated eugenics that justifies the imperial mission have taught those barely out of their teens that the shape of the natives' heads identifies them as being of a criminal type.

These women arrive in the colonies with a ready-made sense of superiority and contempt for the locals carefully instilled in classrooms full of pink maps. The very suggestion that globally whiteness is less natural is seen as an absurd eccentricity. They consider being spoken to by a native as a demonstration of impertinence they are entitled to ignore. Eurasians are the lowest of the low, scorned by the race that is almost too embarrassed to acknowledge them. The natives' customs are the subject of contempt, and as politics is out of the question their conversation is banal and superficial in the extreme. In return manly men of the empire discuss any new arrival as if she is goods on a market stall, making drunken small talk on the subjects of her honour and availability. They marry people they don't love or respect purely for the company so they can be united in their prejudices.

Any local resistance by the natives is soon supressed with a few deaths at the hands of the police. Rumours of a proper rebellion excite those who've yet to kill. They relish the thought of lashing the bare arse of a native with bamboo, rather than allowing them to have it easy in stinking jails.

In the meantime cavalry officers full of racist invective play polo and the rest get their sport by killing any animal that moves, no matter how noble it is, using unsporting shotguns that can't miss. They reduce their servants to pimps and use young local women as concubines (as occupying Nazis took French ones), rob them of their youth and throw them out to disgrace when they are tired of them, even though they grovel like dogs to be kept. Then they go to church like the actors in a Christianising mission they are, half-drunk and blaspheming. There exists such a culture of contempt that even a would-be humanitarian cannot express himself for fear of being blackballed from the Caucasian mafia brotherhood.

The agents of the empire demand unstinting loyalty from those they oppress and the slightest signs of disloyalty among the native administrators is pounced upon and careers are ruined. To resist the occupying overlord is sedition. To the wives of these self-conscious slave drivers the words sedition, nationalism, rebellion and home rule can have only one consequence; their inevitable rape by a succession of black inferiors. Actual rebellion is brutally and swiftly supressed by indiscriminate killing. The white men are aided in this task by greedy natives desperate to be regarded well by their oppressors. The highest honour for the self-aggrandising native man at the fag-end of empire is that he be grudgingly accepted, on orders from above, into the white men's pathetic little European club, a hive of drunkenness, racism, tittle-tattle and bad taste, as a doomed tokenistic insurance against rising resistance; though to actually propose a native for club membership is downright bolshevism.

At the hospital sick natives are given one of three prescriptions from pre-prepared piles by quack doctors, depending on whether their pain is in their head, back or belly. They are then given coloured water by corrupt pharmacists who sell the real medicines on the black market.

Though they don't discuss politics the agents of empire know very well what side they are on. Anyone British who takes the side of an injured native is not only a traitor but a highbrow or a socialist, a Bolshie or Hyde Park agitator, to be categorised with Lenin or A J Cook. Racist unity against the indigenous population is their only prop. They deliberately don't remove their hats for a passing native funeral because they are white and the natives are dirt.

The well-connected army officers despise the non-military population, native and British alike, the cavalry officers despise the rest of the army, especially the Indian regiments. They leave behind them a trail of insulted people, neglected duties and unpaid bills. They consider poor people to be poor due to their own fault and they despise women.

The participants in a pathetic rebellion are punished with banishment and barbarity. In revenge the natives kill and mutilate a white man. 800 people a year were murdered in Burma and the man is of no particular consequence save for the colour of his skin, which means he must be avenged. It is far better that the wrong men are hanged than that no one is hanged.

The upholders of British law abroad want torture, bribes and a return to now prohibited pre-war punishments. They want to raid the natives' villages, kill their cattle, burn their crops, decimate them and blow them from cannon. The white men start lashing out and one of them blinds a boy. When their club is attacked they relish the opportunity to teach the natives a lesson and wish they had guns. Afterward they regret that more of them haven't been killed, guilty or innocent alike.

In the 1920s, as the British Empire fades into an absurd farce, its colonial administrators exist in such decay, loneliness and self-pity that many of them resort to suicide.

Otherwise in marvellous ceremonies with full-dress uniforms, fancy hats and rattling swords the corrupted and the conniving bestow dubious honours on each other as servants of the all-corrupting empire. It's what made Britain great. 'Power tends to corrupt, and absolute power corrupts absolutely... There is no worse heresy than that the office sanctifies the holder of it.'

BRITAIN'S BUSTED FLUSH

The Myth of the British Monarchy – Edgar Wilson

During my brief foray into teaching I was pompously informed that I couldn't properly relate to the students unless I watched the soap operas for the topical issues they raise. If this was true, which it obviously isn't, it would be equally so of the world's most expensive soap opera. Members of the royal family have engaged with mental health, disability, youth schemes, landmines, AIDs, complimentary medicine, architecture, natural disasters, species depletion and climate change. Some of this is no doubt sincere, the rest is designed to endear us to a troupe of very bad actors who should have been booed off the stage long ago. Attempts to secure further episodes have been conscious and consistent.

In the early part of Queen Victoria's reign, royal ceremony was minimal and many writers considered it ridiculous. But Britain's global dominance meant that domestic stability was taken for granted, the royal family became unpopular, republicanism and resistance grew and it was decided that the monarch would become a visible symbol of the nation. 'Disraeli, by a stroke of genius, related the queen to the interests of the nation, *as conceived by the conservative party*. After that it became impossible... to question a conservative view of the nation and the national interest, without being charged with disloyalty to the queen.' A fawning press and a willing Church helped to make royal ceremonial into a national obsession. Through royal weddings, Armistice Day, the state opening of parliament,

Trooping the Colour and Christmas broadcasts the royal family and ordinary families were deliberately conflated, and Elizabeth II has enjoyed more ceremonial pomp than any other head of state. She is meant to represent ideals to which we must aspire, and in old age is the embodiment of the keep calm and carry on culture; not just the head of state, but the head of the status quo.

This we all know, but Edgar Wilson's marvellous book, somewhat belied by its *Spitting Image* cover, also makes it clear what a damaging and dangerous institution the monarchy is. It is well known that Edward VIII, who came to the throne in the 1930s, was a fascist, but the details are perhaps less well known. He had extensively fraternised with Hitler and there were real fears he might stage a coup. He opposed war with Germany, and after he'd been forced to abdicate he urged Hitler to bomb Britain into surrender, probably planning to return as a fascist king following a German victory.

Fascism aside, the monarchy has a long record of obstructing progress. William IV opposed the abolition of slavery. Victoria opposed compulsory education, votes for women and reduced working hours for children. Edward VII hated socialists and would not have the Labour leader at his garden parties. In 1924 George V tried to form an anti-socialist coalition against a Labour victory. He urged Labour to abolish the dole and in 1931 persuaded its leader to cut it and workers' wages. After the war the king opposed Labour's nationalisation programme.

Despite the fact that he was regarded as a god in parts of Vanuatu both Prince Philip and his wife blamed Arthur Scargil for the 1984-85 Miners' Strike engineered by Thatcher. Three of Philip's sisters married senior Nazis and he could easily have been on Hitler's side in the war. He was no friend of democracy and said the privileged would resist attempts to impose egalitarianism. In 1975 his number one son said governments existed by God's permission and those who opposed them opposed God. The heir to the throne is also known to hate the trade unions and has said that farmers are more oppressed than blacks and gays. Princess Margaret was an anti-Semite, a racist and a reactionary, who once said that the Irish were all pigs, and Princess Ann is a climate change sceptic.

It is taken for granted that Her Majesty is above politics and has only symbolic powers. But the monarch's central role is to ensure governments don't engage in 'extreme and illegitimate' actions. The queen is head of the executive, chair of the Privy Council, head of the judiciary, commander in chief of the armed forces and head of the Church of England. She can appoint to offices of state, the judiciary and the military. In the twentieth century the monarch appointed three prime ministers who were *not* leaders of their party, and various republican politicians have been blocked from high office. The monarch can declare a state of emergency and it has been argued that they would be justified in using unconstitutional powers if necessary. In 1967 the *Daily Telegraph* said that if a Labour government attempted to impose equality the establishment would be justified in overthrowing it, and existing powers were used to dismiss the Australian Labour government in 1975.

The monarchy is also harmful to the psychology of the population. Unlike normal theatre it requires us to suspend our disbelief not for an hour but permanently. We are deceived about the real nature of society. The monarchy's massive untaxed and concealed wealth legitimises conspicuous consumption and personal indulgence, sets bad examples of greed, prejudice and lying, encourages fantastic delusions about Britain's place in the world, and promotes fairy-tales and irrationality over equality, self-respect and honesty. As monarchy is dependent upon birth and titles rather than reward for effort it is a denial of human labour. Monarchy doesn't build homes or grow food. It doesn't sell washing machines, teach children or process tax returns. It just *is*.

The idea that human genetics can produce a royal super-species is anti-science, offensive to rational people and encourages the belief that other traits are biological. In any case their lineage is farcical and Elizabeth II is not a direct descendant of the monarchs who took power by force. Ordinary people are degraded by their elitism and condescension and the notion that a family of rich inbred snobs can be used as any kind of moral exemplar is preposterous. The use of God as any kind of justification for monarchy is an abuse of a religion that preaches humility, charity and brotherhood. The British monarchy is arbitrary, unrepresentative, unaccountable, politically partial, socially divisive and overly influential, and its powers are theoretically unlimited. Its existence assumes that ordinary people are stupid; unable to recognise an idea unless it looks like a king or a policeman and it exposes our democratic system as a sham. In parliament questioning the monarchy is seen as bad taste or treachery. The monarchy is *not* a guarantor against extremism as is often claimed, but the guarantor of rule by the right and, if necessary, the far right. It is effectively a branch of the Tory party.

The monarch is meant to be a symbol of stability, security, continuity and traditional values. The gloved hand waving from the golden coach is supposed to mean all is well with the nation. It actually means that our society is rotten. The stability the monarch provides is a delusion, as every strike, protest and riot proves. The monarchy is meant to promote national unity, when every assertion about national unity is a slap in the face for those who come off worst, as well as an encouragement to those who deny class in favour of reactionary nationalism.

The British monarchy is wasteful; if the same efforts had been made to improve public services as have been squandered on maintaining monarchical fantasies Britain would be a fundamentally different place. It is irrational; if it did not exist modern humans would not choose it. Its continued existence depends upon childish fairy tales and questioning the right of these thieves to rule us is the beginning of questioning the entire class system.

There have only been two English monarchs called Elizabeth, one established Britain's imperial reputation, the other has overseen its decline. It is a criminal travesty that the head of a family steeped in imperial conquest, slavery, eugenics, social Darwinism and white supremacism is made to represent the interests of a rainbow nation. The overturning of this deception is at the heart of demands that the educational curriculum be decolonised.

To dismiss the monarchy as mere ornamentation is to seriously misread the situation. The only possible argument for monarchy is that we are as likely to get a good hereditary ruler as a good elected one. This may be true, but the gene pool is bigger and it is our own fault if we *elect* clowns like Boris.

In 1913 a labour leader said the king would be a socialist king if the people wanted it. This is bullshit. The monarchy is anathema to democracy, let alone socialism. It does not become powerless and ceremonial by the mere application of the terms. Rejecting the monarchy as the apex of Britain's class system, its central pillar and its chief symbol is the first step in the abandonment of fantasies in favour of a rational view of the world.

As the free market has inevitably failed there have been calls in some post-'communist' countries for the return of monarchs. Monarchy will only cease to be a focus for conservatism and reaction when socialism is humanity's default system. The Bolsheviks killed the Romanovs for good reason, Edward the VIII remained a danger after he had abdicated and Charles I did not relinquish his claim to rule until his head was unceremoniously removed.

INTERNATIONAL ANTHEM

God who has never been
Does not make people queen
Like some machine
Monarchy is spurious
Theft is notorious
Long to rob all of us
It is obscene

Proles of the world arise
Scatter those you despise
And make them fall
Confound their politics
Frustrate their knavish tricks
On this all hopes we fix
To save us all

Not in this land alone
There will be mercies shown
From shore to shore
Let's make the nations free
Sisters and brothers be
And form one family
This wide world o'er

The choicest gifts in store
On those without will pour
When wealth is slain
When we make our laws
In all our common cause

There will be plenitude
There's never been

Spare not our harmless queen
From history's guillotine
Monarchs must fall
Realise our founding rights
Rid us of parasites
Lackeys and hangers on
Once and for all

WHERE THERE'S LIFE
THERE'S HOPE

A People's History of the Second World War – Donny Gluckstein

A recent article compared the 1994 Rwandan Genocide to the Holocaust, but in underdeveloped Rwanda the victims of ethnic conflict died mostly by machete blows. The Holocaust, an attempt to destroy an entire people, used the administration and infrastructure of several modern states. It was systematic, premeditated and efficient, using the foremost industrial, scientific and technological advances of the day. It was a capitalist genocide, much of it sub-contracted to profit-making enterprises, some of which are still in business.

Commemorations of the Holocaust generally take the form of patronising sympathy. This follows from the rarely challenged view that Jews allowed themselves to be taken without protest from their work and homes and stripped of their possessions, to climb meekly into the trucks that took them to the door of the gas chamber. This picture is incomplete and incorrect; to see the Jews only as passive victims further denies them their humanity.

Hitler's expansionist policy meant the invasion of countries which had large Jewish populations. Many of Poland's Jews already suffered severe social restrictions, but they belonged to mainstream political parties, owned half the banks and were over-represented in the trade unions. Rich Jews were accused of a global conspiracy, working class Jews of a communist plot. Irrespective of their status the Nazis drove them into cramped ghettoes to starve to death. Half of all Jewish deaths occurred in Poland. One in ten Poles were Jewish, but only one in twenty of them survived. Before the war, besides the mainstream organisations, Polish Jews had three political choices; they could support any government that left them alone, they could join the Jewish Bund, a secular socialist movement, or they could join the Zionists, who believed in a separate homeland in Palestine.

In 1936 violent attacks began against Jews. Bund self-defence groups, in conjunction with the Polish Socialist Party, demonstrated, defended their own organisation and protected Jews in general. They rejected the idea that Jews could be saved by the founding of some promised land, in favour of fighting racism where they were. In 1936 a strike by Jews and non-Jews against anti-Semitic violence virtually shut Poland down. In 1937 there was a two day general strike against segregation and the failure to prosecute violent anti-Semites. Many Polish workers and students saw the fight against anti-Semitism as their fight and Polish anti-Semitism was strongest among the wealthy. The Peasant Party recognised it as a scapegoating trick and in return for their solidarity Jews actively supported a ten day strike by peasants. Jews relied for their safety on the working class movement and when the Nazis came many found refuge with Polish workers. This solidarity had to be broken by systematic fascist slander and forced segregation in ghettoes.

The first organised ghetto uprising took place in Lachva, Belarus, when six hundred people escaped into the forests, but the most famous is the Warsaw ghetto uprising. By 1942 100,000 Warsaw Jews had died of disease, starvation and random killings and a quarter of a million had been sent to concentration camps. Three political groups, The Bund,

The Labour Zionists and the Communists formed a united organisation, drove the Nazis out of the ghetto and stopped deportations to the camps. They executed collaborators, taxed wealthy residents and began producing newspapers. 220 ghetto fighters, 500 Jewish ex-Polish army soldiers and some Zionists fought 2,000 German soldiers for six weeks. The Ghetto was only retaken by setting it ablaze. The Warsaw Ghetto fighters could not win, but in choosing to die fighting they inspired others to resist.

In the Bialystok ghetto in north-east Poland the Jewish underground aided Russian POWs and smuggled weapons. In late 1942, encouraged by Warsaw, Bialystok rose up; informers were executed and deportations to the death camps stopped. On May Day 1943 there was a strike among Jewish forced labourers in factories. In August 1943 the Bialystok underground believed the ghetto was to be liquidated. They kept soldiers at bay for ten days and led a mass escape into the forest. In Kovno in Lithuania ghetto fighters backed by the Polish resistance helped five hundred Jews to escape to join the partisans. The population resisted the liquidation of the ghetto and deportation until the Nazis set it on fire. Also in Lithuania a Jewish partisan militia called the Avengers carried out sabotage and blew up military convoys. In Minsk Jews in the ghetto and non-Jews in the city were united in resistance. They ran a clandestine press, harried the Nazis, sabotaged factories and aided escapes. In the most successful resistance of all 10,000 Jews escaped to the forest and most survived the war.

Even in the concentration camps there was resistance. There were underground organisations in six extermination camps and eighteen work camps. In Auschwitz-Birkenau, the underground involved Jews and non-Jews from transit camps, extermination areas and satellite camps, as well as forced labourers from the Krupp armaments factory. In 1944 they destroyed one of the crematoria with explosives smuggled from the factory by women workers. The underground in Sobidor camp was led by a Jew and a Soviet POW. Inspired by Warsaw they killed eleven SS officers and the camp commander, allowing three hundred of the six hundred prisoners to escape. Two hundred avoided recapture, many being hidden by local Poles. A Jewish-Polish army captain led the Treblinka underground. In 1943 they stole weapons, killed the guards, set the camp on fire and destroyed the extermination area. Six hundred of the 1,500 prisoners escaped, many of those who avoided recapture being helped by ordinary Poles. These uprisings led to the closure of both camps.

There was active resistance in a hundred ghettoes and uprisings in fifty. There were revolts in three extermination camps and eighteen forced labour camps. Twenty-five thousand Jews fought with thirty Jewish partisan groups and twenty-one mixed groups. Ten thousand people survived in camps in the forests. Jewish underground groups carried out sabotage, helped POWs, forged documents, published newspapers and distributed arms. Thousands of women couriers worked within the ghettoes. Others, at great risk, kept records of events.

One of the main obstacles to fighting anti-Semitism was Zionism; the belief that the Jews should have an exclusive home in Palestine. The founder of Zionism, Theodore Herzel, said that fighting anti-Semitism was futile. In 1925 Jacob Klatzkin, editor of the Jewish Encyclopaedia, said that anti-Semitism was natural and that to deny it was to deny the rightness of Zionism. He said Jews should reject non-Jews who fought against anti-Semitism. Fighting anti-Semitism was not part of Zionism's plan. In 1937 its leader Chaim Weizmann said, 'The old ones will pass; they will bear their fate or they will not. They [are] dust, economic and moral dust, in a cruel world… only a remnant shall survive. We have to accept it.' This, and Zionism's (correct) belief that imperialists would eventually secure them a homeland, made it absolutely incapable of confronting the Holocaust. The anti-Semites in Poland said 'send the Jews to Palestine' the Zionists said the same. Jews who resisted the Holocaust did so in complete opposition to Zionist ideology. They did so because they came from a pre-war tradition of rejecting Zionism and fighting anti-Semitism.

Poland had the worst punishments for helping Jews in Europe; fifty thousand Poles were executed and thousands were sent to concentration camps for their humanitarian interventions. The country had the only united organisation dedicated to helping Jews, with Socialist, Peasant Party and Bund members, Catholics, students, writers, medical and social workers and boy scouts as members. It helped over half the Polish Jews who survived. Thousands of Jewish children were smuggled out of Warsaw and thousands of Jews were hidden by Poles outside the ghetto.

The mainstream Polish press was anti-Semitic throughout the war. But Socialist, peasant and Catholic papers reported what was happening. The Polish underground told its members that Poles had a duty to help Jews. The Jews who hid, revolted and escaped within Poland did so overwhelmingly with the support of non-Jews. Activists faced a dilemma. Resistance required the participation of the majority, but weapons were difficult to obtain and the ghettos were full of the very young and the very old. Escaping to the forests or to the partisans meant leaving those people to their fate.

Western and Zionist historians have downplayed

Jewish resistance. The narrative of passivity supports the belief that anti-Semitism cannot be defeated. It suits Zionists to say that the Jews were abandoned, though in some places resistance to the Nazis depended entirely on Jewish participation. To acknowledge cooperation and solidarity is to deny Israel its purpose. The Israeli state celebrates the Warsaw uprising, but Marek Edelman, a Jewish resistance veteran, told the Palestinians that the spirit of the Warsaw resistance belonged to them. Two myths surround the Holocaust. The first is that the Jews didn't fight back. The second is that they were abandoned. They may have been abandoned by the western powers, but they were never abandoned by the left.

GUILT BY ASSOCIATION

*I Refuse to Condemn: Resisting Racism in Times of
National Security* – Asim Qureshi (Ed.)

It is perhaps ironic that many indigenous peoples were wiped out by western imperialists' germs rather than by their arms. The plague currently affecting humanity has its origins in wanton deforestation and factory farming, but the octopus of imperialism is apparent in the endless calls for ordinary Muslims and their spokespeople to condemn the actions of others. Like indigenous peoples, stigmatised as being backward, Muslims can only become acceptable by becoming more like 'us', by becoming less Muslim, which, as the Jews found out, is never enough. As well as the outright hostility of the deliberately ignorant, Muslims endure white liberal insensitivity, being endlessly put on the spot by those with good intentions. Anti-racists and anti-imperialists could resent the suggestion that all white people refuse to condemn white violence, but that would be pointless.

In opposition to David Cameron's crass assertion that we 'should understand less and condemn more,' Cyrus McGoldrick reminds us of the cardinal fact; America is the invader, Al Qaida is the resistance. 'Some have allowed righteous anger to lead them to unjust violence. Can we not empathise? ... I won't have to answer for the actions or mistakes of anyone else. I will only answer for what I have done. If I err... I want to say I erred on the side of justice, on the side of the oppressed.' In other words; conquest, occupation, annexation and wholesale theft are the essential problems, not the response to them. We do not condemn a rape victim who injures her assailant or the French Resistance for their violent insurgency. Fundamental to empathy is the assumption that self-defence is no offence.

In *This is not a Humanising Poem* Suhaiymah Manzoor-Khan refuses to prostrate herself before the hypocritical guardians of white respectability and demands that Muslims be accepted for what they are; upright, principled, moral and hardworking, as well as lazy, poor, depressed, unwashed and weeping, unemployed, joy-riding, time-wasting, failing at school and shopping in Poundland, just like the rest of us. Anyone who feels the need to question the humanity of others proves only that they have lost their own. She wants to know on what days of the week she can be regarded as liberal and what the difference is between bombs that kill and those that spread democracy. If exposing injustice is radical, then she is a radical, as we should all be.

Under the Schedule 7 terrorism Act 2000 it is illegal to refuse to answer questions when detained. It is an affront to natural law that anyone should be compelled to answer questions that could incriminate them. It is the responsibility of a state that claims legitimacy to show that it has reasonable grounds for detaining someone and to prosecute them on the basis of that evidence. Anything else is arbitrary intimidation worthy of a dictatorship. The same is true of badgering by the media. Ordinary Muslims are no more answerable for the actions of terrorists than I am for Dresden, Amritsar or Hiroshima (though I am as yet free to condemn them all). Sympathy with a legitimate cause does not imply support for the actions taken by all its advocates, but endlessly condemning them to satisfy the egos of opportunist politicians and overpaid presenters is demeaning and deliberately diverts attention from the imperialist thugs who are usually to blame.

According to research each of us has a one-in-sixteen-million chance of being near an act of terrorism. We are far more likely to die from the effects of austerity, which are obvious and devastating. Should politicians be endlessly pressured to condemn it? Should it be demanded that they repeatedly condemn the selling of weapons to dictators or the propping up of brutal despots? The focus on terrorism deliberately distracts us from these questions. It creates division based on fake unity; struggling rulers have always known that 'with otherhood comes brotherhood.'

Yuval David has said that McDonalds and Coca-Cola are a bigger threat to our lives that al-Qaeda and ISIS. Writer and broadcaster Will Self once said he saw no distinction between those who embark on offensive conflicts and the violent jihadis who try to repel them. Parliamentarian Tony Benn said he saw no moral difference between a stealth bomber and a suicide bomber; they both kill innocent people for political reasons. They could only get away with expressing these truths because they aren't Muslims. Had they been Muslims they would have been pilloried for expressing a crass and unjustifiable moral equivalence; how can the actions of our brave soldiers be compared with those of we choose to define as murderers. Can it really be that simple, or is the distinction dependent upon the level of imperialist propaganda one has absorbed?

In February 2021 the British government announced it was appointing a free speech champion to ensure open debate in universities. In the same week the Greek government imposed a new police force on campuses and virtual dictator Regip Tayep Erdogan made one of his cronies the head of a Turkish university. Last week he called LGBT+ student activists terrorists. The University and College Union says the biggest threat to free speech is ministers trying to police what students can and can't discuss. Integral to this has been an attempt to silence Muslims. The government's own Prevent program has seriously curtailed open debate about American and British foreign policy and the wholesale adoption of the spurious IHRA definition of anti-Semitism has proscribed proper debate about Israel, a touchstone of Muslim concern.

All this is compounded by the advance of the surveillance state and the digitisation of information that incorporates racist algorithms. Lizzie O'Shea says in *Future Histories.* 'By generating technical solutions to the problem of crime, the myth of the state as the indisputable provider of safety becomes a logical, indisputable truth. It creates a category of people it classifies as criminals, which it then polices and trains us to fear.' Our rulers often cite the Enlightenment as our datum, as if the very word encapsulates its goodness. This is what the enlightened Immanuel Kant said; 'Humanity exists in its greatest perfection in the white race... the yellow Indians have a smaller amount of Talent. The Negroes are lower and the lowest are a part of the American peoples.' Spurious science in the form of crude eugenics has for a long time been used to justify oppression. But crude inferences about light and dark, good and bad, modern and medieval suggest we've yet to move on.

Hoda Katebi, an Oklahoma born Muslim of Iranian descent, was asked onto a Chicago TV show to talk about her work as a fashion designer. After it was insinuated that mini-skirts meant freedom and the hijab meant oppression she was asked about Iran's nuclear weapons. She compares this to a white chef being invited on to reveal his latest recipe, only to be asked why he hasn't condemned the violence of white supremacists. Thinking on her feet she places the blame where it lies (i.e. with US aggression) only for the interviewer to say she doesn't sound like an American. Her response should be a lesson to us all; 'That's because I read.' The interviewer then refuses to shake her hand. She says;

'Patriotism ultimately is inherently violent and oppressive; and especially so within ideas of the nation state and Whiteness that were constructed only in opposition to a racist and Orientalist caricature of what is not. Patriotism in stolen land, forced labour, and instructions and borders erected to maintain White supremacy is nothing more than patriotism towards White supremacy. Assimilation into these structures is only assimilation into White supremacy and the associated classism. A image of a visibly Muslim woman in a black *abaya* or a bearded man in *salwar-kameez* could never be the trending image of Muslims in progressive spaces that is being uplifted and pasted on protest signs: unless there is some rejection of identity in order to 'prove' Americanness – like draping an American flag as a hijab – there is a basic understood level of foreignness and incompatibility.'

'Telling a Muslim woman on live TV that she 'does not sound American, is incredibly dangerous. My refusing to play into these aforementioned binary categorisations of the world can not only incite violent harassment and verbal accosting, but even provoke a consistent stream of harassment and threats of violence on line, and (additional) state surveillance... So a simple accusation that I "do not sound American" because, as a Muslim woman, I find this country's colonial history, indigenous erasure, and unending global violence problematic is akin to being flagged by the department of homeland security as a radicalised threat, which, for a Muslim woman engaged in community organising, is no small accusation with lasting consequences.'

In pointing to the concurrence between increasing Islamophobia and rising Muslim representation, much of it patronising and tokenistic, Hoda Katebi says 'Having a seat at the table does not necessarily mean that you are no longer on the menu.'

As I was writing this piece I heard that a cornerstone of liberal British broadcasting, *Woman's Hour,* had been censured for conducting a hostile interview with the first female head of the Muslim Council of Britain.

DAMAGED GOODS

Nemesis – Philip Roth

Philip Roth is the only writer to have his entire works published in a comprehensive edition in the Library of America. Perhaps this is due to his remarkable prescience. As I began reading his 1944 novel *Nemesis* a coronavirus epidemic that had claimed the lives of 130 people, infected 6,000 and forced whole cities into quarantine was spreading across China and certain to spread further. The story is set during an outbreak of polio in New Jersey and concerns the responses of the public and the authorities.

The story is centred on Bucky, a young all-American Jewish man, whose friends are all away fulfilling their patriotic martial duty. Bucky was set on joining the Marines, especially after the personal affront of Pearl Harbour, but he is denied his generational rite of passage and the dubious honour of dying for his country due to defective vision. None of the other armed services are prepared to take him and, diminished as one of the guilt-stricken who didn't go, he is psychologically reduced to less than a man, working as a gym teacher and vacation playground director. His charges are on their long summer break and he witnesses them falling prey to polio one by one.

Jewishness is the lens through which Philip Roth sees America, but fifty pages into *Nemesis* it seems not to matter. The boys' grandfathers have endured anti-Semitism, but that kind of thing has been consigned to the past, except that of course, it hasn't. We are tacitly informed that racism is alive and well in the Land of the Free when the father of one boy refers to some Italians as 'Dagos'. War generally obviates the necessity of divisive and distracting racism. It wasn't until afterward that black men in particular realised that fighting and dying for America still wasn't enough.

Meanwhile, the epidemic kills the younger siblings of those on active service and their distraught parents have to break the news to them by letter. People who have never had cause to consider fairness don't think it fair that the disease strikes people who have always tried to do the right thing. They want to know where the sense of life is if it isn't fair. They have become the victims and as those previously blinded to injustice they can suddenly see.

As with previous epidemics polio throws up questions about domestic pets as well as domestic policy and cats fall foul of ignorance as they did in Pepys's Britain. But the man in the diner believes it was 'the Wops' who introduced polio to the neighbourhood, or possibly the owners of the Chinese restaurant. It gradually becomes apparent that Jewish kids are more susceptible and Roth's 'racial' backdrop becomes relevant. The Jewish doctor is against causing unnecessary alarm; the Jews fled Europe so they wouldn't be afraid and, after all, this is America.

The mourning parents can't blame God because God is protecting their other sons in the war. God clearly saves those who survive, but he's not responsible for those who die. Bucky is alone in blaming God, and considers sun worship as useful as placing faith in that cruel deity. His crisis of faith causes him to question the very nature of God. An omnipotent deity has to will bad things to happen or they would not come to pass. Free will, the faithful's get out of jail card, loses its force when a child dies of disease, and the argument that God wants them to be with him doesn't wash when it causes so much grief. An all-powerful God that lets bad things happen is not a good God. He is no God at all. He does not exist. He is nothing, and no amount of faith can make him be. He may have been necessary and desirable, but he is not contingent. Bucky has been indifferent to his religion, but his indifference turns to anger; if God exists he made the disease.

As the epidemic spreads the desperate community searches for someone or something to blame; it could be the black cleaning women, or paper money passing from hand to hand. It could be spreading through the mail. It could be 'the Chinks', the heat, 'the Wops' or the burger bar. Later people will begin blaming the Jews for the polio epidemic because it is centred on a Jewish area and because blaming Jews is what people do.

Bucky decides to leave polio-blighted Newark to take up a post at a summer camp with his fiancé. He feels humiliation at having to tell his boss he no longer wants his job because he considers himself to be deserting his responsibilities and his self-pride is undermined.

The summer camp turns out to consist in wholesale cultural appropriation. The aim is to manufacture rugged American individuals who demonstrate manhood, fortitude and heroism through a corrupted and vulgar version of Native American self-sufficiency, sanitised for white urban American youth. Naturally the teenage boys Bucky works with are desperate to join up and get some action before the war is over, no doubt assuming as boys do, that war is something akin to a summer camp.

Things go well with Marcia; the romance of the woods and the shore and the moon temporarily distract Bucky from the belief that he has deserted his boys for an easy life in the mountains, his guilt at deserting his boss and his guilt about not fighting in the war, which has been portrayed as being between good and evil. He reassures himself that he hasn't deserted his peers; it is the army that won't let him fight. He's still uncertain about God's role in the unfolding tragedy and jeopardises their relationship by telling Marcia that God must have made polio, which to his devout girlfriend is a preposterous suggestion. Blind faith isn't enough for Bucky. He knows it was only possible to believe in an entirely good God when everything was going well.

At the camp Bucky has everything he needs apart from a conscience he can live with, but he still doesn't go back to Newark. What his discomfort demonstrates is that you can't be truly contented while others are in distress and you can't be entirely well while others are sick. It's not enough for him to keep on pretending; going through the motions of normality in what has turned out to be a far from normal world. His guilt is compounded by the news that one of his best friends has been killed in action in the war he wasn't allowed to participate in.

Inevitably the boys at the camp start falling ill and Bucky is revealed to have brought the virus with him. He eventually succumbs to the disease himself and is ill in hospital when Roosevelt dies and when the atom bombs are dropped on Hiroshima and Nagasaki. As the war ends, and America celebrates, Bucky's massive medical bills are paid for by charities and the formerly fit young man, his life destroyed, is forced to work at a gas station, where the customers call him gimp. Through hard work he eventually secures a government desk job.

God turns out to be no more than chance; Bucky survives, but as half a man, twisted by polio and demoralised by shame, his reduction to the ranks of the less than men is complete. Polio did to Bucky what the war did to thousands of other young American men. Physically and psychologically damaged he consciously distances himself from others for their own good. He is told he doesn't know God and he doesn't know himself. He ends his relationship with Marcia, who wishes he'd been a soldier, believing that then he might then have been better able to deal with the self-pity he disguises as concern for others. Bucky still blames God because he has to blame someone. It would be just as easy to acknowledge that there is no good god and there is no bad god because there is no God at all. As readers we gain no insight into the nature of this non-existent god, but there are lessons on the nature of belief, and even greater insights into disability and resentment.

Bucky is told there are specific stages to be gone through in turn. First the disabled person must physically and mentally adjust to life as a cripple. Having passed that stage they must do what little they can to avoid spiritual extinction. 'Then if you're lucky, five hundred stages later, sometimes in your seventies, you find you are finally able to say with some truth, "well, I managed after all – I did not allow the life to be sucked out of me completely." That's when you die.'

The man who appraises Bucky of this reality takes his own life during stage two, and there's a certain symmetry in the fact that soldiers as well as polio victims find solace in suicide. Like a returning soldier Bucky's guilt is internalised and individualised. Despite the fact that he succumbed to a social disease it is his problem and not society's. The story ends with a picture of what a real whole man should be.

WATER UNDER THE BRIDGE

Economics for the Many – John McDonnell (Ed.)

I wrote this sympathetic review of Shadow Chancellor John McDonnell's 2020 book when Jeremy Corbyn was at the height of his powers and the ruling class had yet to discover the means by which to destroy him, believing at the time that it was mostly pie in the sky. Corbyn was subsequently hung out to dry by the Labour right and the party was trounced in the general election. It is obvious after the 2021 assault on the US Capitol that the most important sentiment is that expressed by Guy Standing.

Within this collection of essays there is much revealing detail about the systemic theft at the heart of the current system. What is suggested is a manifesto for fundamental change; a blueprint that Labour supporters could sign up to. Various left thinkers propose things a Labour government *might* do in response to the instability and polarisation neoliberalism has caused. John McDonnell says he wants to create a socialist society, but I am not sure that all the contributors share the same vision, they certainly don't say so. Instead we are promised an extension of democracy beyond politics and governance into economics. This is said to represent a long Labour tradition encompassing the Luddites, Robert Owen and the Rochdale Pioneers. The Cooperative Movement, with its one billion members, is cited as a positive example of what is possible. As the Coop bank has been sold to venture capitalists and the retail arm is driving through the same kind of attacks on workers' conditions as every other business this seems a little odd.

We are told that 'the economy' is a fairly recent device designed to convince us we share interests with our exploiters. But the suggestion that 'economic illiteracy' is the problem seems patronising; workers do not need to have read Marx to know they are being shafted, or that a whole industry exits to avoid and evade tax. And speaking of Marx – no one does. He simply doesn't get a look in, and nor do the organised working class. All we have to do is wait for Labour and they'll do it all for us.

Ann Petifor tells us that Labour will recruit a well-paid 'carbon army,' funded, like wars, by the sale of bonds. The Fiscal Credibility Rule is explained, which, though it ties Labour to reducing the budget deficit, would have avoided austerity. Johnna Montgomerie explains how 'financialisation' has decimated savings in favour of 'asset based welfare,' made housing a highly leveraged asset and caused a reliance on debt for economic participation. To definancialise the economy Costas Lapavitsas calls for the establishment of public banks. Shadow Trade Secretary Barry Gardiner proposes 'institutional internationalism' as a solution to the twin dangers of protectionism and unregulated trade. Grace Berkeley and Luke Railes argue that London is almost a separate economy and regional devolution is needed to aid regeneration.

As well as a return to municipal ownership of services and renationalisation of key industries it is proposed that Labour encourages workers' cooperatives through a revamp of its 1976 Common Ownership Act. The 'Cleveland Model', which pioneered the concept of community wealth building, is used as an example, as is the radical approach being taken by the ruling Labour group in Preston. Francesca Bria cites Barcelona, which now treats accessible data as a form of public infrastructure alongside roads, electricity and water. In opposition to internet platform monopolies, Nick Srnicek celebrates the recent right to be forgotten and the new 'opt in' to being tracked for advertising. Getting down to fundamentals J. Christopher Proctor explains how 'economics' is narrowed, limiting what students are taught and progressives see as possible, arguing that we have to create our own think tanks where 'heterodox' economics can thrive. Ozlem Onaron argues that 'care' should be properly funded, not least because the positive effects of social infrastructure investment are greater than those in physical infrastructure.

As it comes last we might imply a policy in Guy Standing's case for a 'Commons Fund' and a universal basic income, 'the only welfare policy that has an emancipatory value greater than its monetary value,' which he says would promote freedom, end exploitative relationships and remove the onus on the poor to endlessly prove they are deserving. Standing also says the left needs to ditch Marx's outdated binary notions of class.

This is not a revolutionary document or a concrete manifesto of what Labour intends to do. But there is plenty to learn and some serious discussions with which we should engage. In the final article Guy Standing claims vindication for his 2011 prediction that if the grievances of the precariat were not addressed a political monster would emerge. We can argue about the existence of a precariat separate from the working class as a whole, but the shape of the monster is now clearer. The counter to it is the organised working class. Sadly they do not get a single mention.

I wrote the above when we were going along with the idea that electing the right people to parliament could bring about fundamental change. For the sake of left unity what follows didn't survive the first edit;

John McDonnell celebrates the shift to Labour under Corbyn and says neoliberalism has failed, but he credits it with rules, such as the thoroughly discredited 'trickle-down effect.' This is to fundamentally misunderstand it. Neoliberalism is an attempt to reverse the long-term decline of capitalist profitability *by any means necessary*. The devastating impact of this twisted ideology is obvious in every social indicator. The most ardent neoliberals simply do not care whether working people live or die; they actually believe that wealth is created in the boardroom and the stock exchange. We are engaged in a class war and their side is winning, yet 'Corbynism' consists almost entirely in the personage of one old white man. John McDonnell says Labour will end austerity and repair the damage, but austerity is a smokescreen. We have to do better than helping to save capitalism from itself; rhetoric about increased investment and productivity is platitudinous. It administers treatment to a wounded monster that it may continue to torment us. Furthermore the high priests of Labour's 'broad church' are not singing from McDonnell's hymn sheet. Labour is singularly failing to 'weave a coherent, popular, democratic new narrative for our economy.' What it is doing is fudging and compromising in the name of party unity, just as it has always done.

I am not even sure the ridiculous argument that Labour caused the 2008 crash has been won, far less that academia should be released from its neo-classical economic straightjacket. Wading into the swamp of 'macroeconomic stability' and 'fiscal credibility' only reinforces the view that 'economics' are the province of the clever people who currently run the world and that things change, if they change at all, by us putting a cross on a piece of paper now and again. Working people understand the world only too well. 'Economics' exists to obscure the simple truth that they are being robbed. The privateers who are stealing our public services are only interested in one thing; when a drug company recently increased the price of an anti-biotic by 400% we were told that, 'The Company has a moral imperative to raise prices to what the market can bear.' This is the base *immorality* of the market; the payment of shareholder dividends trumps every human concern.

'Democracy in the industrial field' cannot only mean workers sitting as minority stooges on company boards as their own exploiters in pursuit of the Holy Grail of increased productivity; they must be able to decide what is made and how it is distributed. John McDonnell cannot offer this. Instead he promises incentives for new businesses, the encouragement of cooperatives and jam tomorrow, every bit of it delivered with no input from those who are to most benefit. Aside from occasional tea and biscuits in the boardroom and government help to start yet another café or dog grooming business the majority just have to sit tight and wait. If recent events demonstrate anything it is that the working class are sick of waiting. They are polarised into progressives desperate for leadership, and those so alienated that they are tempted by a political nihilism that undermines the very notion of civilisation. The majority of people continue to support democracy in principle, but they detest the reality.

Capitalism does not, will not and cannot ever operate in the interests of the majority. Even its most dedicated advocates acknowledge that the system is in the dock. Should we overthrow it or not? These essays suggest not. Instead we are offered a kind of second Third Way. I approached this book as a sceptic and soon came to see 'for the many and not the few' as empty phraseology.

In putting his head above the parapet John McDonnell

invites fire from the skilled marksmen of the establishment, but the chances of any working class radical being inspired to anything but voting by this book are practically zero. They would be far better off reading the *Communist Manifesto*. At a time when thousands of angry people are hungry for change and someone tells me every week that we need a revolution, I am sorry to say that I found *Economics for the Many* to be little more than an updated text book on the kind of patronising top-down reformist gradualism social democrats have been preaching since Lenin was a lad.

THE WAY WE WERE

Sniper One – Dan Mills

The personal accounts of the First World War tend not to glorify man's most base activity, but something has changed. Perhaps we can blame Hollywood, Vietnam, Andy McNabb or the politically motivated and populist Cult of the Veteran. There used to be an element of infamy, or at least self-doubt, attached to having been abroad to kill foreigners, especially among those who, during or afterward, realised that they were engaged in a futile waste of life and resources, which is what all wars are. If anything characterises more recent military autobiographies it is *shamelessness*. Some soldiers seem to have interpreted their elevation to socially-distracting demi-Gods as a license to hubristically degrade their adversaries and brag distastefully about the murders they committed while serving as thankless cannon fodder on behalf of brazenly dissembling pseudo-statesmen.

I don't generally read books that glorify murder, state authorised or not, and wouldn't have gone out of my way to read Dan Mills' *Sniper One*, but it came highly recommended. In fact it was thrust earnestly into my hand by an acquaintance. He is a stalwart member of the Labour Party, which despite its pretensions to represent humanity's victims, has backed every imperial adventure since its inception, and still does. In fact the 2003 invasion of Iraq might not have happened but for the support of Labour's most egotistical, self-aggrandising and contemptible leader. I approached the book without enthusiasm; thoroughly expecting a variant on the cheap war comics some of my fellow soldiers used to masturbate over in their bunks: or was that the weapons-grade porn they also consumed?

Sniper One is the true story of British soldiers in Iraq. And here we must remind ourselves what a sniper normally is; he is someone who kills the enemy in cold blood, with a single shot, while he is at his tiffin or toilet. His actions are meant to give the enemy no peace and no relaxation; to keep him in a state of permanent high alert and mental anxiety. Sniping is psychological warfare physicalised.

The book looks and feels like one of Andy McGrabb's interminable offerings, and twenty pages in it's a swaggering account of hyped-up thugs and bar-room brawlers, who are unsurprisingly also sexists and racists. Sergeant Mills claims that snipers can't be mentally deficient, but being able to work out coordinates clearly doesn't make them intellectuals. I soon became convinced that the author was an unmitigated arsehole, with a single self-serving maxim; 'We are the law, they are the criminals.'

It would be foolhardy to paint soldiers as any better than the general population. For the most part they are young, ordinary working class men, as liable to misplaced prejudice as any other public bar bigot; *Loaded* and *FHM* are their favourite reads, dirty films their default entertainment. Workers are condemned for striking, women are judged entirely on their physical attributes and, despite being engaged in a peacekeeping mission, thirty-something Sergeant Mills, says 'If I had only wanted to help the locals I'd have joined Oxfam.' His platoon consists of aggressive hotheads and men who joined the army because they wanted to kill with impunity. They get a rush from combat and lament the arrival of a ceasefire. The Coalition Provisional Authority are 'twats', Iraq's reconstruction is 'tree hugging' and not being allowed to shoot whoever they want is political correctness.

And our heroes aren't blasé about the death they inflict; they positively glory in it while feigning indifference to their victims, not because their work is tedious; every kill is exciting, but because they are tough, macho soldiers who, unlike us over-soft civilians, aren't affected by seeing people endlessly blown to pieces. Except that it's not really like that. I was a soldier for six years, never fired a weapon in the direction of another human being and only carried a loaded one in a public place on a few occasions, but the memory of my service will never leave me and it is an integral part of who I am today. I know it's not the same, but I also I spent three years as a secondary school teacher. It was one of the most stressful periods of my life and I still have disturbing dreams about it a decade later.

How must that be magnified if in your formative years you carried out, or even only witnessed, routine desecrations of the human body? A 2014 *Guardian* article described one young soldier's experiences; 'He was only eighteen or nineteen; he was out on a tour in Kosovo and this little boy, six or seven, would bring them bread and milk. They played football with him and would chat with him, and one day they found the little boy's body in pieces in their water supply. Imagine how you cope with that? They knew it was their fault, because the boy was seen as a collaborator.' Combat veterans report vivid nocturnal flashbacks, during which they can smell burnt flesh and experience the authenticity of death. Still-young men are afraid to sleep because of the terrible nightmares that haunt them.

And there's no wonder; after a colleague blows off someone's head Sergeant Mills says, almost in self-justification, 'The satisfaction wasn't warped bloodlust. It was entirely professional. Just like a bricklayer who's just built his first house, and knowing he can do it – and damn well at that.' Except that the bricklayer has provided someone with a home, whereas the sniper has robbed someone of a breadwinner. Like preposterous posh fox-hunters the snipers rib each other about not yet having killed anyone; someone whose face they could see and their humanity appreciate. After blowing a great hole through someone Mills says, 'He could put his hand through himself to wipe his arse.' These are our sons and brothers, systematically made into killing machines and warped by warfare.

Despite the endless machismo and the graphic descriptions of the enemy in their death throes, there are brief hints of introspection. Danny Mills asks, 'How do you even begin to explain what it's like to watch a bloke get his leg blown off and then pick it up and put it under his arm? How do you then say you weren't actually that bothered by seeing it? ... best to just say nothing.' You can't explain it any other way than by admitting you are some kind of state-manufactured psychopath.

Towards the end of *Sniper One* Sergeant Mills describes seeing himself in action on television while in a pub waiting for a train. There is an abject lack of irony in his belief that the strangers around him probably consider him as, 'just another drunkard in a railway station with mental problems.' In the last paragraph he is preparing to leave the army after twenty-two years' service. The last line is 'I've no idea what I'll do next.' Statistically his options range from the sublime to the schizophrenic.

I expected *Sniper One* to be a load of macho shite; what else could it be? I embarked on it with cynicism, expecting it to be a gung-ho tale of daring do, and that's what it is. The soldiers are doing the job they've been trained and sent to do. Of course they're ruthless and celebrate killing the enemy; it's what they're paid for. They're not nice people, and neither are their enemies. There's no point in blaming them for the situation in which they find themselves; that responsibility lies elsewhere.

As a story *Sniper One* is a compulsive and exciting read. You begin to care about whether the soldiers' beds are going to be destroyed by incoming mortars, and whether the destruction of their mess room and the death of their cooks will mean cold food. But that hardly offsets the impression that some of them are hyped-up and determined killers who joined the army because that's what they wanted to be. Nevertheless, it is difficult to believe that anyone can entirely avoid moments of doubt. At one point the relentless narrative allows a scintilla of sympathy for Iraqi civilians caught up in the unspeakably brutal occupation of their country and the entirely understandable insurgency it caused.

It would be crass to glorify the deranged young men that *Sniper One* depicts, but the book certainly provides an insight into what members of the British army experienced. Having been sent to Iraq on the kind of peacekeeping mission the soldiers belittle as namby-pamby they endure great adversity, suffer serious and fatal daily attacks, and on one occasion lose a battle tank and several armoured vehicles to badly trained and poorly armed tribesmen. Did Vietnam teach our rulers nothing?

Sergeant Mills is relieved when the Rules of Engagement are changed and they can shoot unarmed Iraqis considered to be assisting the enemy. This is not because it will lead to a just resolution, but because they consider themselves to have been hamstrung by the kind of bleeding-heart liberalism that prevents them from doing what they think they should be doing; killing anyone who happens to pass through their sights, or, as the message across the beer-bellies of armchair warriors says when their 'These colours don't run' T shirt is in the wash, 'Kill 'em all and let God sort 'em out.'

Sergeant Mills makes a bold attempt to convince himself and us that what the British army did in Iraq was worthwhile. He is compelled to do this, despite copious evidence to the contrary, because unquestioning faith in Britain's noble and civilising mission is the timeless soldier's only salvation. The alternative is the spiralling, destructive guilt and self-recrimination that leads to sleeplessness, suicide and vagrancy, via strong drink and domestic abuse. I wonder how Danny Mills and his trigger-happy old pals really get through each day. I think I'll stick to reading about the First World War. Can it be that it was all so simple then, or has time rewritten every line?

A THOROUGHLY
AVOIDABLE DESCENT

One Man's Terrorist, A Political History of the IRA
– Daniel Finn

Northern Ireland is one of Britain's last colonies. Imperial rule has consisted in brutality, dispossession and repression. In 1921, following sustained attempts at national liberation, the island was partitioned. The northern state was gerrymandered to ensure a permanent loyalist majority and Catholics were systematically marginalised. Opposition was guaranteed and the question for Republicans was always whether the Irish people should be liberated from Britain or from capitalism first. In December 1956 the IRA began attacking police and military targets in the north, believing it could drive Britain out. When the general population showed little interest the leadership attempted to build a workers' movement capable of replacing both northern and southern states with an all-Irish socialist republic. Some IRA members considered this plan a distraction from the armed struggle, others that they were making a grass-roots revolution and that picking up a gun and acting *on behalf* of others was an easy option.

As part of the 1960s upsurge in international working class resistance an effective civil rights movement could have transformed the lives of Northern Ireland's Catholics. Its modest demands for universal suffrage, fair government and an end to sectarianism did not threaten the union with

Britain, but the possibility of non-sectarian working class unity was sabotaged by unionists who branded it a subversive conspiracy. The state responded to civil rights marches in 1968 and 1969 with bans, extreme brutality and further repression. Republicans were forced to defend themselves and their homes from a police force on the rampage. The argument shifted from civil rights to police repression and a non-sectarian future slipped away as opinions hardened.

The Official IRA knew violence would license further attacks on ordinary Catholics. It called for a bill of rights, democracy in the north and a peaceful transition to a united Ireland. The Provisional IRA quickly recruited those who disagreed with this strategy. Its leadership condemned 'red infiltrators' and turned its back on the republican socialist tradition. Catholic families became the victims of mass pogroms and by the time British troops arrived with armoured cars and machine guns ten people were dead. The struggle became one between the Provisional IRA and the British army. The British Labour government did not impose its authority on Northern Ireland; Unionists demanded the restoration of law and order and the army resorted to its well-practiced tactics of colonial repression.

The Northern Irish premier refused to ban Orange marches and the army facilitated them. The Provos declared themselves the defenders of nationalist areas, but escalating repression united the two wings of the IRA in confronting the British state. In response to limited stone throwing the army invaded the nationalist Falls Road area, drowned the area in tear gas, fired 1,500 live rounds and killed four civilians. To complete the show they paraded two gloating Unionist politicians around the area in their Land Rovers. Overnight the Catholic attitude to the security forces went from neutrality to hatred. The army's own account of The Troubles regards the

Falls Road invasion one of its greatest miscalculations.

As the army made the situation worse by subjecting the Catholic population to clouds of teargas and arbitrary arrests young civil rights activists transferred to the armed struggle, believing social questions could be postponed pending a united Ireland. In February 1971 a Provisional IRA sniper killed the first British soldier to die in Ireland for fifty years. To stop an exodus of members the Official IRA also sanctioned attacks on British soldiers.

In August 1971 soldiers began kicking down doors, smashing up Catholic homes, dragging away young men and subjecting them to colonial torture methods, while refusing to arrest loyalist paramilitaries. In Ballymurphy the army killed ten civilians in thirty-six hours and recruitment to both wings of the IRA rocketed. The nationalist population was united in supporting the resistance as the army kidnapped and imprisoned innocent people. The Civil Rights Association called for total non-cooperation with the state and nationalist residents barricaded the army out of their estates.

The descent into open war was ensured by the Unionists' belief in their God-given right to rule at the expense of ordinary Catholics, their willingness to use repression to enforce that rule and the unwillingness of the British state to confront them, in favour of the timeworn blunt instrument of colonial style military force to prop up a blatantly unjust and unfair status quo. The unionists refused to share government with nationalists and Edward Heath continued to back them.

At the end of 1971 mass civil rights protests returned. After weeks of escalating confrontations IRA recruitment was massively boosted by Bloody Sunday, when the British army killed fourteen civilians. Every witness to the massacre contradicted the army's version of events, but the Home Secretary backed the army's lie that it had acted in self-defense. The official whitewash of Bloody Sunday, which effectively upheld the army's right to summarily execute peaceful civil rights marchers, caused unmitigated fury. It also gave the IRA a legitimacy that would have previously been unthinkable.

While the British state fostered relationships with 'moderates' the IRA made itself unpopular by turning from a war against imperialism to one against other Irishmen. British army casualties fell as those of UDR soldiers and RUC officers rose. This saved the British government from public resistance to high casualties and made loyalist paramilitaries even more determined. The IRA considered launching its own Tet Offensive, which it would almost certainly have lost, but it was scuppered by people within its own ranks. Any credibility it gained by its bombing of infrastructure targets was lost when it targeted a Warrington shopping centre.

The bombings meant that the IRA engaged in ceasefire negotiations from a position of strength, but as talks began loyalist paramilitaries were colluding with the British army in the murder of republicans.

As a condition of peace talks Gerry Adams insisted only on eventual reunification by public consent. Britain refused to commit to full withdrawal, but as troops left Catholic areas loyalist hit squads moved in and attempted to scupper the talks. The document that emerged contained no real commitment to a united Ireland. Sinn Fein accepted vague promises about cross-border institutions, which it saw as a precursor to eventual Irish unity, and equality in the north that would make a state based on the oppression of Catholics irrelevant. This was essentially a reversion to the strategy of the civil rights movement of the sixties without the movement. Tony Blair agreed to Sinn Fein participating in peace talks prior to the IRA decommissioning its weapons, the

Good Friday agreement was eventually signed and after much wrangling a power-sharing assembly was formed.

In the IRA's own terms their three decade war had ended in failure. Many advocates of guerrilla war had known all along that armed struggle alone was not enough, but Gerry Adams was given credit for tactfully ending an unwinnable war. Tony Blair was accused of gullibility but the careful handling of Sinn Fein meant Adams stayed in charge and splinter groups did not revive the armed struggle. The IRA finally agreed to decommission its weapons in 2003 and power sharing began. Some hoped for a revival of the civil rights movement. Instead Sinn Fein became a conventional political party, substituting the suited politician for the gunman, neither of whom rely upon the self-activity of the masses and neither of which will deliver necessary radical reform.

In the 1970s Irish republicans rejected spectator politics, the peace process signalled its return. Sinn Fein stole the SDLP's clothes and then its vote. Its rhetoric sounded radical in the conservative south and it did well electorally, aided again by the 2008 crash, but it didn't back civil disobedience against water charges and prevaricated over abortion rights. As the situation becomes ever more complicated, the solution in the radical tradition of Irish republicanism becomes ever more obvious.

In 1918 the Irish people voted for self-determination. The failure to respect their democratic will created the IRA and launched a war for independence, to which imperial Britain typically responded with targeted assassinations, collective punishment and partition. While cynically pretending to be protecting a minority, it privileged its elite beyond their wildest dreams and gave ordinary Protestants a farthing more than Catholics, the better to rule them both. In doing so it sowed interminable division, just like it did in every corner of its stinking empire. It is impossible to exaggerate the contempt Northern Ireland's social, political and economic usurpers have for the Catholic population. As I write their *de facto* leader has resigned for not being bigoted enough, to be replaced by a man who believes gay people are an abomination to God, Catholics are six times more likely to contract and transmit coronavirus and the world began 6,000 years ago. Surely their days are numbered.

GUILTY UNTIL
PROVED DEAD

Death on the Rock – Roger Bolton

It will come as no surprise to many that among the noble professions of politics and journalism are many liars, or that life can become very uncomfortable for people who try to tell the truth. So it was for Roger Bolton. As a conviction BBC reporter he cut his teeth in Northern Ireland and notes how BBC programmes were banned or censored and the corporation accused of aiding the terrorists. In 1977 journalists who attempted to expose the mistreatment of Northern Irish prisoners were subject to a state sponsored witch-hunt, during which they were accused of inciting the IRA to murder police and prison officers. There may be two sides to every story, but Labour's Northern Ireland Secretary Roy Mason insisted that only the British state's side should be told. Despite threats to the BBC's charter and funding and to journalists personally the BBC reiterated its policy of open reporting.

'If it is to be maintained that change is brought about by the ballot box and that we are a civilised state with high standards we must not deny [those who represent, or seek to represent, sections of the populace] a voice, whoever they are, or allow those high standards to be reduced under provocation. That way the state is in danger of becoming what those who wish to destroy it say it already is, a tyranny, which can only be changed by force.'

In 1979 news editors, judges, senior police officers and civil servants met to discuss how broadcasters would modify their reporting in the interests of the status quo. The BBC had previously been willing to broadcast an interview with a leading republican whose organisation had murdered an MP outside parliament. This kind of thing is dangerous as it can lead to greater public understanding. Rather than hear what *their* enemies think the upholders of liberal democracy and the free press have decided that the public must 'understand less and condemn more'.

Consequently the BBC was accused by foreign diplomats of reporting human rights abuses abroad while ignoring them in Northern Ireland. This didn't bother Margaret Thatcher, who believed that opponents of the British State had no right whatsoever to have their opinions heard, and that anyone who facilitated the airing of their opinions was as good as a terrorist. She told the BBC to get its house in order and the Labour leader, James Callaghan, 'no defender of the press, nor a believer in open government' and a former advisor to the Police Federation, backed her up.

BBC journalists never believed the IRA and the British State were morally equal, but they did believe that the public had a right to know what republicans thought and that they would discredit themselves by expressing it. For this they endured a government sponsored media campaign of lies that culminated in hate mail and death threats. Roger Bolton's programme, *Panorama*, was lauded for scrutinising the powerful, but he had to sue the *Daily Telegraph* for alleging he was a subversive who had colluded with the IRA. Political interference was not exclusive to matters Irish; Bolton was invited to lunch with an MOD minister who asked him how 'we' (the government and the BBC) were going to defeat the anti-nuclear campaign of CND.

During the Falklands War the BBC again came under government pressure to report entirely from the British side. Bolton quotes Michael Leapman from his book *The Last Days of the Beeb.*

'It meant, in effect, that the BBC was not free to pursue a line that diverged to any significant degree from the jingoism that the government's information machinery was encouraging. Its editorial independence could be exercised only within defined limits – and one of the factors that defined them was Parliament's responsibility for setting the licence fee.'

The BBC was told it could not interview the widows or parents of the dead. The entirely Christian assertion that there was no difference between a widow in Portsmouth and a widow in Buenos Aires incensed people like Thatcher and Tebbit. When Thatcher was asked about the sinking of the *General Belgrano* on live TV she said only the BBC could ask about the right of a Prime Minister to protect 'our boys' from the threat of an enemy ship. As a member of the public pointed out, Thatcher was lying. The *Belgrano* posed no threat to British forces when it was sunk.

During the 1980s journalist Paul Johnson said; 'The BBC not only lies, it lies for the left. It not only rapes, it rapes for the revolution.' Johnson also referred to trade unionists as 'fascists', defended Augusto Pinochet, wrote speeches for Thatcher, was decorated by George W Bush, opposed 'moral relativism' and declared himself unimpressed by Nelson Mandela.

In reality BBC employees are vetted and it was unlikely that anyone with left-wing sympathies would be employed by the corporation, to whom 'left-wing sympathies' meant buying a copy of the *Morning Star,* out of personal or even journalistic interest, or acknowledging someone who might know a member of the Communist Party. The death of McCarthyism is greatly exaggerated.

In 1988 three IRA members were shot dead by the SAS in Gibraltar. It was claimed that the victims had been armed, that there had been a gun battle, and that a car bomb had been planted, defused, or destroyed in a controlled explosion. When all this was exposed as lies the MOD leaked that the soldiers thought the IRA three were going to detonate a remote controlled bomb which did not exist.

The Labour opposition applauded the murder and it took the *Times* to speak for reason; 'It is an essential aspect of any successful anti-terrorist policy to maintain the principles of civilised restraint which obtain in a democratic society. A failure to do so, argues that terrorism is succeeding in one of its critical aims: the brutalisation of the society under attack.' In other words if the state arbitrarily executes suspected terrorists and criminals it becomes as bad as the terrorists and a criminal state itself.

It had been discussed prior to the killings in Gibraltar whether the SAS was immune from prosecution and decided that they were not above the law and did not have a licence to kill. Nevertheless, off the record, journalists agreed that the deaths were part of a deliberate 'shoot to kill' policy. Asked why they didn't report this they said it didn't matter what they wrote, their editors would change it. Even Enoch Powell said the SAS must operate within the law and weren't entitled to kill someone on the basis that they were planning a crime.

When Roger Bolton posed serious questions about the Gibraltar operation on *This Week* he was smeared and slandered as unpatriotic and pro-terrorist by government and tabloids alike. One Tory MP referred to the report as 'the cringing limp-wristed antics of the wet liberal pacifists in the TV establishment.' Without even seeing the programme

Thatcher said 'trial by television and guilt by association is the day that freedom dies.' While Tories and tabloids engaged in blind patriotism the broadsheets gave the programme a fair review and all legal opinion was that the journalists' enquiries had been genuinely aimed at seeking the truth – except for Rupert Murdoch's *Sunday Times*, which slandered and misquoted all the witnesses. Its downmarket sister paper, the *Sun,* fabricated a story that *This Week's* main witness was an anti-British ex-prostitute with a criminal record. The broadsheets were attacked by Thatcher's press secretary, the odious Bernard Ingham. Both he and the Prime Minister sought to remind journalists of their responsibilities; to either print and broadcast the government line or say nothing.

It was revealed at an inquest that no attempt had been made to arrest the three IRA suspects; they had been shot in the back and 'finished off' from four feet away while on the ground. One of them had twenty-nine rounds in his body. The following day the *Sun* explained to its readers 'Why the dogs had to die', and 'have their brains blown out', bragging that one 'IRA fiend [had been] cut down by sixteen bullets.' The paper referred to the SAS killings as 'a super-smooth away-day mission'.

Roger Bolton was told off the record by an ex-cabinet member that the IRA suspects were already dead men when the cabinet decided to send the SAS, and that in the Iranian embassy siege released hostages held onto the legs of a young terrorist to prevent the SAS taking him back inside to finish him off.

For daring to question the right of the British State to carry out illegal targeted assassination Roger Bolton and his *This Week* team were effectively put on trial themselves, with the tabloids baying for their blood. The team were vindicated by the subsequent enquiry, but the *Sun* still found them guilty.

Thatcher also rejected the findings of the enquiry. *Death on the Rock* won a BAFTA and a Broadcasting Guild award for best documentary. An ex-soldier politician told Roger Bolton over dinner 'Of course there was a shoot to kill policy in Gibraltar, just as there was in the Far East and Aden. But it's none of your business. There are certain areas of British national interest that you shouldn't get involved in.'

Thank goodness we live in a democracy with a free press and not under some kind of junta that practices extrajudicial execution and where the news is censored.

THE GUARD DOG AT THE GATES OF PERCEPTION

Captive State – George Mombiot

George Mombiot's *Captive State* is about the corporate takeover of Britain. He paints a picture of a society under siege, whose very institutions are threatened by a power greater than any government, a power so great that only the risen people can confront it;

'The struggle between people and corporations will be the defining battle of the twenty-first century. If the corporations win, liberal democracy will come to an end. The great social democratic institutions which have defended the weak against the strong – equality before the law, representative government, democratic accountability and the sovereignty of parliament – will be toppled.

If, on the other hand, the corporate attempt on public life is beaten back, then democracy may re-emerge the stronger for its conquest. But this victory cannot be brokered by our representatives. Democracy will survive only if the people in whose name they govern rescue the state from its captivity.'

Our problem is largely that we have taken our rulers' rhetoric at face value. We no longer believe in Father Christmas, fairies at the bottom of the garden or that the moon is made of green cheese, but we are unable to shake off the misguided notion that what goes on in the mother of all parliaments is an example of democracy, perhaps because the alternative is too awful to contemplate; no one likes to admit they've been taken for a ride.

George Mombiot knows full well that the responsibility for stopping the corporate juggernaut lies with ordinary people, but his starry-eyed portrayal of a liberal democracy that in some golden age represented the people and no longer does is self-delusion. It has actually always defended the strong against the weak and ensured that the law was *not* equal. The MPs most of us didn't vote for demonstrably *do not* represent us, they are in no way accountable and parliament is sovereign for only so long as it represents the interests of the powerful, who have at their command the means to overthrow it should it cease to do so.

The setting up of some new scenario in which liberal democracy is under threat from corporate vultures obscures the fact that it was never intended that the interests of the majority be represented. Lenin called parliament a committee for the management of the affairs of the whole bourgeoisie, someone else said that if we could do anything with a vote they would never have given us one. The idea that we could actually instigate fundamental change by putting a cross on a piece of paper once every five years is a fantasy. The party system is a machine for ensuring that our electoral choice is effectively restricted to three people who all believe the same thing. A real democracy wouldn't need to parachute centrally schooled party hacks into unwilling constituencies, constantly invoke bogeymen or resort to jingoism.

The regular use of the term Britain PLC should leave us in no doubt that ordinary people are mere cogs in a corporate enterprise, facilitated by national governments, over which we have absolutely no control and they have very little. The words 'business' and 'back-room deal' are synonymous; the back-handers, lies cover-ups and profiteering at the heart of capitalism make it and democracy anathema. The whole pseudo-democratic system is riddled with corruption, nepotism and back-slapping. Politicians are interchangeable with the directors of obscene industries dealing directly in death and in the parasitical manipulation of markets that deprive people of the necessities of life. If we lived in any kind of democracy we would have a completely different set of priorities.

Instead, as Mombiot tells us, the corporations control all universities, thereby making independent science impossible, and they control all government committees, making honest assessment of the benefits or dangers of science impossible. In a 1999 government white paper on Public Health the only environmental pollutant mentioned was radon, which occurs naturally. At the largest ever ministerial meeting on the environment and health in the same year the links between industrial pollution and cancer were dropped from the agenda. There is no longer any independent oversight of drug and foodstuff introduction and usage.

Furthermore the 'Academic freedom' which 'is a guarantor of our wider liberties' has been undermined to such an extent by corporate sponsorship that 'Business now stands as the guard dog at the gates of perception.' The thinking person's first question about any research should be who funded it and what did they want to prove.

Right down to the level of the individual, what is good for the economy is automatically assumed to be good for us all, even if it means subverting the whole purpose of human learning into a twisted caricature whose sole purpose is the manufacture of unquestioning off-the-shelf business-ready workers. Under this criterion the only point of the arts is clever advertising and the only point of social science is in determining consumer dynamics.

What goes for education goes for health. The jewel in Britain's crown, the envy of all nations, is its National Health Service, but the resort to the Private Finance initiative '...demonstrates unequivocally that the government's plans for the NHS spell the end of accessible, affordable, universal healthcare in Britain.' We are heading for the American model for those who can afford it and charity for those who can't, if they're lucky.

Behind the corporate assault on health and education are international trade agreements that Mombiot calls 'the greatest threat to representative government on earth.' As an example he cites the Canadian authorities, who banned a petrol additive that had been shown to cause nerve damage in human beings. Under the terms of the North American Free Trade Agreement the producers of the additive sued the Canadian government for loss of revenue. The powerlessness of national government in the face of corporate dominance was demonstrated in Canada's forced out of court settlement and the reversal of the ban, which involved lying to the Canadian people that a serious threat to human health and wellbeing was after all harmless.

What is agreed at an international level is inevitably implemented at a local one, often against the wishes of those involved. We do not have to travel to the indigenous regions of South America to see people being side-lined by the corporate steamroller. In a chapter on the destruction of a community in Southampton in favour of developers Mombiot describes the council being bribed, public meetings rigged, petitioners branded as criminals and residents' leaders having their property set on fire.

We might console ourselves that in the two decades since this book was written the greedy short-sighted thieves who control the world have begun to realise that they too are in danger of going down with the ship, but it is quite obvious that the cure they envisage entails more of the disease; electric cars, carbon trading scams, smart meters and other profit-generating technological fixes for obviously political problems.

We could of course waste our lives waiting for the men in suits to rotate once more, in the vain hope that one day will rise through the normal channels some messiah who isn't in the pocket of big business, who can singlehandedly confront the corporations and reverse four centuries of environmental rape and human exploitation. We could even put some well-intentioned individual on a pedestal and point them in the right direction. But as sure as Christmas comes we will see them succumb to the back-scratching brotherhood or be systematically annihilated. History shows us that when we elect our potential saviours through a rotten system designed specifically to nullify their childish opposition we end up with the calming hand of the self-proclaimed sensible who promise us better things tomorrow if only we wait passively. We must ignore their appeals to reason, and we must never, ever line up with those who condemn the resistance while being blind to the actions of the real criminals. George Mombiot quotes Frederick Douglas;

'Those who profess to favour freedom, and yet deprecate agitation, are men who want crops without ploughing up the ground. They want rain without thunder and lightning... Power concedes nothing without a demand. It never did and it never will.'

Those of us who long ago lost all faith in the ability of deliberately undemocratic institutions to guard us from the poverty, starvation, war and environmental destruction that are the inevitable consequences of a system based on ruthless competition already know that 'those seeking to contain corporate power will be forced to confront not only the corporations themselves but also the states which have succumbed to their dominion. They will suffer privations, vilification and, as the law is further distorted to accommodate business demands, even imprisonment.' This has forever been the case, and yet people continue to resist.

FROM THE HORSE'S MOUTH

Policing Controversy - Ian Blair

On page three of Ian Blair's autobiography we discover that while he was Commissioner of The Metropolitan Police he was good friends with Rebecca Wade, the editor of the *Sun* newspaper, which was at the centre of the phone hacking scandal, and that his son was doing work experience with the paper. This cosy relationship with the editor of a reactionary tabloid doesn't exactly inspire confidence in police impartiality. However, Ian Blair wants us to know that he was on the right side of history in being among the millions of British people who questioned the wisdom of declaring a 'War on Terror'. This sensible position seems to form part of his case that he was forced from office for being too liberal and independent.

The ex-commissioner would have us believe that the police were not designed to be agents of the state, merely the enforcers of law and order, but this hackneyed defence begs a fundamental question; whose law and whose order? The modern police force certainly consists in the 'bodies of armed men and their equipment' that Lenin saw as the public face of the state. Despite Ian Blair's protestations the role of the police was always to control dissent from below. His innocent assertion that the bloodthirsty butchers of Peterloo, who were unequivocally the representatives of the rich, were merely 'attempting to control a demonstration' when they drove their horses into a crowd containing women and children wielding unsheathed sabres is no more believable than when applied to modern protests.

Ian Blair sees the 1985-85 Miners' Strike as a watershed, though it was far from the first time phalanxes of state thugs had confronted the working class. The watershed was actually in the strike's defeat by a vindictive and deeply ideological Tory government, which enabled it to drive through its neoliberal assault on the entire working class. For a generation of people it blew out of the water any notion that the police are not political. They were obviously working for the capitalist state in the interests of its ruling class and against the interests of those they exploit.

According to Ian Blair a large number of police officers in the 1970s were Labour voters because police work inevitably opened their eyes to the realities of a deeply unequal society. Something must have changed in the subsequent decade because there isn't a great deal of evidence that they had any sympathy for the miners whose lives and communities they helped the Tories to trash. Perhaps they were all taken in by the propaganda put about by Ian Blair's friends at the *Sun*. Or perhaps they were encouraged by the Tories' consistent favours to them as a conscious bulwark to their political and economic plans.

There are also scant grounds for any belief that the police are sympathetic toward the unhappy victims of the sick system they help to uphold. Many of the hundreds of people who have died as a result of contact with the police have been on society's margins and many an activist can attest to progressive protesters being insulted and assaulted by officers without provocation.

Ian Blair was in charge when armed Metropolitan Police officers fired six rounds into the head of the completely innocent and unarmed Brazilian man Jean-Charles de Menezes on an underground train. According to the ex-commissioner naïve people only asked why Jean-Charles couldn't have been arrested in his home on the basis of concrete evidence because they did not understand police operational methodology. We can certainly understand that the police constructed an entirely fictitious story to justify their actions and obscure their abject incompetence.

It is quite apparent where the ex-commissioner's sympathies lie; after the police killing of Roger Sylvester he said he felt the trauma of his assassins and after the killing of Jean-Charles de Menezes he advocated withholding details from the Police Complaints Authority on dubious operational grounds. Not only that, he confirms along the way what has always been rather obvious; that if armed police officers were ever truly held accountable for their actions they would refuse to carry arms.

In fact, when the completely innocent grandfather Harry Stanley was shot dead in the street two police firearms officers were suspended. One hundred and forty others, out of a total of four hundred, handed in their firearms cards. The authorities gave in and the suspensions were lifted. Only five years later did the authorities decide that the officers concerned had no charge to answer. Police officers have not and will not be prosecuted for shooting people dead, no matter how wrong they may have been in doing so; the risk of alienating them is too great.

Ian Blair was well aware the Met was riddled with corruption and it seems he made a serious attempt to tackle it. His claim is that he was brought down by a media interested only in sensational headlines and politicians aiming to make capital from the shooting of an innocent man, whose death, given the existence of the terrorist threat, he was powerless to prevent. He may have been the victim of the kind of sustained media campaign no public figure can survive, but he was hardly blameless. He claims he tried to bring a degree of social and racial justice to London's policing, but the *Daily Mail* said, 'Every day that Ian Blair clings to office seriously damages the Metropolitan Police and its ability to provide safety and security in the capital.' By some twisted logic the paper decided that the undermining of public confidence in the police force made another terrorist atrocity more likely.

In 2017 Bernard Hogan-Howe used his last speech as Metropolitan Police Commissioner to defend armed officers, calling the accusation that they are trigger-happy an urban myth. But two things are clear, firstly that British police forces now operate a deliberate shoot to kill policy and secondly; it is simply not possible that every killing on an increasingly long list was justified.

The Met dragged its flat feet all through the inquiry into the corrupt and obstructed pretend investigation of the murder of Stephen Lawrence, it spied on members of his family seeking justice and it considered it unreasonable that all its undercover officers be called to give evidence.

Cressida Dick oversaw both the Stephen Lawrence case and the killing of Jean Charles de Menezes and was promoted for it. She has now become the first female Commissioner of the Metropolitan Police. Her appointment is effectively a reward for both. Ms Dick is proud to inform us that she has always turned down desk jobs, preferring 'to be out on the street working shifts in the rain and the blood and guts.' In pen painting her past the BBC says her officers 'accidentally' shot Jean Charles de Menezes; that's 'accidentally' in the head, six times, at point blank range. The Menezes family says the appointment shows that the police can act with impunity, an assertion which is demonstrably true.

Meanwhile we are invited to celebrate the assent of a thoroughly establishment female Oxford graduate to the dizzy heights of the establishment, thereby proving that any woman from a humble background who doesn't make a glorious success of her life has no one to blame but herself. One could be forgiven for thinking that Ms Dick has been rocketed to stardom, irrespective of her disgraceful record, purely to prove that the Met is a right-on employer keen to reflect the demographic, and not a gang of largely white, ex-school bullies and social inadequates infected to the core with racism, sexism and homophobia.

Like most Metropolitan Police commissioners and chief constables Ian Blair was knighted for doing his job. What that job is depends mostly on one's political perspective. Those on the political right never tire of telling us that those who have done nothing wrong have nothing to fear. It is no doubt their opinion that the police exist to prevent crime. Given that we live under what is clearly a criminal system it might be suggested that they exist to facilitate its continuance.

Every new scandal is met with promises that the police have learned lessons and will change. And yet the police remain essentially the same. There is one simple reason for this; they are a necessary component in a society divided by class.

It would be difficult for a socialist to write an account of the Metropolitan Police in the 1970s and 80s more damning than that of its own former commissioner. Sir Ian Blair quotes one detective inspector, responding to attempts at reform, saying, 'The trouble with these plans and targets is they assume my CID office is full of swans. Some of them are not swans. Some of them are arseholes, even when they are sober, which is not very often.'

HOPE, DOPE AND DISAPPOINTMENT

Something Understood: Hope in an Age of Adversity
– Mark Tully

I can't deny that my reading regularly takes me into less than appealing areas of human existence, but Christmas Day came while I was compiling this volume and in the spirit of the season I really wanted to include something positive, optimistic and uplifting, something in praise of the human spirit and potential that brought us kicking and screaming to the point when it all started to go wrong, whenever that was, because wrong it has most certainly gone.

Struggling to find anything inspirational on my sagging contemporary veneered chipboard bookshelves I resorted to the wireless and Mark Tully's *Something Understood.* The velvet-voiced veteran has presented his religious-philosophical Sunday morning program for a quarter of a century and, despite my entrenched atheism and otherworldly ignorance, I have in the past found it edifying and entertaining. The eminently suitable festive topic was *Hope in the Age of Adversity* and I settled down for a lesson in life-affirming positivity and the optimism I am regularly accused of lacking.

The chronological element of the program's title; 'age', suggested that we are enduring something together, or at least at the same time (though hopefully not the crass assertion that we are all in it together, *it* currently being a pandemic whose disproportionate impact is obvious).

However, quick as a flash, while our attention was diverted, the celebrated broadcaster and inveterate God-botherer elided positive expectation into personal comfort, collective distress into private adversity, for which there is obviously only an individual solution, and hope into faith; preferably faith in God. In retrospect I should have perhaps expected the latter, but if religion isn't a collective enterprise it isn't anything. The fact that faith can be considered a solitary affair is a product of a pro-capitalist protestant individualism far removed from any notion of an outward looking Christian community. It is not one that 19th century English Methodists, anti-arms trade Quakers, South American liberation theologists, or for that matter modern Muslims, would recognise.

As hope dissolved like liver salts on the morning after we were left with nothing more to hold onto in a world that is clearly collapsing around our ears than the comforting sound of bird song and the sight of the rising sun. Nature is indeed marvellous and there is nothing at all wrong with celebrating it, but as a substitute for serious engagement, let alone a philosophy of life, ornithology and heliotherapy, like campanology and philately leave a little to be desired.

It is in the nature of human beings to ask why. A conscious refusal to face up to fundamental questions is self-defeating diversionism worthy of the ostrich who puts his face in the dirt while hoping that no one kicks him up the arse to bring him to his senses. The sun rises just the same on the sated and the starving, on the free and the oppressed and on the settled and the war torn. As a medicine abstentionism is a placebo easier for some to swallow than others. Birds sing on battlefields and borders; they'll keep singing until there's none left. The comfort we find in them can only be relative to our willingness to face facts and our belief in the ability of human beings to act collectively, as we always have done, even if it's only to stop species depletion.

When objective reality is reduced to our subjective attitude to it we are entering a swamp from which there is no escape. The belief that personal attitude is at the heart of human fulfilment is the beginning of a slippery slope through selfishness and victim blaming to corrosive bootstraps individualism, where the problems of the world cease to be in the world but in the minds of the dissatisfied. In a western context pseudo-Buddhist mysticism, along with all other forms of contrived inner-peace, are the refuge of the privileged who have decided they can live with other people's discomfort. Changing our attitude to the world absolves us of the much more difficult task of changing the world itself. Birdsong cannot drown out reality and pretending otherwise is like putting your fingers in your ears when others raise what are considered to be political questions. In reality no one abstains from politics because politics is life. The opposite of politics is death.

One contributor to Mark Tully's comforting Sunday morning pap wanted us to believe that 'sureness', i.e. being confident in one's beliefs and opinions, was a problem which led to confrontation, asserting in hackneyed inevitability, no doubt to the groans of philosophical materialists and social progressives who hadn't already switched off, that we only had to look at Northern Ireland. This seemingly inoffensive claptrap is an insult to generations of justifiably aggrieved activists and to the intelligence of anyone over the age of five. One of the things that sets human beings apart from other animals is that we have a history. We didn't spend countless millennia developing an intellect in order to refuse to use it. In Ireland there have been victims and perpetrators, progressives and reactionaries. The suggestion that cocksure opinions are behind a century old campaign for social equality and national liberation and not the desire to throw off the repressive imperial power behind them is asinine. Intransigence and belligerence are indeed factors in Northern Ireland, but they aren't causes. Behind than are real human concerns that need to be assessed accordingly.

To assert otherwise is to deny marginalised, disenfranchised and poverty stricken people, in the Irish case Catholics, in America black people, the right to assert their civil rights. It is to recommend that they put up and shut up, make the best of a bad job and attribute their intolerable situation to the almighty and his mysterious ways. In circumstances of explicit social and economic disparities, backed by institutional repression, conscious philosophical aloofness ceases to be neutral and becomes taking sides. The religious man at peace with the world who calls for peace and love between implacable antagonists, only one of whom has a just cause, is the obverse of the unthinking atheist who makes facile assertions about religion causing wars. Both have refused to grapple with the reality of the very real situations in which other people find themselves.

To bolster the belief in all-conquering hope Mark Tully sought the patronising opinions of a wealthy stud farm owner, who had conveniently discovered meditation as a means to reconcile the fact that her pointless enterprise was threatened by the coronavirus pandemic and she'd have to sack half her staff. By this time we were so far away from a collective solution to our collective problems and into the nauseating territory of navel-gazing individualism that it made little difference that Sam Cooke, whose *Change is Gonna Come* is widely viewed as a call to collective action, was enlisted as a harmless advocate of hope, passivity, faith and contentment.

The owner of the stud farm said she had faith in the mercy of God, celebrated love and selflessness and that we should get rid of our egos; that is, according to one definition, the part of the mind that reacts to reality, or according to another, our self-esteem. It was just one more thinly veiled repetition of the tired and disabling suggestion that we change the world by changing ourselves; that is we learn to live with a world full of poverty, injustice and cruelty, rather than upsetting ourselves by thinking about it, let alone pointlessly resisting it. It is nothing more than a recipe for the maintenance of the obviously obscene, unjust and unequal status quo. But worse than that it was put forward by someone who has directly benefitted from material inequality.

Among the program's platitudinous references was 'All will be well, all will be well and all manner of things will be well.' No doubt for some people, such as stud farm owners, they will, but it is unlikely they will have attained the material comfort upon which their new found mental comfort is based by pretending the world didn't exist.

In the end a Sunday morning program ostensibly designed to sooth the troubled soul, but which in reality serves to mollify righteous indignation, caused me severe irritation by asserting that the opposite of hope is despair. Empty hope based on a refusal to face up to the causes of and solutions to the world's problems is despair. It is resignation in the face of a challenge. It is giving up. The opposite of despair is resistance. Humanity is on a bus being driven toward disaster by people who have shown themselves to be ideologically incapable of changing direction and all will not be well unless we collectively wrest the steering wheel from their suicidal grasp, and no amount of inner peace can alter that fact.

Mark Tully's main residence is in India, where inequality is at its greatest. Can he really have come to terms with it? Christmas is a time for peace and love, a time for forgetting our differences. A time for football matches in No Man's Land. Next week we can resume blowing each other apart. Meanwhile, half an hour of disabling psychological introspection dressed up as spiritualism was enough to drive me to drink.

THE RETURN OF THE PRINCE

Lenin for Today – John Molyneux

Vladimir Lenin, the Marxist theorist and leader of the 1917 Russian Revolution, died in 1923 to be succeeded by Joseph Stalin, under whom the Soviet Union became a brutal and oppressive dictatorship. Entirely due to the danger that enlightened convulsions pose to their continuing existence our rulers and their servants have since disingenuously claimed that the USSR was the embodiment of Karl Marx's ideas. The maintenance of this fiction was greatly aided by much of the world's left, who deluded themselves for decades about the reality of Stalin's regime.

Three and a half centuries after absolute monarchy had been overthrown in Britain, the downfall of the tsarist autocracy was long overdue. All the progressive Russian political parties knew revolution was coming, if they disagreed about the form it would take. Lenin rejected the kind of politics that made ordinary people passive observers and called for a workers' revolution and a workers' government.

At the beginning of the twentieth century, as every European socialist party abandoned its anti-war principles and Europe descended into carnage, Lenin argued that imperialism represented the forced export of excess capital and that the conflict was about the division of the world in the interests of capitalist robbery. He said socialists should work for the military defeat of their own ruling class and a subsequent civil war for the progressive transformation of society. What pro-capitalist ruler wouldn't despise him?

The pre-war world had been divided into power blocks for the purpose of exploitation. Germany had overtaken Britain in capital accumulation, but had no colonies. In order to export its capital it attempted to steal colonies from its rivals. The First World War was therefore the necessary consequence of capitalism. For this reason Lenin insisted that only socialist revolution could end imperialist wars. He slated short term multi-national solutions as only truces between periods of war and in 1939 was proved correct.

Naturally smaller countries sought liberation, and Lenin made a distinction between oppressed and oppressor nations. He proposed an alliance between the workers of advanced countries and the oppressed peoples of minor nations *and* a temporary alliance with the rulers of such nations, while insisting on the independence of any workers' movement within them. Such international solidarity is clearly anathema to organised capitalist pillage.

Lenin believed that the appeal of reformist parties like the British Labour Party was in their ability to bribe the working class, which could not continue. As the Labour Party still exists he was clearly incorrect. 'Bribery' is an unsatisfactory term, but capitalist expansion through imperialism made it possible for trade unions and labour parties to obtain concessions from capitalism without overthrowing it. These organisations also disciplined the working class under tolerable conditions, but events since 1979 have demonstrated that progressive reformism is dependent entirely upon capitalist prosperity.

Lenin dismissed attempts to transform society by winning a parliamentary majority, in favour of the destruction of the state apparatus and its replacement with properly democratic workers' councils. He rejected the idea of the state as neutral, saying it arises from the division of society into classes and reflects irreconcilable antagonisms and interests. He insists that even in 'democratic' countries, the state is an instrument for the oppression of one class by another and that elections only allow workers to decide which member of the ruling class is to repress them.

Even if it were possible by bourgeois elections alone for progressives to capture the existing state machinery it would mean the working class being reduced to a passive role. Destroying the capitalist state means a risen and engaged working class driving the police off the streets, seizing police stations, winning over soldiers, forming local committees and commandeering public transport.

Some of Lenin's detractors pretend current elections are really free and that government exists to mediate between various interest groups, others parody the ruling class argument that he was an authoritarian. The most pathetic argument is that Lenin's opinions are now out of date. Pythagoras' theory is 2,500 years old and though Copernicus said the earth went round the sun in 1543 it still does.

Lenin's party, the Bolsheviks, was not authoritarian and unlike establishment parties was not dominated by its leadership. It argued regularly, made its decisions democratically and then put them into practice united. Lenin was often in the minority and outvoted, but he remained committed to socialist revolution and opposed to any compromise with reformism. He emphasised the need to take up all cases of oppression and tyranny and his party participated in the day-to-day struggles of the working class.

Some recent movements have declared political parties unnecessary, but Lenin said repudiation of the party principle meant disarming workers in the interests of their exploiters. Marxists take their politics seriously and have no interests apart from those of workers as a whole. Leon Trotsky, who was expelled from the Soviet Union and then murdered by Stalin, said there was no substitute for a revolutionary party. He saw nine separate national uprisings and the only success was in Russia, where the party was systematically built over decades. Since Trotsky wrote there have been fourteen revolutionary upheavals. None of them involved a mass revolutionary party and none of them succeeded.

Lenin had no patience with those who thought politics should be left to politicians, saying that a proper working class consciousness involves responding to all cases of prejudice, injustice, violence or abuse, no matter what class is affected. The times in which Lenin lived meant he had no experience of resisting women's oppression, and though the revolution decriminalised homosexuality, he did not analyse gay oppression. He did not mention disability rights, and the struggles against racism came after he was dead, but Marxist and Leninist principles apply equally to these struggles.

The Soviet Union existed for over half a century. It was a nightmare in every respect, a disaster for workers, women, LGBT+ people and minorities. It is in the capitalist class's interest to say that Lenin led directly to this authoritarian tragedy. To characterise Stalinist Russia as socialist or communist is to damn socialism and communism, as those who do so are well aware.

The belief that Lenin led to Stalin rests on the idea that capitalism is natural and corresponds to human nature (though this is refuted by thousands of years of egalitarian societies) and that socialism is unnatural and can only be imposed by force and dictatorship. This is strengthened by the idea that there has always been social and political hierarchy and that ordinary people are incapable of running society. Consequently an equal or classless society is utopian and doomed to fail.

The Lenin led to Stalin argument is often asserted as a historical fact, without evidence, and uncritically accepted. If evidence is produced it is that the Bolsheviks became authoritarian and all existing communist and socialist regimes are authoritarian. The latter claim is easy to refute; there are no existing communist or socialist regimes. Lenin would not have agreed that any regime brought to power without a workers' revolution was socialist and it is dishonest to claim Leninist principles drive regimes, such as that in China, which are Marxist or Leninist in name only.

The Bolsheviks *did* become authoritarian, but they did so due to circumstances outside their control, which are conveniently ignored, though Lenin explained them fully. The revolution could not be defended without committing mistakes and even crimes, and these too have been acknowledged. When the revolution came under threat from internal and external forces the Bolsheviks had two choices; they could hold out for revolutions to occur elsewhere or surrender to the counter-revolution, which would have meant unspeakable mass repression. We know this would have happened, because it has happened after every other failed uprising.

Lenin insisted that the revolution could not succeed unless it spread to other countries. Stalin's theory of socialism in one country was not a continuation of the Russian Revolution, it was its denial and a rejection of everything Lenin stood for.

A Leninist is someone who champions the working class and agrees with Lenin's theory of imperialism, his theory of the state and his theory of the party. They believe that to stop hunger, poverty, endless wars and climate change it is necessary to bring down capitalism and establish workers' power. They celebrate Lenin because he was right, not as a hero they long to replicate. No modern revolution that has not taken on the power of the state, understood imperialism and built a mass party has succeeded, but one must; the future of humanity depends upon it.

TRAVELS IN MY PANTS

Neither Here nor There – Bill Bryson

When Bill Bryson toured Europe twenty years ago he approached the continent's capitals with the jaded realism of a weary traveller, determined to allow credit only where it was truly due. It is difficult not to see his travelling in order to write about it as a conscious alternative to a character he himself universalises; the man, and it is always a man, women have other concerns, who has no one and spends his time staring into space with an untipped cigarette and an unusual hat. Of Bryson's caricatures this is one of the most attractive; a man at peace and a worthwhile persona to cultivate. Less attractive is his facile resort to national stereotypes and his obsession with seemingly ubiquitous sex shows and sex magazines.

I personally resorted to vicarious and unnecessary travel in Bryson's easy-read and fact packed books as a break from pointless and unnecessary metal work, only to quickly come to the conclusion, as he seems to have done without knowing it, that travelling round the world to see things you don't really care about and failing abysmally to enjoy yourself while doing it, like building silly bicycles, is fucking pointless. You may as well expect to enjoy yourself by obsessively commenting on the never ending bad news in an old school exercise book, only to waste even more of your life by typing it up for posterity under the illusion that you are some kind of modern day Pepys.

Bryson even acknowledges that the only possible reason for going to Lichtenstein is to be able to brag that you've been there, and this truth can be expanded to all foreign travel, though he stops short of doing so. It is debateable whether it takes a wise man or a fool to admit that what he fills his life with is utterly pointless; at least the man with the untipped cigarettes and the funny hat has ceased pretending. Not only do I know that I only build silly bicycles so I can brag about them to people who don't give a shit, I also know that they invariably have no concept of what making something from scratch actually entails and I am wasting my breath. More than that it's indisputably clear that the world, culture, integrity, communities and individuals have been ruined by tourism, with its McDonalds, chain coffee shops, fake Irish and Olde Worlde bars, endless stores full of bastardised pseudo-traditional tat and overpriced restaurants.

All this is innocent enough, but Bill Bryson, who travels the world spending a fortune on what most people consider luxury, precisely so that he can make a good living by writing about it, finds it necessary to take a swipe at Trotsky for being perpetually idle. This is the same Trotsky who dedicated himself to an often unpopular cause for no personal gain, held political meetings in garden sheds when he was teenager, chaired the Petrograd Soviet, led the Red Army, stood unswayed in his beliefs until he was murdered for it, was the author of numerous books on everything from manners to modern art and penned both a massive autobiography and the magisterial, thousand page *History of the Russian Revolution*. Coming from fellow writer Bryson, whose travel based offerings, along with his cultural and scientific popularisations, have all benefited from the obvious help of a large team of researchers, this is a bit rich.

If Trotsky is regarded with suspicion in Great Britain he is doubly so in the Land of the Free and the home of the McCarthyist witch-hunt, and it takes a very brave American to reject more than a century of bible-bashing patriotic conflation and boot-straps individualism to recognise that what Trotsky stood for is only the true realisation of utilitarian principles with which most people can agree. It is perhaps asking a lot for Americans even to be critical of the endless shit that blights the modern world, given that the administration they are sometimes sickeningly loyal to is ultimately responsible for much of it. To give Bryson credit he is vocally anti-Nazi. We can only hope this isn't only liberal lip service and that he also supports their necessary physical grass roots confrontation.

Perhaps the story of Bryson scabbing on a strike while working as a journalist at Wapping is apocryphal, but when he uses loaded phrases like 'the dead hand of central planning' it speaks volumes. There is patently nothing wrong with democratic central planning, railways and scientific research would be much the better for it. The western objection to central planning has nothing to do with its effectiveness and everything to do with generating private profit. It is disingenuous to pretend that the five year plans of the Soviet Union had any other purpose but to build up its industry at the expense of the people for the sake of pointless competition with the West. Any discussion of central planning is incomplete without the identification of its overseer. In the Soviet Union it was ultimately Uncle Joe, who didn't have to work in a tractor factory or rely on public transport.

The same prejudice is evident in Bryson's identification of 'monuments with crushingly socialist names', the opposite of which are presumably monuments with liberating capitalist ones, such as the equestrian imperialists that litter London in stone and bronze, along with those of history's great humanitarians such as the incinerator of Dresden Bomber Harris, the starver of Indians Winston Churchill and the ruling class thug and butcher of Argentine conscripts Margaret Thatcher.

In the last few pages Bill Bryson calls communism a noble experiment, as if it was concocted in a laboratory and handed down from on high. This grudging concession is only a reiteration of the bar-room philosophy that communism is a good idea but it doesn't work. It reminds us of Gandhi's retort when he was asked what he thought about western civilisation; it would be a good idea. Communism is a very good idea and we don't know whether it works or not because it hasn't been tried.

Despite what experts would have us believe there is no extant socialist society and there never has been. The noble experiment was strangled at birth by people who are happy with the world just the way it is. The working class men and women who overthrew the Tsarist autocracy no more wanted it to be replaced with the Stalinist dictatorship than the men and women who overthrew Hosni Mubarak's regime wanted it to be replaced with the brutal military dictatorship of General Abdel Fattah el-Sisi or the men and women who made the Iranian revolution wanted the western-imposed Shah to be replaced by the rule of medievally-minded mullahs. The Chinese people have had no more say in the ideological somersaults of their so-called communist rulers than the man in the moon. The only way the paranoid and obsessive opponents of communism can get away with their lies is by pretending that communism is the opposite of democracy, when it is actually their own corrupt and corrupting system that makes real democracy impossible.

Bryson almost laments that our rulers believe, or say they believe that 'the only system that seems to work is one based on greed and self-interest.' It is of course increasingly obvious that it only works for a very select few. If it worked in any real progressive, humanitarian, democratic, just or equal sense we wouldn't currently be choking the world with cars and shopping centres, polluting the seas and the skies, melting the ice caps and allowing billionaires to hide their wealth in off-shore tax havens while half the global population suffers from famine, disease and war. It only seems to work because we don't live in Syria or some other sibilant centre of extreme discomfort.

In my sixth decade I know exactly what Bill Bryson means when he talks about 'the sudden weight of not knowing what to do with myself.' That's why, like so many other people, I'm reading his book. I just wonder why I didn't find it as hilarious as those who are quoted on the back cover.

CLERICS, COPS AND CAVEMEN

Misogynies – Joan Smith

Joan Smith grew up in a progressive and equal home but saw Peter Sutcliffe's notorious campaign as more reflective of daily reality. She mistrusted the police and believed contrived theories about the Ripper's motives only obscured a hatred of women. She realised equality was not imminent, that the penalty for being female was sometimes death and asked the believers in biologically based sexism if they were happy with its consequences.

Before 1991 marriage equalled sexual consent; rape within marriage was impossible and the opponents of change feared for the reputation of perfectly normal men. Eminent judges said that rape victims had asked for it, women out late at night were probably prostitutes and that those who said no didn't always mean it. One feudal throwback gave a derisory sentence to a man who killed and cooked his wife on the grounds that he had been exceptionally patient with an impossible nag. Michael Douglas defended *Fatal Attraction*, declaring himself sick of feminists, whose unreasonable demands had caused men a terrible crisis. As in other 'male revenge' films, the intent was to show women that their unwanted intrusion into public life at men's expense has dangerous consequences. The flip side was the way Diana Spencer was constructed as a carte-blanche compliment to the worldly king in waiting. A fantasy close to child abuse was sanctioned even by the Anglican primate and badly needed a sequel, in which the fairy-tale princess turned grown-up woman was driven to an early death.

There is of course a biblical precedent in the story of Mary who, in her lack of resort to the reproductive advice and legal abortion we know existed, provides a timeless reinforcement of biological determinism and established women's inferior status forever. Her acquiescence is part of a veritable catalogue of theological opposition that was mobilised against female ordination, to be backed by Neanderthals like the *Sunday Telegraph's* Peregrine Worsthorne, who said it would be no more welcome than a foreigner on the throne. The Bishop of London joined those who deliberately conflated biological gender and socially constructed femininity in a way that not only disallowed women priests but would have precluded the Iron Lady's elevation. He went on to assert that the man-God had chosen a patriarchal society for his creations, presumably in perpetuity.

In the beginning God punished Adam for taking notice of a woman, a tendency which the godly should clearly avoid. Across Europe the guilty Eve became the guilty witch and the unspeakable church-led persecutions can only be attributed to a pathological hatred of women, in which the pious did not scruple to invent versions of history blaming the guilty daughters of Eve for every misfortune.

The ancient world was no paradise, but the prejudices of Roman men have been deliberately magnified by social conservatives claiming to be objective historians. They cite Cicero, who used women as pawns in internecine power struggles and branded them prostitutes in court to discredit them. They portray Roman women as being infected with irresponsibility, because they no more agreed with female freedom than the Roman men they distort.

Nowadays fifth century Greek democracy comes with a caveat, but it seems being unable to vote was the least of Athenian women's problems. Many were denied a social existence by men who regarded homosexual relationships as far superior. Old Etonians are expected to grow out of this kind of thing. Those who don't may resent being forced into disingenuous heterosexuality and literature can provide examples; WH Auden was comfortable including 'women' in a poem about fascists, a gay Compton Mackenzie character believes he can pass for a Victorian woman hater, not least because he is one. Admirable assertions about the right to be gay can hide a future for women not unlike Plato's Athens.

Two millennia later Czech novelist Milan Kundera was lauded for novels in which female characters are calculatingly disparaged, to be repeatedly 'tamed' by men exercising their power, none of which seems to have bothered Ian McEwan or Salman Rushdie. *The London Review of Books* praised Kundera's *The Art of the Novel*, which lists every important European male author and not a single woman, even though they explored new territory long before the men he credits with doing so.

The territory Marilyn Monroe explored was equally well-trodden. She self-manufactured a living sex doll with the voice of a child who never tells tales. Her stardom relied on the self-delusion that her fans saw her and not her sex. In a visit to troops in Korea; half-dressed, in freezing cold weather she worked US Marines into such a frenzy that she had to be asked to tone it down. In her autobiography she denies all responsibility for what men saw, but her only value was in her lack of value. The persona she created had a limited shelf life and like Dianna she had to die early.

In a semi-fictional account of a slave revolt William Styron gratuitously inserted a would-be serial rapist. He went on to write *Sophie's Choice*, ostensibly about a female Holocaust survivor, in which a parade of degraded females act as stimulants to the author's *alter ego*, Stingo. Sex is interspersed with the violence of the concentration camp and the abuse Sophie suffers from her boyfriend. Once Stingo has had wild sex with her she returns to her violent partner and they die in a suicide pact. Those who see the story as one man's noble attempt to save a severely damaged woman ignore the fact that in attempting to possess Sophie Stingo shows no regard for her psychological needs and his sole driver is perverted lust. The clue is in the first mentioned book, where Styron also used historical events as a vehicle for his own fantasies about female discomfort and death.

The military sex-death conflation is encapsulated in the song book of Oxford-based USAF bomber pilots who, in the true military elite spirit, consider everyone else to be human scum. In their songs of freedom these self-declared free men express crude right-wing politics, overt racism and the degradation of women. In *I fucked a Dead Whore*, for example, sex and death are intertwined. It seems that in denying allegedly feminine emotions military men need to degrade women themselves.

And so to Margaret Thatcher, whose very existence proved that anything was possible, even that being a woman was an advantage. Leaving aside the anti-women policies and the refusal to accept that she had benefited from feminism, Margaret Thatcher was a liar. She lied about her own self-sufficiency, she lied that it was possible to combine a career with selfless dedication to motherhood and she lied that child care was just a matter of better organisation. All of it; the live in nurses, the nannies and the posh public schools for her children was dependent on Denis's money. Pure and simply Margaret Thatcher married a rich man and it allowed her to dedicate herself to ruining the lives of others while dishing out contemptuous Tory morality.

Coming full circle; the main difference between the original Jack the Ripper and Peter Sutcliffe was that one is a compound myth and the other was a truck driver from Bradford. West Yorkshire plod wasted months looking for a man unlike themselves when they should have looked in a mirror. They interviewed Sutcliffe nine times and ignored mounting evidence against him. They constructed a motive based on a hatred of prostitutes, whom they defined by their own spurious criteria, when what Peter Sutcliffe really hated was women. They categorised his victims as either innocent or prostitutes, whom it was normal to hate and whom they spoke of with transparent distaste. They created the story that the killer had strayed from an understandable task and the papers went along with it.

Far from demonstrating what can happen when a deranged man acts on a message from God the case actually concealed something deeply troubling in society. Sutcliffe was a third generation misogynist inculcated with Catholic denigration of women and his violence was largely on the parts of the body that signify gender. He had a history of disparaging prostitutes and cruised red light districts to abuse them. He believed that women were either deities or damned and when women seemed to let him down he decided they were all whores. Yet the *Daily Mirror* blamed his quiet career-minded wife for dominating him and one senior detective said his victims were a substitute for her.

When northern football fans proudly sang 'There's only one Yorkshire Ripper.' They were only half right. Misogyny is at the heart of our culture, but rather than looking in men's heads for the solution we need to look at how society is organised. Masculine and feminine behaviour are not natural, they are a necessary means for the maintenance of an unstable and unjust system. Masculinity is harder to live up to than femininity, but its very promotion is the denial of female status. An equal future can only be assured when men and women confront this truth together. The best way the twenty-first century man can demonstrate his manhood is by showing some humility. If that means being put in his place by women, so be it. It is not something he should resist or criticise; in recognising centuries of oppression it is something that, as a decent human being, he should celebrate.

MUD, SWEAT AND SELF-JUSTIFICATION

Running Free – Richard Askwith

The BBC made no bones about why the Tokyo Olympics are going ahead during a dangerous global pandemic – money. If they are cancelled Japan will be liable for billions of pounds in compensation. The country is experiencing economic stagnation and political careers are riding on the white elephant of the Olympic legacy. Sport has for a long time been the precursor to spending by spectators and participants alike; someone new to running can apparently spend £1,500 on 'essential' gear before taking a step, running alone is worth twice as much as football.

Without overtly criticising the blatant marketisation of what is essentially free Richard Askwith counter-poses his brand of off-road running to often-reluctant, relentless, soul-destroying tarmac pounding; every step of which is recorded, analysed and uploaded. Obviously one could splash out as much running off-road as running on it, but having himself been the victim of extreme kit fetishism Askwith has turned over a new leaf and demonstrates the zeal of an ex-addict. Getting soaking wet, covered in cow shit, nettled and lacerated are all positive aspects of his personal return to what he sees as the primeval roots of his chosen pastime. It is immaterial that running off-road is not the opposite of running on-road. For what appear to be literary purposes the antithesis of his personalised discipline is a conflation of elements, all of which he is careful not to directly condemn.

In speaking for what he sees as back to basics running Askwith is well aware that he expresses wider concerns about our contemporary existence. Referring to less cossetted generations he says 'Their whole relationship with the physical world was different. They understood how things worked: their machines, their homes, their factories and, not least, the natural world around them. They knew how to make things – rather than just buying cheap packaged things that other people have made, cooked or grown for them... What, meanwhile, does our twenty-first century sophistication really amount to? Most of us are pathetically dependent on technologies we don't understand, fuelled by resources we don't have and paid for with borrowed money... Take away our oil, our electricity, our credit, our... telecommunications networks... and many of us would barely be able to function.' This clichéd contrast only goes so far because it involves a kind of rose-tinted revisionism. If modern society is individualistic then past societies must have been more inter-dependent. Medieval peasants did not make their own ploughs or shoe their own horses, Victorians did not by and large build their own homes or dig up their own coal; specialists did. Human beings have always had to depend upon the skills of others because we are a collective and cooperative species. The entirely self-reliant individual Askwith idealises is largely a fallacy.

I am not a runner, but my predilection for single fixed-gear gear bicycles has seen me accused of deliberately making life difficult for myself by people who regularly take part in organised sporting challenges, while consoling themselves that they are in some way subverting their ethos. Partly by shunning organised events Richard Askwith imagines other people seeing him as 'some kind of crazed survivalist, wilfully depriving [himself] of the protections of civilisation.' In reality no one cares what he does, any more than they care what I do. But for the record I crave a simpler past, in which cycling was new, and a technology I understand: a technology that until recently I could recreate in my own modestly equipped workshop, on machines made by others.

Askwith insists that his intention is not merely to handicap himself the better to enjoy the challenge, but that in taking to the fields he enjoys 'a powerful feeling of reconnection as well as empowerment when you rediscover simple skills... I feel the texture of the earth... read the landscape with as many senses as I can... I feel the wind and the rain... I encounter the kinds of inconvenience that comes from nature rather than from man. And, each time, there comes a point when I realise that they don't really constitute a reason for feeling sorry for myself. I suppose you could call it self-conquest. But perhaps that's making too big a deal of it... more simply; I've discovered that there's more strength in me than I thought.' Many of us enjoy a challenge, but some of this comes very close to self-flagellation, engaged in only because it's good when it stops.

I read *Running Free* while riding a bicycle I'd bought on eBay two hundred miles home. In my hotel room a TV program featured the restoration of a boneshaker and it reinforced my plans to convert the bike to a single fixed gear. Richard Askwith says 'It's an understandable urge, yet the older I get the more futile it seems... The precious things in life are moments: the experience itself, not the tweeting or posting about it... not ticking off achievements but doing things for their own sake.' The news was dominated by the epitome of vicariousness in an England-Germany football match. It must have been difficult for those endlessly referencing the Second World War to restrain themselves.

After hearing that the woman who developed the Oxford vaccine had been given a standing ovation at Wimbledon by people who will never do anything nearly so exciting I had a twenty minute engagement with the psychopaths on the A9, before taking a rolling road for Appleby in Westmorland. 'There's a boost to be had from the act of taking the plunge: into the weather, or into the discomfort zone created by aching muscles and joints... the world may be full of threats and sorrow, but it's also unimaginably rich in interest, consolation and beauty. And so, perhaps, are you.' Many of the cyclists who passed me were power assisted, yet nothing since the invention of the first safety bicycles has made cycling better; only different. Richard Askwith's 'illusory protections of civilisation' may as well be the illusory advantages of carbon fibre, electric motors and effective brakes.

Askwith idolises those who survived the First World war for their fearless sporting prowess, quoting Wade Davis; 'They were not cavalier about death – they all wanted desperately to live – but they had seen so much that it had no hold on them. What mattered was how one lived.' Considering that off-road running is not remotely dangerous in a death-defying sense this is all a bit over the top. But while lamenting 21st century risk aversion Askwith goes on 'we are, after all, still going to die, health and safety or no health and safety. Aren't moments of magic and delight worth at least as much as an illusory sense of living in a risk free world?' Perhaps they are, but he also constructs a scenario in which he is accused of irresponsibility and of having failed to grow up. 'We can be immature for all sorts of reasons; and sometimes there is a nobility in our immature moments – just as there can be ignobility in the habitual caution of maturity.' These sentiments apply as much to politics as personal behaviour;

there is certainly nothing noble in condemning youthful idealism, or in demanding that the future of humanity be left in the hands of the responsible adults in the room.

There is an oblique allusion to why we should find pleasure when and where we can; 'Life is short at the best of times, *and these are not the best of times.*' (my emphasis) 'Of course, we cannot be made fundamentally better people by behaving recklessly... I doubt, however, that we are often made worse people by our moments of childish fearlessness.' If only the childish fearlessness Richard Askwith believes he displays in his off-road running were extended into the arena of public affairs we might find the key to our collective salvation. The problem is that many of us expect someone else to provide our excitement, recreational and political, instead of just getting out and doing it; the tendency extends far beyond our leisure activities. If we allow someone else to run our lives for us they will; often in their own narrow minority interest. Some of them will pretend to provide services for us, all the while prioritising profit for themselves.

On-road runners tend to wear headphones, possibly to block out reality. Those who run in the countryside notice what's going on. Richard Askwith can see for himself the ever-increasing urban encroachment manifest in plans to 'kick-start and unleash dynamic potential' as part of the plan for economic growth at any cost. The construction industry's priorities are not those of the potential homeowner. Sports equipment manufacturer's priority is profit; 'When I see an industry making money hand over fist... I instantly assume that the consumers concerned are being taken for a ride.' That's because they are, but Askwith almost lets them off; 'One can hardly blame [an] industry for seeking higher profits... but... you'll be struck by the subtly different language that advertisers use in their product descriptions when addressing industry insiders; "builds incremental sales"; "presents attractive margins and repeat sales"; "translates to repeat purchase and increased profitability"; "perfect impulse item for consumers"'. To be an unquestioning consumer, whether what we are consuming is manufactured leisure experiences, material products or mainstream politics, is to be a means to someone else's end.

PRUDES, POLLS
AND PAXMAN

The Victorians – Jeremy Paxman

Jeremy Paxman is an overblown and overpaid political interviewer who once drew attention to the lack of support offered by modern underpants. Russell Brand is an entertainer who has written a naïve book about the necessity of a serious social uprising. Interviewing Brand the legendarily probing Paxman was uncharacteristically dumbstruck at the comedian's excoriation of the current political system for its obsessive concern with the wellbeing of the capitalist class and open contempt for the unwashed hoi polloi.

Brand explained that he and others didn't abstain from the cosy tripartite charade that stands in for democracy out of apathy, as is often claimed, but from a conscious belief that all its participants were pissing in the same pot, it was a waste of time and that only revolution could end their deliberately obfuscating reign. Used to disingenuous intellectual sparring with like-minded Oxbridge alumni Paxman failed abysmally to belittle Brand for rejecting the cross on a piece of paper once every five years ruse.

The interview stimulated much debate, not least about whether a diversionary 'none of the above' box should be included on British ballot forms. In Spain, for example, 'votes' of those who decline to choose between the Siamese twins of capitalist conspiracy are entered in their own column as people actively expressing dissent. An electoral returning officer was moved to describe the spoiling of UK ballot papers as 'a growth industry.' Even octogenarian national treasure, squeaky clean conservative comedian and tax dodger Ken Dodd found it necessary to castigate Brand for his stupidity in discouraging people from exercising the democratic privilege they have been so benevolently granted, possibly lest the entire theatre be exposed for what it is.

Thoroughly establishment figure Paxman, (Charterhouse, Cambridge), has also penned a popular history, the title of which is a misnomer, in which he graciously admits that any such work says as much about the period in which it is written as about the one it purports to portray. Despite the title, and the fact that primary school children are consciously misled by the National Curriculum, there was no such thing as 'the Victorians'. Furthermore, there was no such thing as 'the Romans' and there is no such thing as 'the British'.

Some Romans did indeed gorge themselves while prostrate (and take themselves to vomitaria following over indulgence). The rest fought in the army and worked in the fields, manufacturing and the service sectors. Canting, sex-obsessed middle-class 'Victorians' may have covered up their piano legs, but the majority lived in damp, airless, rat-infested slums with very little furniture, managing to labour long hours in mines and factories on little more than sweet tea and bread and margarine.

The only purpose of appending an eponym derived from a privileged royal parasite is to obscure the reality of class society. It is an insult to the industry of those who actually created Britain's obscene wealth. If they belonged to anything it was the timeless working class, not a contrived, bizarre and anachronistic monarchical cult.

Paxman's class position is emphasised by the fact that he chooses 'Victorian' paintings as the vehicle for his exposition. Such art apparently 'taught the Victorians to celebrate the places they were now living and connected the whirling, noisy present to a suddenly distant ancestral past.' We can almost imagine the Lancashire mill worker longing for the oil painted and idealised peasant paradise his fortunate chattel forbears enjoyed.

Without irony Paxman explains that 'Victorians' did not always live up to their own moral standards. Osbert Lancaster described them as good husbands. Yet William Powell Frith, who had a family life 'the picture of Victorian propriety' and who painted *Many Happy Returns of the Day* 'with its moral and improving tone', for many years ran two households; one with his wife and twelve children and another with his mistress and seven. Frith's domestic arrangements were well known in his circle and tolerated, but he was snubbed by the queen, the consciously constructed epitome of staid Victorian morality, and perhaps its only real practitioner; though unspeakable amorality was practised in the wholesale repression and butchery of her imperial subjects.

As Britain sought to replicate itself abroad the primeval act of robbery which had separated the mass of people from the means of production through the enclosures and clearances was carried on in different forms across the globe. Nevertheless, popular artistic depictions gave a lie to any notion that the middle class was ignorant of the lives that were being lived around them. 'Rather the reverse – awareness of the awful lives of the poor was a reason to keep earning.' Though painters were also prepared, on demand, to present a sanitised present and a mythical past, where each man was his own master.

Samuel Smiles was born in 1812 and spent his early years agitating for parliamentary reform. Put off by Chartism's threat of violence he became convinced that the solution to society's ills lay in each man improving himself. He wrote the bestseller *Self Help,* 'a hymn to Victorian values, to enterprise, self-reliance and hard graft.' In it a working man makes good through personal heroism and hard work.

Nowadays the self-improvement industry is worth billions. The worse the world gets, the more atomised and individualistic society becomes, the more people turn to internalised personal panaceas and the Victorian ruling class, no less than our own, saw the advantage of reinforcing the benefits of self-reliance and boot straps individualism.

The naturally cooperative working class populates and pervades Paxman's text, but always as some kind of collective threat; they are at the same time the source of all wealth and the source of all worry; better it always is to divide them with the fake philosophy of individual liberty.

Today Formula 1 boss Bernie Ecclestone, former property speculator and loan shark (net worth $3.9 billion) says women aren't strong enough to be F1 drivers. Ruskin and others believed that women were 'physiologically different to men, and that if women were taught Latin and Greek, valuable brain space might be used up that could be better used to hone sewing and home-making skills. Women... possess only a finite amount of strength and the physical demands of menstruation and bearing children means they have less energy for mental activity.' There was also 'a persistent notion' that educating women could make them sterile. The female monarch, like the Iron Lady, deplored the mad wicked folly of women's rights, a tradition preserved by our tabloids.

The age of consent was only eleven when Victoria came to the throne and there were brothels where Victorian men could avail themselves of children, but the Victorian elite, like their ruling class descendants, tended toward moral inconsistency. They celebrated the family while baby farming took place and prostitution soared; they celebrated progress and comfort while the majority lived malnourished in squalor, or took the queen's shilling, where;

'The events of the Crimean War showed officers of the British Army to be snobbish, stupid and incompetent, and regular soldiers often breathtakingly courageous...'

'The most pressing and pervasive problem... was an invisible one – the problem of class. Ordinary soldiers usually came from the lowest strata of British society; generally illiterate, they would often join as a last resort to avoid prison or the dreaded workhouse. Wellington called such recruits "the scum of the earth", and they were treated accordingly.' And for what?

'General William Butler remarked in his autobiography that "It is a misfortune of the first magnitude in the lives of soldiers today... that the majority of our recent wars have their origins in purely financial interests or sordid Stock Exchange ambitions."' How different are today's noble aims. While the west carries out its humanitarian interventions revisionist historians attempt to impose a civilising aim on the ruthless Victorian imperialists whose descendants are Bush and Blair.

After the Indian Mutiny Charles Spurgeon, an evangelical preacher, told 25,000 people at Crystal Palace that 'holy war' must be made on the Indians. Stories of rape were manufactured and scenes created of soldiers departing to avenge the dead. Soldiers, former malnourished inhabitants of slums returned as heroes, having taken part in the ransacking and looting of villages, the forcing of prisoners to lick up the blood of the dead, the smearing of the condemned in pig fat and the blowing apart of people by cannon. To his credit Paxman says 'There was nothing particularly civilising about it.'

History is too much about the ruling class and the dictionary defines 'Victorian', by which it means the important and influential people of the period, as 'exhibiting the characteristics popularly attributed to the Victorians, especially prudery, bigotry or hypocrisy.' None of which, as ruling classes go, makes them particularly special.

WHERE THE HEART IS

At Home: A Short History Of Private Life – Bill Bryson

Like most Victorian country parsons the original owner of Bill Bryson's 1851 home received as much in pay and rents as a senior civil servant and the richest parish in the land produced an annual income today worth about £5 million. These posts were sinecures for the sons of the gentry, who had no formal training and paid lip-service to religion, leaving them plenty of time to be linguists, palaeontologists, botanists, hot air balloonists, mathematicians, historians and social reactionaries.

Privileged Victorians generally considered the Chartists' campaign for universal suffrage a threat to civilisation itself. In 1848 it was feared a chartist rally might descend forcibly upon parliament. Sadly it fizzled out, allowing the *Times* to describe 'the mob' as cowardly, unpatriotic, ignorant and dirty but essentially good-natured, an unfortunate tendency that allowed our rulers to obstruct enfranchisement until they discovered in the Labour Party the means to make it worthless.

Of Britain's famous invaders, the Jutes probably didn't exist, the Angles made no more impression than a Cotswold coach party and the Saxons took over by trespass rather than terror. They lived a simple existence and any changes in farming were imperceptibly smooth. For centuries there were two types of ordinary people; serfs tied to the land and freemen too poor to leave it. Eventually changes required bigger fields; the poor were forced off the land by act of parliament and into ever-expanding factories. Some rural communities didn't revive until the Range Rover was invented.

As the rich became ever richer they demolished ancient villages to erect grand palaces to their vanity and an urban middle-class sought splendid town houses. In 1851 a third of London's young women were servants, whom Virginia Woolf denigrated and others regarded as less than human. Casual humiliation was routine and it was recommended they be ritually humbled in front of children for the good of them both. Mrs Beeton warned against sentiment or Christian charity being shown to servants and Victoria, empress of ever-expanding dominions, forbade them to look directly at her.

Raping the globe came at a cost; between 1500 and 1850 two million sailors died of scurvy. Captain Cook discovered how to stop it, but it was many years before the British navy took his findings on board. It has long been known that without salt we would die, so people died fighting over it. Many more died fighting over pepper and other spices, which became the world's most valuable commodities. They drove the great voyages of discovery, during which Columbus didn't discover America, nor even suspect its existence, and Vasco de Gama meted out unspeakable and gratuitous violence toward every native population he encountered. Crossing the Pacific Magellan's crew were reduced to eating rat shit and wood shavings and he was killed in the Philippines. Columbus failed in his quest for spices, only discovering dozens of other foods Europeans didn't want, but which now form the basics of world cuisine. In exchange the Mesoamericans got meat, cheese, forced relocation, the suppression of culture and diseases that nearly wiped them out.

Britain turned to tea, a classless beverage that allowed

the East India Company's private army to advance British capitalism abroad. Both were claimed to confer impossible health benefits, unlike sugar which ruined people's teeth, but provided ample career opportunities for Africans who didn't mind travelling. Such was the trade imbalance that Britain had to force opium addiction on the Chinese and convert India into a cash crop economy, possibly saving its empire, the purpose of which was the theft of raw materials from the colonies and the forcing of finished goods on the inhabitants. This was bolstered by a law requiring all New World imports to be made in, or pass through, Britain. America took endless tons of stuff that had pointlessly crossed and re-crossed the Atlantic, making the fortunes of numerous British merchants. Adam Smith was animated by the deliberate suppression of free trade and it was a contributory cause of the American Revolution. As America advanced industrially thousands of millionaire philistines built gigantic palaces and toured Europe buying every cultural artefact they could find. They also married their daughters to hard-up British aristocrats, producing such fine, upstanding citizens as Winston Churchill and Harold MacMillan.

When Britain had cornered the market in tea it turned to cotton, deliberately ruined India's indigenous industry and carted the stuff off to Lancashire, where, thanks to modest men like John Kay and James Hargreaves and ruthless opportunists like Richard Arkwright, the machines developed to process it began the industrial revolution, wholesale child labour, long working hours, mass poverty and the reinvigoration of slavery, which until then had been in decline. Children were forced into mines, to become stunted and vitamin D deficient, into potteries to be poisoned by lead and arsenic and, from the age of five, up chimneys, to contract testicular cancer and be ruined before they were teenagers.

Until the 1830s no one had any idea what made plants grow and crop yields were falling as soils were depleted. Then someone discovered big bird shit deposits and guano-mania gripped the globe, creating great wealth, the founding of banks and inevitable war. In Britain it killed the trade in human waste and night soil men began dumping it in rivers. Farmers became hooked and chemical fertilisers were discovered just as guano sources were depleted and the price rocketed.

The Victorians' obsessions were sex and death. The former stigmatised anyone able to amuse themselves in private, completely denied feminine sexuality, led to much wedding night surprise and made the proper medical treatment of women impossible. The latter led to bizarre formalised rules about mourning (by women) and paranoia about being buried alive. There was also justifiable concern about having their bodies stolen from their graves as a trainee surgeon-ready corpse could fetch ten times a skilled worker's wage. Poor people held onto the remains of their loved ones until putrefaction and maggots made them worthless. This only added to the stink of the grossly overcrowded slums they were forced to inhabit. They had no option but to shit in cellars and yards and murderous epidemics such as cholera were ignored until they began killing wealthy people.

It wasn't an accident that the Victorian poor lived in appalling squalor amid municipal and individual ostentation. The rich and the poor exist entirely in relation to each other; the poor were poor *because* the rich were rich. Britain's greatness relied on the organised robbery of one class by another. Consequently, very large numbers of the working class were unable to adequately feed themselves, rickets was endemic, up to 100,000 children were fending for themselves on London's streets and working class life expectancy was reduced to levels not seen since the Bronze Age.

It is quite possible that wealthy Victorians had been inured to the suffering of others by the buttoned up, buttock clenching self-reserve that was inculcated in them as children, and was complemented by the sadistic regime at public schools. But, excuses aside, the general attitude to the poor was that they were meant to be poor and every misfortune they endured was their own fault. The cruellest of all theorists was the clergyman Thomas Malthus, whose contempt for the poor has not been exceeded except by the most ardent advocates of neoliberalism. Poverty and ignorance are not accidents of nature they are means of control and the Victorian working class lived as it did because that was how the ruling class wanted it to live. They considered ordinary people neither suited for nor entitled to education and almost universally opposed it, lest they got ideas above their station.

With Britain at its economic zenith and visibly able to waste great wealth it must have seemed to many people that life couldn't get any worse. But the government made sure that it did with the Poor Laws, which established a system of workhouses intended to be so horrible that no one would willingly enter them. The half-starved and demoralised people who fell to the ultimate indignity were prone to dangerous epidemics and had their meagre food *and water* rations further reduced when they couldn't complete the largely pointless work they were given. Those unable to find a place in these hell-holes were subject to paltry 'outdoor relief' which was regularly withheld on spurious grounds comparable to today's bureaucratic benefit sanctions regime.

In the 1860s a handful of wealthy and influential members of the exploiting classes suddenly noticed the poor and began to patronise them. There was a sudden surge in domestic missionaries, among them Dr Barnado, who wasn't a doctor and may have been a charlatan. His homes bore direct comparison with the workhouses, he stole children off the street and shipped hundreds off to Canada. Nevertheless he was despised for denying natural class hierarchy and undermining the poor laws.

Bill Bryson makes scant reference to working class resistance, but it is unlikely the people who had overseen criminal inequalities for centuries suddenly discovered a conscience. What Bryson does say is that entirely justifiable unrest in America, combined with natural disasters, including successive waves of locusts, might easily have led to socialism. Bring on the crosses and the holy water.

AN INAPPROPRIATE APPELLATION

The Psychopath Test – Jon Ronson

In *The Psychopath Test* Jon Ronson seeks to establish whether there is a preponderance of psychopaths at the top of the corporate and political worlds. As the definition of a psychopath is a person with a severe chronic mental disorder, especially someone exhibiting abnormal or violent social behaviour this seems superficially unlikely. But one of the symptoms of psychopathy is a lack of empathy, and obliviousness to other people's discomfort seems like an advantage in both fields. The right-wing politician, the imperialist, the corporate exploiter and the parasitic futures trader would surely sleep easier if they were able to ignore how their decisions affect other people. If Tony Blair, for example, had a grain of empathy he'd have to do far more than take his smug self to the Catholic confessional, he'd have to hand himself in for trial as the mendacious charlatan and warmonger he obviously is, to be found guilty as charged in the court of all reason.

Unfortunately the picture is complicated by Ronson's intertwined notion that 'we spend our lives self-referencing, over and over, in a strange kind of loop.' I once thought this sounded quite Proustian, and as a literary theory it has its attractions; people see in books statements that confirm their own opinions and disregard those that don't. As a social theory it might mean that 'we' keep doing things the way we do because that's the way we've always done them or, more fundamentally that the system we live under has a compelling force that is beyond our control.

In other words we are all on a turning roundabout we can't get off. Of course there are those who like to pretend that we don't live under a 'system' at all, and that our society is the entirely natural and neutral product of human evolution, even that this is the best of all possible worlds. Were this true we should have good reason to be depressed, not to mention very disappointed with ourselves.

Ronson says he once believed society to be a rational thing, but now wonders if it might in fact be built on insanity. As applied to social, economic and political ideologies and the activities of their respective adherents, adjectives referencing mental health are perhaps not entirely appropriate. In any case the erection of such a dichotomy is misplaced and unnecessary. Capitalist society and the free market to which its ideologues pretend to subscribe are perfectly rational, if extremely anarchic. The real question is not about their rationality, nor about the sanity of their advocates. It is about in whose interests they operate.

The problem with beginning our analysis where we are is that we are carrying so much baggage it is difficult to leave it behind and examine things objectively. Psychiatrists who diagnose people as having a psychological dysfunction do not do so in the abstract, they do so within the constraints of the dominant ideology, which means they take a great deal, maybe even the whole status quo, for granted. Those who analyse society do the same; how else could a subsidy-harvesting gun-runner enjoy the title of entrepreneur or a semi-elected international murderer that of statesman, while others go to jail for not paying their TV licence?

The truth is that the current state of affairs is neither

normal nor natural. It may have come about by a series of happy or unhappy accidents, but it is maintained by deliberate and conscious policy, and extreme force where necessary. The brakes have been applied and humanity is in a period of arrested development. Capitalism has fulfilled its historical role in bringing our species to the point where everyone can be fed and housed. We now need to advance to a more egalitarian system so the benefits can be properly enjoyed, instead of being squandered by a minority on questionable profit-generating schemes and personal ostentation.

Anyone with a materialist conception of history is rightly suspicious of psychology, because it looks for the solutions to social problems inside people's heads, but they might be surprised to discover that they share their suspicion with the Church of Scientology. In fact the Church's main focus is its hatred of psychologists and it has a whole division dedicated to unmasking them and their entire discipline as fraudulent. It brought down the famous TV psychologist Raj Persaud by denouncing him as a plagiarist, presumably unable to get him for tax evasion or misusing the photocopier.

Their founder L Ron Hubbard's suspicion of psychology is understandable given, for example, that Samuel Cartwright in 1851 discovered a mental disorder in slaves, the symptom of which was 'a desire to run away from slavery.' The fact that slavery was a state-sanctioned and institutionalised reality meant that anybody who opposed it was clearly off their rocker, as are 'the Loony Left' and others of equally dubious sanity who, for reasons best known to themselves, oppose capitalism. It makes no difference that the desire to take humanity forward is perfectly rational; the rules are made by the people who run *this* society not a just one, and they have shown time and time again that there is no level to which they will not sink to defend it.

Ronson's book is celebrated for taking the reader on a journey from the funny to the disturbing, and we clearly have cause for concern; but anyone who previously considered our rulers to be selfless, well-balanced individuals uninterested in a lucrative career, who only have the best interests of the general population at heart, hasn't been paying attention.

More worrying is that in ascribing to politicians the psychopathic traits of glibness and superficial charm it seems Ronson is leading us towards the frightening conclusion that the only current politician who isn't a psychopath is the apparently unreconstructed oaf and serial sell-out merchant John Prescott, Tony Blair's favourite pseudo-left stooge.

I have misplaced my copy of the Bob Hare checklist for identifying psychopaths, but I am fairly certain that Vladimir Putin would meet the criteria, along with many other world leaders. It has often been said that the last person who should be given power is someone who seeks it and there are very few of them who wouldn't cling to office given half a chance.

Among the tell-tale signs that might identify a psychopathic business leader are statements revealing a belief that the human world is made up of predators and prey, suggestions that it is foolish not to exploit the weaknesses of others and the expression of 'callous jubilation' when big companies re-organise, i.e. sack lots of people, perhaps when it makes the price of their shares rise.

Jon Ronson says it isn't easy to understand why the CIA would have wanted to back murderous anti-democratic death squads in Haiti, but there are only a limited number of reasons why they might have chosen that course of action. Perhaps they wanted to keep the current leader in power to prevent the rise of a progressive government that would imperil their strategic and economic interests without getting bogged down in messy military invasion which might get Americans killed and upset the public. This is the usual reason, and it worked to very good effect in Indonesia *et al*.

The bumping-off of opponents is not of course exclusive to tin-pot dictatorships. The Israeli secret service Mosad has made it an art form and the spy David Shayler revealed MI5's role in targeted assassinations, which amount to the same thing. Unfortunately he went on to claim that no planes were involved in the events of 9/11 and that 7/7 didn't happen, and then that he was the new Messiah. The suggestion that holograms were used to make it *appear* that planes had hit the twin towers isn't without foundation; the US Department of Defense has been carrying out research into the use of holograms for deceptive purposes. When asked why the US authorities might use holograms to fake an alien invasion Shayler said, 'To create martial law across the planet and take away all our rights.'

The former head of a computer anti-virus software company John McAfee has raised concerns about the extent to which mobile telephones can be hacked. His primary concern is the possible harvesting of information by the security forces. The BBC's John Humphries asked was it not justified on the grounds that it helped to catch criminals. McAfee said there had always been criminals but that it hadn't always been the case that the rest of us had to suffer intrusions and restrictions that they might be caught. It appeared that the BBC was treating him as a crank crying wolf, because, as Jon Ronson says, madness is newsworthy, normality isn't. Taking government policy at face value sometimes requires having the holders of unorthodox opinions on to make them look daft.

The Psychopath Test doesn't really come to a conclusion, rather fading away into a discussion about the very high number of children in the USA misdiagnosed as being bipolar when they are just oppositional, an unacceptable attitude in the land of the free and the home of the brave. The back cover blurb says the belly laughs come thick and fast. Unfortunately ridiculing the calculated ruthlessness of our rulers doesn't seem to be making them any more willing to alter their ways.

JOHN DOE AND THE MESS
IN MESOPOTAMIA

The Soldiers Who Say No – Peter Laufer

Howard Zinn hopes that *The Soldiers Who Say No* will be read by young people likely to be enticed by false promises or misguided patriotism into fighting their rulers' wars. Michael Ratner, who has written on the injustices of Guantanamo Bay, says that when soldiers who refuse to fight in Iraq get medals he'll know society is just. Ann Wright, a retired US Army colonel and diplomat says it is moral cowardice to follow illegal orders and real courage lies in resisting them and facing the music; after all it is the soldiers themselves who have to live with having carried out state murder in a conflict that has nothing to do with national security.

This post-facto encouragement to mutiny would mean armies couldn't function and wars couldn't be fought. The reality is that while some soldiers and civilians resist every war, only to be forcefully silenced, sometimes terminally, most do as they're told.

In her introduction Clare Short sympathises with parents who've lost children to a war without honour and based on lies. Such a selective critique conveniently ignores the fact that all wars are based on lies and there is honour in none of them. War is politics by other means and politics is distilled economics. The Iraq war was about oil (and global dominance), all other claims are disingenuous obfuscation.

Peter Laufer rejects the state preferred appellation of

'terrorist' to describe the Iraqis who resisted the US-led invasion because the term applies equally to the actions of the American military, from the initial 'shock and awe' to the indiscriminate assaults on cities. He decides upon 'enemy' and quotes a US soldier; 'We have met the enemy and he is us.'

When the war began the French newspaper *Le Monde* said we had all become Americans, and the British press agreed. Decency, morality, belief in the rule of law, fairness and justice should have made us insist we were all Iraqis, but war doesn't work like that. We lied to ourselves about the reasons for the invasion and we kept lying to ourselves all the way through the inevitable atrocities. We were as guilty as the naïve, brainwashed and impressionable young men who did the killing. The only difference was that, unlike them, we didn't get to find out what war really entails.

A US soldier who escaped to Canada says '...that's the problem with war. Your president, your generals, and... your commanding officers, they don't go out there with you. They send you out there to fight and do the crazy shit and do the dirty stuff. You're the one who has to live with the nightmares from it. You come back, you're nothing you know? Guys are living on the streets that fought in Iraq just as well as I did. I mean it's horrific... I had to do things for the wealth of other people. I blame them because they made me do it. You can lie to the world, you can't lie to a person who's seen it. They made me have to do things that a man should never have to do, for the purpose of their gain, not the people's – their financial gain. George W Bush should be the one to go to prison – but that ain't never going to happen.'

Another soldier says, 'In October of 2004 they said there's no WMD, and I just sat down and cried. That was the last straw. It was for absolutely nothing. I felt totally worthless. I sacrificed part of my humanity ...for what? For what? I can't point to a single thing. We're going to liberate the Iraqi people by killing them?... I'm a veteran of Operation Iraqi Plunder. I think it is important to tell it like it is. I refuse to call it Operation Iraqi Freedom. There was no freedom over there. It was not a war to liberate Iraq. It was a war to make it safe for US business interests. It was a war of aggression and occupation. To call it Operation Iraqi Freedom is an insult to the Iraqi people and it is an insult to humanity.'

'People were saying "I'm proud of what you did over there," and I'm saying, "God I'm not. Why are you telling me you're proud of me? You don't even know what I did."'

Some people think British troops are heroes; but they too don't know what they did. They don't want to know what they did. If they knew they'd be horrified at the wholesale murder of civilians and the destruction of whole towns, or incapable of basic humanity.

One deserter turned activist says; 'The United States wasn't founded on oil. It wasn't founded on the fact that everyone has a right to lay a pipeline in Afghanistan. It wasn't founded on the fact that some guy can make money from Haliburton building things in Iraq.' Unfortunately, while the countries and the companies might be different, these are exactly the principles on which the US is founded. It was built on genocide and slavery under a political system deliberately designed to prevent real democracy and since World War Two it has invaded over fifty countries and helped destabilise and topple numerous progressive regimes. Like the fundamental values Britain is keen to ram down the throats of immigrants the glorious principles on which the US is founded are a fantasy.

One US soldier's reasons for refusing to go to Iraq can be applied to any of the US's foreign adventures; 'I object to the Iraq War because it is an act of aggression with no defensive basis.' Nevertheless, it was quite obvious that Iraq had no weapons of mass destruction and that those who said it had them were lying. There was no evidence whatsoever to back up the Bush administration's bizarre claim that the secular Baathist government was working with a fundamentalist terror group and the notion that the US wanted to export democracy is laughable. But none of this is the point; the US had decided to attack Iraq long before 9/11 and the British government knew this, all it needed was an excuse.

A barrister acting for soldiers says, 'If you had an actual government based on people who learned something from the Vietnam War, you'd be in a better position. But the government is those who didn't serve and didn't learn.' Governments aren't like individuals who learn from their mistakes; they act out of economic and political expediency. The Vietnam War wasn't 'a mistake'; it used up lots of armaments, tested new technologies and made some people lots of money. It would have been better if the US hadn't been humiliated by a peasant army using bicycles and bamboo, but you can't win 'em all. The Iraq war wasn't a mistake; the US has been defeated, but they're getting the oil and the rebuilding contracts. What's a few, dead, fucked up and crippled working class Americans and a few hundred thousand Iraqis when there's profit to be made?

When it was suggested to US soldiers who refused to serve in Iraq that they were volunteers and knew what they were getting into they said they were lied to by recruiters who promised help with financial problems and said they wouldn't be sent to Iraq or would be given non-combat roles. Their advocates reject the whole volunteer idea; '...young Americans are compelled to join the army because of an "economic draft" and a "poverty draft."' Soldiers whose contracted period of service is nearing its end are also prevented from leaving in wartime; 'The net effect is not much different than conscription.'

One of them goes further; 'Iraq is where the US has to be defeated – categorically defeated. We have to impose the kind of limit on the US ability to conduct mayhem around the world that was imposed by the Vietnam defeat. There's only a few ways that can happen. There has to be a refusal within the military to participate, and obviously there has to be a refusal around the world to support it.'

Darrel Anderson joined the US Army because he needed healthcare, money to go to college and to take care of his daughter. Joining the army was the only way he could get them. He swallowed the bullshit about protecting his country and he wanted to be a hero. He soon realised the Iraqis didn't want the US in their country. He heard other soldiers bragging about kicking Iraqi prisoners to death and he deserted. He says that if he was an Iraqi facing an invader that destroyed everyday life, threw innocent people in prison and killed with impunity he'd do exactly what the insurgents did. He didn't want to live with being a murderer.

I have never spoken to my brother and his wife about the death of their son in Afghanistan. I suspect they would like to believe he was doing something useful at least; perhaps even that he was a hero. The sad fact is that his life was wasted in another senseless, futile and illegal war fuelled by greed and vanity and the people who launched it should be in jail for crimes against humanity. The chasm that has opened up between Muslims and non-Muslims around the world and the political drift to the right across Europe is entirely their doing.

It is unlikely that most parents consider their sons to be heroes, and that they know, like the rest of us, that 'hero' is a label assigned by opportunist politicians and armchair militarists who seek only to bathe in the reflected glory of someone else's misfortune. There was nothing heroic or glorious about the Iraq War. It was just the latest in a litany of imperialist adventures perpetrated by a country that has somehow managed to obtain a reputation as the world's policeman. If the US is the world's policemen it is the biggest bent cop ever and Britain has perjured itself by backing up its lies, thanks in large part to Tony Blair, a persistent offender obsessed with his own statesmanship and reputation.

BUGS, BUSINESS AND THE ABNORMAL NORMAL

There is no Outside: Covid 19 dispatches

This collection of essays begins; 'The best safeguard against the novel coronavirus is the ability to withdraw oneself from capitalism.' Would that it were possible. The opportunist application of the tired austerity-era 'we're all in it together' rhetoric is undermined not least in Modi's India, one of the most unequal countries in the world, where the proto-fascist Hindu nationalist BJP has used what it calls 'the Muslim virus' to reinforce its scapegoating.

But the racism begins in Trumpland, where a shyster real estate dealer and his coterie of right-wing sociopaths belligerently insist in referring to the Wuhan or Chinese virus, even, like stupid adolescent boys, to 'Kung Flu', and demand that China pay for what it has done to the US (economy). It is nothing but the continuation of Trump's dangerous divisiveness.

Racism and inequality are also evident in the casualty figures; Covid 19 is intrinsically connected not only to institutional racism, but to neoliberalism, environmental destruction, precarious employment, mass incarceration and the rise of authoritarianism. The pandemic is only highlighting the inequalities of an unjust and unfair world.

Governments recognised the potential health crisis. They equally understood the threat to the economy. Those who wanted to ignore the death and suffering for the sake of profits were temporarily defeated, only for herd immunity to return in a different form. Diseases are only real when rich people start contracting them. In health and wellbeing, as in other areas of life, class is key. Our rulers have systematically downgraded class as a useful concept while capitalising on our gullibility, but it hasn't disappeared. The affluent can withdraw themselves from danger, but in the richest nation on earth there are millions of people who without work cannot eat, let alone pay for health care.

A proper response to coronavirus is anathema to the endless production and consumption ideology of capitalism. Lockdowns prevent spending, and saving working class lives is bad for business. Gross inequality, poorly paid, insecure work and an abysmal healthcare system in the US are the consequence of a weak labour movement. With the help of Tony Blair's New Labour it has taken the British capitalist class forty years to reduce us to the same state. The pandemic has entrenched inequality, with the rich getting richer through nepotism and spurious emergency procurement mechanisms, which is why it has become a referendum on the whole political and economic system.

The US health system is built on denying people basic care and amassing vast profits. Elevating British health workers to heroes is an attempt to politically neutralise them as they battle the same ruthless priorities. Those on the front line know poverty is at the heart of health inequality. The fight by often poorly-paid, migrant and marginalised NHS workers for better PPE and improved conditions is inextricably linked to the fight for decent homes, meaningful education, improved public health and climate justice. Putting health workers on a pedestal only detracts attention from decades of widespread, systematic negligence.

A US sex worker writes. 'To be scared of the sick is to

be scared of the living... arguably we should be more fearful, but to take on risk with a partner – to alleviate the loneliness of their anxiety by making it both of yours – is an act of dumb love.' She goes on, 'Thinking about that month now, I feel stupid, and lucky, which is how I feel about a lot of the things I've done.'

She reports an interview in which a man is asked if he's political. He has an adversarial relationship with authority; 'He hated cops. Not this or that cop. Cops.' 'Because of what they represent' asks the interviewer, 'Because they're cops.' She says, 'Fags, dykes are expendable in this country' and to the expendable can be added whores, one of whom points out that. 'One cannot become a criminal, one can only be labelled a criminal by the state.' Pinochet killed thousands, Bush and Blair killed millions. Looting gets you locked up, being black in the US gets you shot. It also gets you a much bigger chance of dying from shitty diseases that are the fault of the same system that oppresses you. The sex worker says, 'Workers in this country are treated like shit, a reality that grows more starkly evident everyday as unemployment climbs and rents are not forgiven.' But like many others at the bottom of the heap, prey to all kinds of dangers, she gives timeless advice; 'Don't involve the police.'

Whatever happens the pandemic had a silver lining in the Black Lives Matter movement. Following the murder of George Floyd the Minneapolis local authority voted to defund and disband the police force and replace it with a new community-run body. Naturally the mayor, having reached the dizzying heights of municipal stooge, opposed such extreme pronouncements; after all they threaten to undermine the whole purpose of the police; to protect the rich from the poor and uphold the capitalist status quo, at a time when people could see that black people weren't just being killed by the cops, but by callousness and contempt.

As human interface has been reduced to dodgy digital connections the pandemic has also raised legitimate concerns about accelerating mass surveillance. The Indian track and trace system is based on CIA and Israeli Defence Force systems used to track militants in Afghanistan and Gaza. More generally such systems have made us all aware of just how much we are being watched. Not just by the cameras that are everywhere, and in America are subsidised by the police and given away as prizes, but by the tracking of our phones.

We are assured that the information the authorities collect will be used only for infection prevention purposes, but we all know that's bullshit. The virus will cause a massive recession and those already reeling from a decade of austerity will inevitably resist being made to pay for it. We are expected to believe that the authorities who tapped phones, opened and read mail and carried out witch-hunts in the past won't use what they've got at their disposal to undermine resistance and pinpoint activists. Thanks to Covid 19 the digital economy has been given a massive boost and wherever we go we leave tracks for Big Brother to follow. What communications technology has given us by the spoonful it has taken away in truckloads. Its freedoms are illusory; they used to make petty criminals wear electronic tags and now we all carry one voluntarily, making us like dogs on retractable leads.

Meanwhile, between the Zoom meetings, 'We walk to escape the trauma of the pandemic, only to relive it all again by walking.' ' I magnetize myself to walls or duck into the oncoming traffic whenever someone approaches in the opposite direction, pause to let other pedestrians pass whenever a sub-six foot collision course is looming, speed up, slow down, cross if things look emptier on the other side... other people are suddenly, surprisingly threatening – not quite enemies, but potential sources of deadly infection. This is a strange feeling everywhere but especially in New York...'

Who'd have thought we'd find birdsong an antidote to isolation, disease and death. Were it not for the lockdown we wouldn't be able to hear it; it would be drowned out by traffic. No wonder people have seen how the world could be and demanded no return to the insane, diesel-stinking, car-obsessed, consumer-crazy normal. One writer suggests America's novel should be *One Hundred Years of Sodom and Counting* because the coronavirus has afflicted the already afflicted, but that implies intrinsic wickedness and depravity when the culprit is an evangelical attachment to a ruthless political and economic ideology.

Lots of people who have died of Covid 19 in the US had asthma. Asthma is caused by traffic pollution. It's caused by cars. It just happened to be Covid 19 that killed them. Car drivers don't want to talk about traffic pollution and most of us drive cars. Motorists are to be given endless incentives to trade in their cars for electric vehicles to stimulate the economy, while politicians pretend their concern is the environment. The disease came from primeval forests due to the mad demands of the capitalist economy. The politicians have known it was possible for years and they did nothing.

Any disaster could have befallen the marginalised people who have died. It could have been redundancy, rent arrears, gun crime or depression. Like World War Two bombing ordinary people can't control the virus, they can only endure it. They have to go to work in places where social distancing is not possible. They have to do often poorly paid front-line work.

Coronavirus is a manmade disaster, both in its creation and in its administration; the latest cull of the poor in the interests of the rich. A return to the same kind of politics will only ensure it happens again.

In the UK, amid endless complacency and wishful thinking about our unilateral exit from the pandemic, ordinary people are returning to work, perhaps shielding themselves against something that obviously isn't present but which will be practically impossible to avoid when it is, if not this time, the next.

AUNTIE AND THE
POWERS THAT BE

This New Noise: The Extraordinary Birth and
Troubled Life of the BBC – Charlotte Higgins

It is Charlotte Higgins' stated mission to discover the real BBC behind an often polarised debate. She begins by celebrating the corporation as the embodiment of our civilisation and an intrinsic accompaniment to modernism. Its early employees; ex-army officers, spies and aides to politicians, are portrayed as fitting representatives of the fledgling state broadcaster.

The BBC's first boss, the repressed and profoundly religious son of a Presbyterian minister John Reith, was a school bully, an insubordinate soldier and secretary to a Tory MP, with inflated ideas about his own destiny. A conservative and a traditionalist he was dismissive of avant-garde artists, thinkers and writers, and represented the elitist wing in the interminable cultural debate. He had a tendency toward obsessional relationships with young women, to asking prospective employees if they accepted the teachings of Jesus Christ and he admired the efficiency of Hitler and Mussolini.

Nevertheless, for the first time in history the British people could enjoy a simultaneous experience. The BBC is characterised as giving us everything and attempting to sell us nothing. It has become fashionable to claim 'democratisation' in what everyone can theoretically access, but listening to the radio was consumption nonetheless, and it was proudly declared that it helped to make the nation one. There were edifying talks and, after a ban on 'controversy' was lifted, discussions between politicians. Even women were reassured that they had a stake in the running of the country.

The BBC was born with its famous impartiality, which one early program maker, Hilda Matheson, described as Reith's avoidance of anything to which 'business magnates' might object. He developed a dislike for Matheson, who another employee noted was seen as too left wing. After Reith was told at his London club that he was being dictated to by 'a gang of reds' Matheson was forced to resign, and HG Wells noted that Reith was loyal to those above him, rather than to the liberal possibilities of the BBC.

Reith retired in 1938 believing that Churchill had blocked his advancement in reprisal for the BBC's coverage of the 1926 General Strike, which some saw as the possible precursor to revolution. To his credit Reith resisted Churchill's demand that the BBC speak for the government and allowed the broadcast of TUC statements, but he blocked an appearance by the leader of the opposition, the BBC failing the first real test of its impartiality.

The 'talks' were downgraded during the Second World War in favour of news and the BBC's reputation was greatly enhanced, mostly on the basis that it told the truth where others didn't. At the same time radio was described as 'the most powerful single instrument of political warfare the world has ever known.' The notion of truth-telling played into the long-held and largely undeserved myth about British exceptionalism, and one writer has compared the BBC's truth to that of the Delphic Oracle, which famously 'locked the truth inside slanted speech and tricked the unwary with riddles.'

In 1950, when the BBC began its coverage of elections, it saw itself as democratising democracy itself and avoided making predictions. Afterward current affairs presenters were discovered in MPs who had lost their seats and royal ceremonial became a staple. By the late 1950s it was being noticed that the BBC wasn't always as impartial as it liked to pretend.

Thirty years later Alasdair Milne was forced out by Thatcher to be replaced by John Birt, who appeased the free market Tory right by overseeing the forced marketisation of the BBC. In doing so he made it a microcosm of Britain; cuts and redundancies at the bottom, overpaid consultants, bloated salaries and the prospect of ennoblement at the top. A new broadcasting act compelled the BBC to outsource 25% of its program making, and 'entrepreneurs' made millions at the public's expense. Birt is credited with saving the BBC by doing what Thatcher wanted before she asked for it. His style was Stalinist and morale plummeted, but he brought the BBC reluctantly into the neoliberal age.

Some BBC programs have looked at the world from the point of view of the powerless and they invariably get people's backs up, but it has been around war where the BBC has become most unstuck. In the 80s Thatcher demanded that the IRA be denied publicity and eventually the opinions of Sinn Fein were entirely supressed. In July 1985, the Tories got wind of a documentary featuring paramilitaries and ordered that it not be screened; everyone knew that Thatcher was censoring the BBC.

Tony Blair's PR thug Alastair Campbell personally rang the BBC during the invasion of Afghanistan threatening reprisals if 'crap' about civilian causalities wasn't taken off air and New Labour's endless references to impartiality were a cover for coercive self-interest. An impartial BBC might have said openly that the country was being taken into an illegal war with Iraq on the basis of lies. Instead it muffed it and the fallout led to David Kelly's suicide and the resignation of the

Director General.

Director General Tony Hall said 'I think the reason the vast majority of people in this country support the BBC is because we are independent, we are impartial.' A BBC employee says 'the BBC is at its highest levels concerned with not offending the establishment, not making enemies in high places. Its core purpose – independent and impartial journalism – clashes with its survival instincts.' Another said, 'When push comes to shove, senior people at the BBC consider themselves part of the establishment.'

When Robert Peston broke the story about the failure of the Northern Rock building society he was accused by politicians of attempting to destroy the British economy. He says, 'we have also been too worried about what other people think... there is no institutional bias to the left – if anything, it is a bit the other way.' A senior journalist laughed when asked if the BBC had moved to the right, saying, 'undoubtedly, you're not supposed to read the *Guardian*... it confirms everyone's prejudices [it is] more important... to be seen reading the *Telegraph* or the *Times*.

The right-wing commentator Quentin Letts says the BBC is 'full of lefties', even though he has had a series on Radio 4 and well-known BBC employees have resigned to take up posts with the Tories and UKIP. But the BBC's most prominent critic is the *Daily Mail*. Its editor, Paul Dacre, says the BBC's 'cultural Marxism' undermines the conservative values held by millions of Britons, particularly their (racist) attitude to immigration. He also accuses the BBC of 'a closed thought system operating a kind of Orwellian Newspeak', which is 'perverting the political discourse and disenfranchising countless millions' and of being responsible for political apathy. He calls climate concern a 'blood sacrifice to the BBC God.' It is no great wonder then that *Daily Mail* loyalists, who every day imbibe a distorted picture of Britain and the most closed world view possible, think the BBC is too left-wing.

Dacre also said he would 'die in a ditch defending the BBC as a great civilising force' because like most sensible critics he doesn't want the BBC to disappear. Free-marketeers hate the BBC's paternalism, its bureaucracy and its intellectual self-satisfaction. They hate the licence fee and they think the market should decide what programs people get. One Tory critic has compared the licence fee to church tithes being paid by atheists. Others have made careers attacking the BBC and providing anti-BBC quotes for the tabloids. One of Thatcher's former aides said he couldn't understand why people rioted against the poll tax but have never rioted against the license fee, but even Thatcher, who saw it as politically useful to attack the BBC, and imposed her man to bring the corporation to heel, wouldn't have wished for its demise; it has a vital role in dissipating minority opinion in a safe and controlled way and she loved the God-bothering and distracting ceremonial.

The BBC is alleged to be part of what makes Britain great and to bind us together in that intangible impossibility, a singular British identity, but the transparency of this mendacious and dispiriting guff is ever more apparent.

In February 2021 a caller to Radio 4's *Feedback* bemoaned the failure of the BBC to hold the government to account during the pandemic. A writer to the *New Statesman* took on the question of its political bias and the widespread belief that people's opinions cancel each other out, saying the BBC is politically conservative, while being culturally 'woke' and that these are not opposites.

I love BBC radio in the same way that I love the NHS, but in the year of my birth Director General Hugh Carleton Greene said that while the BBC tried hard to be impartial, it made no pretence to impartiality on questions of morality and political extremism. As a radical realist living under a political and economic system of which I do not approve, I do not expect the BBC to reflect my views. The problem is that those on the political right demand, often vociferously, that it reflects theirs, and the BBC, as an integral part of the establishment, reliant on the good will of ministers for its funding, invariably capitulates. Anything else would be biting the hand that feeds it. It has been said that there has never been a popular movement against the BBC, but perhaps the greater danger, especially for the establishment it represents, is that it becomes irrelevant.

CRIME, CONSENT AND CORRUPTION

Accountability and a Pair of Blairs

Thirty-four years ago the private detective Daniel Morgan was found dead in a pub car park having been attacked with an axe. In June 2021 a panel that had spent eight years looking into several separate bungled police investigations into the murder released its findings. We need not trouble ourselves here with the details of a complicated case, in which serving or ex-police officers were probably complicit in murder, we need only note that due to their inability or unwillingness, the victim and his family were failed abysmally and that the police force of our illustrious imperial capital is discovered to be rotten to the core. The specific finding is that the Met's first objective was to protect itself and its reputation (such as it is) and that due to institutional corruption, collective incompetence and the venal behaviour of individual officers they failed to properly investigate the murder and, furthermore, that they obstructed the work of the panel. Not only that; their failings continue to this day and go right to the door of the current Metropolitan Police Commissioner Cressida Dick, a woman not unfamiliar with the riding out of controversy.

It was entirely appropriate that the day after all this came to light the automatically ennobled ex-commissioner Lord Ian Blair, whose downfall was itself caused by police murder, was invited onto Radio 4 to pass comment. In his autobiography, appropriately entitled *Policing Controversy*, the former commissioner made what on the surface seems like a startling admission; he said that a third of his own officers were corrupt, a third of them knew there was corruption and a third were too stupid to see that anything was going on. For many people there was nothing shocking about the statistics, and while the frank acknowledgment of a universal truth may have taken aback those who considered the police to be the saintly guardians of a law and order system unparalleled in the free world, they have had plenty of time to absorb a reality that many others already took for granted.

Nevertheless, the latest entirely unexpected revelations have left politicians and the media uncharacteristically bereft of excuses. The Home Secretary, who has clearly not read Ian Blair's book, says it is one of the most devastating episodes in the Met's history and that the panel's findings undermine democracy and threaten our very civilisation. In fact it would be quite easy for someone with ten minutes to spare to compile a top ten of those individuals the force has failed abysmally, starting with Jean Charles de Menezes and Stephen Lawrence, two completely innocent young men, both of whose murder investigations were also marred by systematic lying and corruption.

It has been noted previously that West Yorkshire Police were unable to catch the Yorkshire Ripper because they manufactured a perpetrator entirely different from themselves, when they should have been looking for someone who shared their entire moral and social outlook. A very similar denial of reality is evident in the refusal of the semi-elected administrators of the current rotten system to acknowledge that the people they daily idolise and reward handsomely to uphold it turn out to share their distorted, sociopathic values.

In the wake of the kidnap, rape and murder of Sara

Everard by a serving Metropolitan Police officer the BBC has discovered that there have been 829 allegations of domestic abuse against police officers and other staff in the last five years, very few of which have been prosecuted. As the three biggest forces in the country didn't bother to respond to the reporter's freedom of information request it is likely that there are many more. In response *Woman's Hour* received various calls from victims inside and outside the police force, including a serving female officer who said she didn't know what was going on in her own force, and a woman who said her husband changed after he joined the police and became ever more arrogant and bullying. On the same day it was announced that with very few regional exceptions the police have also singularly failed to use their powers to protect the victims of stalking. The next day Dame Vera Baird said that the moment women report rape they are subject to prejudices and stereotypes that render them dodgy citizens who may have been flirting. The obvious presumption that the victim should be believed has been thoroughly undermined by one or two false allegations and things seem to be back where they were in the 1980s.

The current Tory Home Secretary is, not untypically, a nasty piece of work who has been willing to stigmatise women, fleeing migrants and anti-racists for cynical political gain. Given that she is nominally in charge of the police her brief would almost certainly include some background information, which might include a biographical synopsis of the comments of previous leaders. As she has never expressed any desire to reform the police we might assume that she is happy with them as they are; and why shouldn't she be? They perfectly reflect the values of the unequal and unjust society she champions. They are a capitalist police force whose job it is to uphold capitalist values.

Of course the police are corrupt. You can't have a semi-autonomous extra-societal fraternity, whose job it is to protect a corrupt system, and whose first allegiance is to each other that is anything *but* corrupt. The present system doesn't just make corruption possible, it makes it necessary and inevitable. In a grossly unequal society the police's entire role is to *not* notice crime. Leaving aside the crimes of poverty, hunger and homelessness, it is a fundamental requirement that they turn a blind eye to massive tax evasion, arms sales to dictators, going to war on the basis of lies and, in Boris's case, manslaughter by extreme negligence, to focus on the petty crimes of the already marginalised. There can be no such thing as a police force that stands above and outside society, and is so selective in its interpretation of crime, that isn't corrupt. Taking money to ensure that the corrupt system continues *entails* moral and economic corruption. The only question is of whether police corruption aids or disrupts the smooth day to day accumulation of capital by its official paymasters. Along with Ian Blair's frank admission that the Met was corrupt to the core the force has also been found institutionally racist, another necessity for a social system founded on divide and rule. That judgement caused very little to change and nor will this one, irrespective of the fact that if the Met were a secondary school it would face certain closure.

Daniel Morgan's family knew within three weeks of his murder that police corruption was central and repeatedly told the investigators what they undoubtedly already knew. Following the latest devastating findings the victim's brother, Alistair, said he'd like to see the police adopt a whole new ethos. Unfortunately, like many people, though his confidence has been shattered more than most, he possibly still labours under the illusion that the police exist to protect the public from crime and not to protect state authorised criminals from public scrutiny. A Metropolitan Police spokesman was bold enough to acknowledge that they hadn't got the balance right, usually between them they are successful in pulling the wool over our eyes.

If I remember rightly the philosopher John Locke argues that by allowing the authorities to empty our bins we are sanctioning all the other things they pretend to do on our behalf. There are undoubtedly members of the 'if you haven't done anything wrong you haven't got anything to fear' brigade who will sanction any police action as long as the baddies are caught (or killed). For an equal number of people the idea that we are policed by consent is a sick joke. In many cases the police *are* the baddies, they are just better armed, better organised and operate under the cover of a legal system designed to protect them from prosecution and administered by a judiciary entirely biased in their favour.

Several years ago anonymous police officers summarily executed Yassar Yaqub on a motorway slip road. He was by all accounts no saint, but then who is? Certainly not those who allow children to go hungry, sell arms to ruthless dictators, award government contracts to their friends and walk out of lucrative parliamentary careers and straight into fantastically more lucrative careers in the very organisations for which they have lobbied. There is unfortunately a residual and lamentable belief that in this country the police produce evidence against wrongdoers, to present it to a court that they may be judged accordingly by their peers. This was never entirely true and it is increasingly mistaken. It is therefore most appropriate that on a bridge over the same motorway someone has posed the apposite question. 'Who owns the police and the government?' They have also thoughtfully provided the answer; 'Not you.'

The corrupt un-convicted war criminal Tony Blair and

his contemporary, the lamentably honest if equally corrupted ex-Metropolitan Police Commissioner Ian Blair, deserve each other. Neither being the head of Britain PLC nor being its chief bouncer entails acting in the public interest. Come the day of reckoning it will be difficult to decide who to arrest first.

THE WHITE MAN'S BURDEN

The Descent of Man – Grayson Perry

When I extricated *The Descent of Man* from its secure packaging it fell open where Grayson Perry describes his youthful frustration and his tendency toward smashing things that failed to perform. Having been in my youth similarly impetuous I was instantly on his side. His broken home and violent step-parent caused him to flirt with the armed forces (whereas mine took me less than voluntarily to the army careers office herself). Despite his eventual decision not to take the queen's shilling Perry only narrowly avoids arguing that today's wayward youth should be compulsorily enlisted in the mincing machine of militarism, and he comes worryingly close to the old man's mantra that we need another war. In selling the armed services as an outlet for superfluous laddishness he fails to note that ex-soldiers are grossly over-represented in our jails, on the streets and on the lists of successful suicides. The army only made me a racist National Front supporter; it got my delinquent nephew killed.

Naïve comments about the army aside this is a worthy attempt to challenge men's sillier and sometimes self-destructive attitudes, because it would improve society and make them better people. In a world generally dominated by men this has to be a good thing.

We are introduced to Default Man. He is white, middle aged and middle class. He rules the world and by his standards all other men are judged. Despite the fact that these men represent a social class, and are not mere representatives of dominant masculinity, class has no part in Perry's exploration. In his schema the Ministry of Masculinity controls the on-board guidance system by which modern man runs in timeless tramlines, requiring a self-motivated change that appears essentially to be against his nature. It seems that everything from car envy through sexist banter to ostentatious quotations is reducible to male machismo, but, as Karl Marx was keen to point out, 'being creates consciousness, consciousness does not create being'; the lives we are forced to live make us think the way we do, not the other way round.

Unfortunately the *Descent of Man* doesn't take us far beyond the misplaced notion that (learned) masculinity, is responsible for war and other nasty things. Men need to change their ideas in order to make the world nicer. For the solutions to real problems in the real world Perry looks not at the world, but in men's heads. This idealistic reductionism is no substitute for a materialist analysis. It is as if Marx never bothered his arse to extract the materialist kernel from Hegel's idealistic nut.

It is nowhere acknowledged that millions of men resist being competitive, combative and complicit in Default Man's world, while striving tirelessly for a change of direction. White middle aged men might be part of the problem, but like everyone else they also are part of the solution. Half of the two million people who demonstrated against the disastrous and unjustified invasion of Iraq were men and some of us were guilty of being white and middle-aged.

There's nothing wrong with trying to change men's attitudes to themselves and other men within the confines of capitalism. But I can't help thinking that Grayson Perry has missed the target. He's arguing for a paradigm shift within a socio-economic system that thrives on competition and division. Capitalism is not about to relinquish one of its historically most effective tools; hence the current assault on abortion rights.

This is essentially a psychology book and it wouldn't be fair to expect a psychology book to argue for a revolutionary transformation of society. Except that at one point Perry says he hates to use the 'R' word, meaning he doesn't like it. What Perry is effectively advocating is reformist psychological tinkering rather than revolutionary behavioural therapy.

The book closes with a Freudian resort to sex as the locus of all men's problems. I didn't need a psychology book written by a well-known artist to tell me what an old bricklayer told me thirty years ago; to the effect that the male penis is not a moral compass.

I like Grayson Perry, but the *Descent of Man* constitutes an avoidance of the reality that only in struggle are dominant notions about masculinity really challenged. British miners did not remove the topless picture from their magazine during the Great Strike because some rich well-meaning artist said they should. They removed it because they were supported selflessly, unceasingly and without preconditions by the women of the pit communities and beyond.

THE BENEFITS OF BELGIUM AND BICYCLES

The Land of Second Chances – Tim Lewis

The Land of Second Chances is ostensibly about the formation of the first Rwandan cycling team. It begins with what is claimed to be a Rwandan proverb; 'You can't know where you're going unless you know where you've come from.' This universal axiom is daily denied by politicians and misguided proletarians alike, who, despite reams of evidence to the contrary, regard human progress as an inevitable one-way street, while attempting to rationalise the actions of individuals and communities without proper consideration of their history.

It is no surprise then that in his introduction Tim Lewis takes two things for granted. Firstly, that the Olympic Games are an intrinsically good thing for humanity and, secondly, that 'entrepreneurship' is the answer to all our problems. This vacuous orthodoxy is everywhere expressed, even when it is contradicted by reality. The NHS was not created by entrepreneurship; it is being destroyed by it. Free and universal access to education was not achieved by entrepreneurship; its future is denied and threatened by it.

As we skate over the region's history it soon becomes obvious that the encouragement of entrepreneurship under King Leopold of Belgium was responsible for wiping out half the population of Congo, some ten million people, in the search for profits from rubber; just as entrepreneurship, shortened to 'oil', is responsible for the current carnage in the Middle East. The real name for entrepreneur is 'exploiter' and his real game is the ruthless pursuit of profit, irrespective of the fact that foreign aid from guilty Belgium and generous Switzerland helped bring Rwanda out of the post-colonial doldrums and into the shiny nirvana of modern market capitalism. Fake generosity and conscience money cannot expunge what has gone before, and there is no more reason for anyone to be proud of Belgium's bloodthirsty imperial past than of Britain's.

Where entrepreneurs fear to tread the Church goes clothed in lies. In Rwanda, taking its lead from the British racist John Hanning Speke, it helped to consolidate the divisions between Hutus and Tutsis who, prior to colonisation, had lived side by side under a relatively fluid social structure with much intermarriage. This deliberate and conscious division of the people on the basis of spurious eugenics led directly to the 1994 genocide, from which Rwandans are still recovering.

Into post-genocide Rwanda, like some saintly saviour, comes Tom Ritchey, multi-millionaire inventor of the mountain bike, who has belatedly discovered that money isn't everything. 'It can be very lonely when you're just driving ahead,' he says, 'you look behind and there's no one there.' The heart bleeds, as it does for all the lonely millionaires out there. Like them, and all the other affluent middle-aged men in crisis, Ritchey has a garage full of all the things he thought he wanted. He's tried the psychology and the self-help books; he's taken long rides in the hills to figure out what was happening to him, but answers came there none. His was the kind of debilitating ennui that only privileged westerners can contract. It cannot be explained to people who are fully occupied with getting the essentials of life. Then, Like Paul on the road to Damascus, Tom Ritchey found purpose in Rwanda.

Underlying his magnanimous plan to provide produce-transporting bicycles for the coffee growers of Rwanda (and buy up all the coffee for Starbucks), is the patronising notion that the people lack ingenuity themselves and it can't be done from the bottom up because they are too stupid. Not only do they need Paul Kagame, the dictator in all but name, they need western millionaires to tell them how to go on. And behind this is the notion that a people, a country, has to be profitable, measureable by capitalist standards, a competitor on the world market, not just happy or self-sufficient. In other words it has to conform to a tired model which has without fail proved disastrous for those at the bottom of society.

More insidious yet is that a man who realised that money doesn't make you happy has got over his resulting depression by going to another country to foist what failed to fulfil him onto other people. Through their 'charity' westerners get good coffee and a clear conscience. The Rwandans get a bicycle, a cash crop instead of food security and a foothold on the ladder that will make a handful very rich and the majority into alienated appendages of the machine, with less connection to the world than when they were peasants.

'Tom also felt there was potential for adventure travel and eco-tourism (based on flying), building hotels (based on thousands of tons of concrete) and running cycle tours (based on flying).' And a cycle team that could be 'a marketing tool'. And all this makes him feel much better about himself, as it no doubt has every other magnanimous philanthropist who personally sacrificed nothing.

'When I give food to the poor they call me a saint. When I ask why the poor have no food, they call me a communist', said Brazilian Archbishop Dom Hélder Câmara. Bezos, Gates,

Ritchey *et al* ignore such obvious questions and keep their millions, while patronising the poor and prolonging the myth of trickle down.

It turns out that *The Land of Second Chances* isn't about second chances for Rwandans but for Americans who have lived a life of excess with no thought for others. Jock Boyer, the coach of the Rwandan cycling team is a convicted paedophile and a Christian like Tom Ritchey; both of them Seventh-Day Adventists. Having deep religion doesn't appear to be a barrier to moral turpitude and there is no sense that Boyer feels he's doing penance. But with the self-righteousness of a Christian zealot he says the good he does now affects the bad he did then. As one reporter said, 'I hope the victim is doing as well.'

All of us are capable of doing anything given the right or wrong situation. If we don't admit that we are not honest with ourselves. The good American college boys who went to Vietnam didn't imagine that they'd end up raping and mutilating civilians, but that's what a good number of them did. Any one of us *could* murder our neighbours, molest a child or betray our friends for a scrap of food in the right circumstances. Until we understand that we'll never understand anything. It's not a question of good and evil, these barren concepts take us nowhere. The Holocaust and the Rwandan Genocide were not random aberrations, they are explainable historical events.

The descent into communal violence begins with the denial of the collective purpose pre-capitalist human societies needed to survive. It is manifest in the corrosive anti-social expostulations of the rabidly anti-equality thug Margaret Thatcher, who used uniformed state mercenaries to wage class war, in the process destroying industries, communities and lives. She did her best to realise for others Rousseau's pessimistic 'nasty, brutish and short' life and make it every man for himself. 'The individual life – as you have in Europe, we don't have that here,' says a Rwandan. Rwandans still have 'umuganda' days, when everyone is obliged to do their bit for the community, thereby tying it together. It's a bit like David Cameron's Big Society, only without the callous Tory hypocrisy.

The single-minded Rwandan cycle team trainer doesn't care about the genocide, or what part members of his team played in it, and is therefore unable to appreciate what it takes for a people to recover from such horror. He's suffered for sport and he's here to make them suffer in the name of sport. He's just one more sadomasochistic sportsman with a trailer of baggage. Disgraced racer Lance Armstrong was a troubled youth. When he was asked what pleasure he got from cycling. He said he didn't do it for the pleasure. He did it for the pain. Top level sport is punishment, and vice-versa.

Eventually it occurs to the writer of *Land of Second Chances* that not all Rwandans want life changing experiences, fame, jet-setting in planes and hotels. They are western aspirations not theirs. Team Rwanda members also had to learn to eat with a knife and fork to avoid being accused of eating like pigs, even though half the world eats with their hands. I eat with a knife and fork at home, but I wouldn't dream of eating a curry with them. A third of the population of Bradford is of Asian extraction. I wonder how many of them have picked up the tools of western refinement and civilisation as a symbol of their self-improvement. I have been to Rwanda and I can still feel the humiliation of poverty-stricken dancers presented by affluent westerners with a thank you meal surrounded by stainless steel cutlery they didn't know how to use.

Before the genocide Rwanda had its own bicycle factory and informal races must have taken place. Now every piece of two wheeled transport, motorised or otherwise; and there are millions of them, is imported, along with the countless white pick-ups of charity-funded NGOs. The west has been interfering in the country for a century and a half and yet most Rwandans still live in abject poverty.

Paul Kagame holds together a fragile dictatorship, but within it women hold 55% of parliamentary seats, something we seem incapable of replicating here. Rwandans deserve a second chance, where they've come from is all too apparent, but sporting success driven by bored Americans on an ego trip is irrelevant to those struggling to stay alive.

FASTER, HIGHER, STRONGER

The Olympics: Profit, Sport and Politics

The Brazilian favela of Vila Autodromo was built around a fishing village on a lagoon and in 2005 was declared an area of special social interest. It lacked proper sanitation and the drug gangs that terrorised other parts of Rio. When Brazil won its Olympic bid in 2009 it was decided that the Olympic Park would be built next to the favela. The regeneration plans included paved roads, proper sewers and renovated homes. The winning design by a British firm won an international award for urban planning. Under the slogan 'A New World', and a public-private partnership, Rio's Olympic facilities were built by two construction companies with a record of corruption. They were bribed with large areas of land beyond the Olympic facilities on which to build upmarket housing. The leading real estate company had big holdings in the west Rio Suburbs and in 2015 its billionaire boss made it clear that poor and indigenous Brazilians were not wanted in the bright new neighbourhoods.

Despite protests against greed and social cleansing, collusion and corruption ensured Rio's west-side became a maze of highways, shopping malls and luxury flats. Amid hypocrisy about irregular constructions and unhealthy conditions 60,000 people were duped, bullied and threatened out of their homes and Vila Autodromo and other communities were wiped off the map. The last residents were driven out by rubber bullets and percussion grenades as the bulldozers moved in. The British media reported that preparations for the games were being hampered by people who refused to leave areas required for construction, and then that disagreements were forgotten once the games began.

Rio is a divided city. Away from the Olympic glamour the young, black and poor in almost invisible communities face daily repression by a corrupt and dangerous police force. Human rights are ignored and the justice system is a joke. When activists made links with the Black Lives Matter movement in the U.S and highlighted increasing police violence ahead of the Olympics the interim president banned protests and accused them of terrorism. The public relations director said sponsors' investments needed to be protected and their expectations met; 'The idea is to promote inclusion and unity. Political demonstrations create divisions.' Nevertheless, the Olympic flame, portrayed as a symbol of inclusion and unity, was derided as a symbol of repression and as it toured cities there were attempts to extinguish it. The whole games were widely seen as a waste of money and protests took place inside and outside the stadium. Visitors had to drive past hastily erected 'walls of shame' that hid the favelas and denied the existence of their residents. Behind the ceremony and the fake claims about sustainability Brazil was a country in economic and political crisis.

Most of the hundreds killed by the police prior to the games were young black men and nine out of ten were deliberate executions. The police invariably cite self-defence or 'resistance followed by death.' They blame victims for their own deaths, interfere with crime scenes, remove bodies, plant weapons and smear victims and their families. Community activists and those who give evidence against the police are risking their lives. People go out to buy bread and don't return.

Admittedly the Metropolitan Police have yet to descend to such levels, but the 2012 London games required the biggest security operation since the Second World War, involving 13,000 police officers, 17,000 service personnel and 10,000 G4S staff. The Navy took to the Thames and Typhoon jets, radar, helicopter snipers and surface-to-air missiles were deployed at a cost of £553m. Newham Council was accused of social cleansing and of forcibly relocating five hundred families to Stoke-on-Trent. The private rental market overheated, exacerbating existing housing problems, as landlords evicted ordinary people to cash in. The Clays Lane housing estate, home to 450 tenants, was compulsorily purchased and many of those evicted were in temporary accommodation for years, all of it to make way for a new, affluent population. The Olympics gave the council an excuse to destroy communities and it was a godsend to developers, who grabbed large areas of land at knockdown prices in the name of regeneration.

Regeneration is a Thatcherite term based on the fallacious 'trickle down' theory of development, for which the Olympic Games are the perfect vehicle. They allow developers to fast track the dispossession of the poor and marginalised as part of a plan for capital accumulation. The requirement for a spectacular show is an overarching device that allows for wholesale destruction, the trampling of people's rights and a restatement of for whom and for what cities exist.

Beijing is normally subject to heavy policing and the permanent presence of soldiers, but prior to the 2008 games, while the British media reported a 'clean-up', hundreds of citizens living a marginal existence were socially cleansed from the city, to be held in specially expanded camps. One and a half million people were evicted and human rights activists were arrested. Prior to the 1988 Seoul Games the

South Korean dictatorship turned a multi-owner city into a corporate one owned by an affluent elite. 720,000 people were evicted and those who resisted were beaten and imprisoned. Some of the dispossessed were forced to survive in caves, street vendors were banned, the homeless, alcoholics, beggars and the mentally ill were rounded up and put in camps.

The 1992 Barcelona games were used to rid the city of large Roma communities. The council swept the city of beggars, prostitutes and street sellers. Four hundred poor and homeless people were subject to 'control and supervision' measures. House prices more than doubled as the Olympic districts were gentrified. Three quarters of the public housing stock was either sold off or demolished and 59,000 people were driven out of city by rising prices. Soon after Atlanta won the Olympic bid for 1996 the numbers at the city's soup kitchens fell, as homeless people were locked up, scared off and put on buses. Redevelopment led to the closure of many homeless hostels. Ahead of 2004 Games in Athens 2,700 Roma were forcibly evicted. And so it goes on; over 2 million people have been driven from their homes since 1988 for the Olympic Games.

The slogan for London 2012 was 'Inspire a generation.' The organisers boasted that they could achieve what no other games had. The economic benefits didn't materialise and the numbers participating in sport sank to their lowest level since records began. The Olympic legacy is a myth.

The Rio games were sold as a means by which the country could reinvent itself, revitalise its infrastructure and restore its finances. Instead they reduced the quality of life for many Brazilians and reinforced the country's divisions. The water was still not fit to drink, the bays were still full of sewage, and the rain forest was still being cut down. An unnecessary Olympic golf course was built in an

Environmental Protection Area containing flora and fauna unique to Brazil. The games turned out to be the perfect symbol of decline and double standards and cost Brazilians $12 billion, the highest figure in Olympic history, most of which found its way into the pockets of the already rich.

It has to be asked why cities keep bidding to host the Olympics. The IOC's mantra is that they bring tourists, put cities on the map and stimulate business and investment, but private consultants produce exactly the projections the IOC wants. The games actually cause huge public debt and laughable claims about environmental sustainability. There were four bidders for the 2024 games. The existence of effective protest movements in the host cities is a problem for the IOC and there are predictions that it will choose cities where dissent can be quashed without causing public outcry. This may mean the games go to countries under oppressive regimes.

It is regularly claimed that sport is above politics, but the marching, the flags, the national anthems, the alliances with corporate sponsors, the labour exploitation; the treatment of indigenous peoples, the marginalization of poor and working class and the selection of the host cities are all deeply political. The games are a focus for protest because they represent everything that is wrong with the world in the twenty-first century. Any disruption is nothing compared to the destruction, displacement and death entailed in capitalism's greatest showpiece.

There will still be those who say the athletes are above all this. But they have chosen to ignore the oppression and the corruption in favour of a winning is everything culture, big sponsorship deals and the possibility of security for life. At the London Olympics in 2012 forty percent of the British medals and fifty percent of the gold medals went to privately educated athletes. In Rio a third of British medal winners had attended public schools, which educate seven percent of the country's pupils. Is it worth all the waste, the evictions, the brutality and the repression to see the world's privileged running and jumping? Sport is fundamental to the existence of modern human beings. Thousands of people play amateur sport every week. The Olympic Games have nothing to do with this. As one Rio de Janeiro resident said, 'These are the exclusion games... It is an event by the rich for the rich.'

THE SWINGING SIXTIES

At Her Majesty's Pleasure – Robert Douglas

Robert Douglas was brought up in a one-room Glasgow tenement. His grandmother came from a coastal fishing background and migrated to Glasgow to work as a domestic servant. She became alcohol dependent after her husband died and ended her life in the Salvation Army hostel. His mother died when he was fifteen and he left his violent father to join the RAF cadets, going on to do his national service in the army. In 1962, after briefly working in a coal mine, he began work as a prison officer at Birmingham jail.

On the fly-leaf photograph Douglas looks like a hard man, but it might be the cap with the army style slashed peak and he claims not to be. Nine out of ten of his colleagues are ex-servicemen and some of them certainly are. The older ones are Second World War veterans who wear their medals to prove it. Some have endured privation in prisoner of war camps and escaped to live off the land. The younger ones have been brutalised by national service.

None of the military veterans are prepared to take any nonsense from prisoners and, having done his bit for his country, Douglas considers himself entitled to pass judgement (and occasionally sentence) on those who resort to crime rather than doing an honest day's work. Within half an hour of his arrival he witnesses a prisoner being dragged into a cell by officers and given a kicking and blithely says he has no moral objection to such summary justice. Some of the officers are capable of great kindness, and Douglas is not a man without feelings, but after seeing a couple of violent prisoners in action he decides it is best to get his retaliation in first where necessary. The ex-Special Forces officers don't go in for displaying their medals; they are identifiable by their speedy resort to violence. Douglas tells the story of a Special Forces double veteran jumping on the back of a struggling prisoner and deliberately breaking his shoulder blade to immobilise him.

The prison officers work a twelve day fortnight, with every other weekend off, and until nine o'clock two nights a week. Prisoners are allowed one half hour visit every twenty-eight days. Prior to 1967 they were housed either one or three to a cell to prevent homosexual activity. Only after homosexuality was decriminalised for consenting adults were two prisoners allowed to share.

As an avid reader of espionage novels Douglas is familiar with the history of exposed spies and knows the media sensationalise clandestine cold war activity. He is delighted that a convicted Russian spy, believed to have been a colonel in the KGB, is serving a twenty-five year sentence in the jail and relishes the possibility of meeting a single-minded secret agent to find out the truth.

The prison doesn't really know what to do with the spy. He is categorised as someone liable to escape and placed 'in patches', meaning he is identified by a yellow square on the back of his uniform and yellow stripes down the legs. He has to be officially handed over from officer to officer, his every movement recorded in a book that accompanies him.

The KGB colonel becomes friends with a convicted member of the IRA as neither of them consider themselves to be criminals. Their superior status is reinforced by their jailers, who regard principled 'political prisoners', as being worthy of more respect than common criminals. Despite his curiosity Douglas regards both men as enemies of his country and idly wonders if he would receive the same five star treatment in a Russian jail.

Prison officers also do duty at Birmingham assizes and Douglas, a fan of courtroom drama, is excited at the prospect of his first murder trial, in which a man is accused of stabbing his wife to death. The experience lives up to expectations. The man is found guilty and given a life sentence. For civil cases, such as divorce, the officers are supposed to be in civilian clothes, but this only means wearing a civilian jacket over their uniforms. Their jangling keys and truncheons make it obvious who they are.

The single officers are placed in local bed and breakfasts and Douglas is joined in his lodging house by a big Welshman who seems destined to be placed in charge of the punishment landing. Another officer is nicknamed Sticky due to pre-emptive use of his truncheon.

Douglas is told to bring slippers for his night shift when all the men are locked in their cells, not so the prisoners can sleep, but so they can sneak up on them. When their cells are unlocked in the morning the inmates slop out *en masse*, emptying their chamber pots and filling up their jugs with hot water while it lasts. The slopping out recesses are a favourite place for assaults. If the warders see a well-known trouble maker being assaulted they leave the assailants to it. They also stand back if they suspect a prisoner has started a fight believing it would soon be stopped. Douglas doesn't like bullies and intervenes on behalf of the victim, but if a fight is between two hard men who pose a threat to the warders they let them wear themselves out before stepping in.

After slopping out the razor blades are handed out from numbered slots in a box so the prisoners can shave. When the inmates have been given their breakfast: porridge, fatty bacon and bread, the officers retire to their canteen for a full breakfast. The prisoners wear a grey battle-dress uniform over a striped shirt and are required to have the tunic fully buttoned. Douglas considers it part of making a name for himself to ensure that they do. The most persistent transgressors are a group of West Indian men all convicted of living off immoral earnings.

When a prisoner asks Douglas how he can bring himself to be responsible for other people's incarceration, in order to embarrass him, he believes he has disarmed the man by saying he enjoys the job and has never made as much money.

For employment the prisoners sew mail bags, just as they did in the same Victorian jails while the imperial queen was alive. The longer serving prisoners don't speak to each other in the workshops because they haven't got used to the recent lifting of the no talking rule.

One night Douglas is on night duty in the hospital ward reserved for disturbed men, some of whom are convicted murderers. At midnight a recently arrested and respectable young man is brought in on remand, accused of the murder of his girlfriend. Douglas gets him tea, shares his own sandwiches with him and muses that he only missed being hanged by two years. By 1962 capital punishment was reserved for those who killed policemen or prison officers, those murdering a second time, and those killing someone during a robbery.

Later in his career Robert Douglas guarded a condemned man for a month, becoming good friends with him. Officers who had fulfilled this duty were not expected to officiate at the execution. Nevertheless, he breakfasted with the executioner and provides us with a detailed description of a hanging, which took place in a special room at the jail.

The last hanging in England took place in 1964. The British prison reformer Elizabeth Fry said that punishment was not meant as revenge, it was intended to reduce crime and reform the criminal. Perhaps for this reason even God's Copper James Anderton who, being a devout Christian must have believed in redemption, dismissed capital punishment as a deterrent. He said there was no purpose in shortening one person's life when we are all going to die. Elizabeth Fry also asked 'Does capital punishment tend to the security of the people? By no means. It hardens the hearts of men, and makes the loss of life appear light to them; and it renders life insecure, inasmuch as the law holds out that property is of greater value than life.'

Among the wealthy protectors of (their own) property who would reinstate the death penalty is the hard-hearted present Home Secretary Priti Patel, a proud Thatcherite and loyal supporter of Israel, who is prepared to score political points by allowing desperate people to drown in the channel. She is also a bully who has denounced 'lefty lawyers' for frustrating her racist immigration policies, called climate activists criminals and, without noticing any irony, dismissed Black Lives Matter supporting footballers as engaging in gesture politics.

Robert Douglas ended his working life a rural meter reader in an already disintegrating energy supply industry, who knows what dizzying heights the humanitarian Home Secretary might attain.

A CLASH OF IDEAS

I Fought the Law – Dan Kieran

Dan Kieran's thesis is that the Blair government did all it could to turn the citizens of Britain into unquestioning consumers. As he quotes the economist Milton Friedman saying that it is illegal for any corporation to put the public or the planet above the interest of its shareholders, it might be suggested that these ideas predate the honourable member for Sedgefield, envoy to the Middle East, advisor to dictators and doyen of the lucrative after dinner speech circuit.

Kieran is unimpressed with alleged economic prosperity obtained at the expense of massive consumer debt, overwork and depression, by people in the grip of fear about terrorism, violent crime, poverty and global warming, and goes in search of those who have suffered for their refusal to conform. His main example is concrete and concerning. In its wisdom the Blair government decided that it should be illegal for anyone to protest within a thousand metres of parliament without prior police consent.

The proposal, as part of the Serious and Organised Crime and Police Act, was promoted by Peter Hain. As a young man Hain campaigned vigorously against South African apartheid, and you might imagine he, of all people, would consider the right to protest sacrosanct. But that would be to misread how the parliamentary system works and how it is in the interests of those who make careers in it to forget that they were once young, idealist and principled. The proposal was instigated by the commons speaker Michael Martin, who has opposed a woman's inalienable right to choose when to terminate her own pregnancy, and was intended entirely to rid our elected representatives of an inconvenient little man who had been conducting an individual four-year anti-war protest in Parliament Square.

The Labour government drove through the law despite widespread concerns that it undermined fundamental freedoms and afterward pretended they'd done so for security reasons, 'security' being the magic word that silences all critics instantly, for who could be against security? Subsequently a woman received a criminal record for reading out names of the war dead at the cenotaph and the Defence Secretary said those concerned by this injustice were being hysterical; that is by exhibiting wild, uncontrollable emotion or sentiment, rather than just stating forcibly that it was wrong.

The threat of terrorism is undoubtedly real, as those cowering under endless western bombs would no doubt testify, but many of the domestic threats imagined by the media and taken up by politicians are not. However, when their alarming stories turn out to be bullshit they invariably remain silent. To admit to scaremongering would be to concede that they are unjustified in removing our rights.

It is reassuring to be told that our chances of being the victims of a terrorist attack are spectacularly low, but less so to be told that 'only renegade states determined to throw their weight around can obtain nuclear weapons'. This suggests that the US, Britain and various other respectable and largely Caucasian countries ought to be regarded as renegades, i.e. as having departed from recognised principles, which indeed they should; for the only principle on which their empires were built is 'Might is Right'.

Dan Kieran makes the obvious, but often overlooked, point that if a terrorist is determined to carry out an attack then no undermining of British citizens' fundamental rights is going to stop him. However, he goes a long way further by saying in the same sentence that only a change in the direction of foreign policy can do that. This is a bridge too far for the unquestioning patriot, who struggles to accept the fallibility of his own beloved country. To question British foreign policy is to open the door to the suggestion that terrorism is inevitable so long as the west backs up its global theft of resources with military action, support for dictators and the undermining of progressive governments. It is to assert that terrorism is a response to western aggression and not the other way round.

The right of the British people to resist war has always come a very poor second to the rights of those who wage imperialist war on behalf of those who want to make money. After the 7/7 attacks there was a call for Londoners to show their defiance of terrorism by carrying on as normal. As attractive as the patronising 'keep calm and carry on' culture is, it means nothing more than continuing to go to work and go shopping to make profits for someone else. At the time there were about 3,500 suicides a year, nearly ten a day, many of them will have been of young men destroyed by war, because that is the way of things. Many more were of people who had got into an inescapable spiral of debt doing what the government wanted them to do above all else; spend money they didn't have.

For Dan Kieran there was some mythical period in our history when much of this didn't happen. His idealisation of the past has convinced him that today's politicians are special in that they no longer fight for the long-term interests of the people who elect them, but for the short term interests of those who want to amass personal fortunes. Unfortunately, it was ever thus, but Dan decides to see how bad it is by becoming part of the resistance. As a law abiding citizen who generally respects authority and the police he does this with some trepidation, knowing that if he is arrested on a protest he will be forever regarded as a troublemaker and probably prevented from entering the United States of America.

His chosen protest, a picnic in Parliament Square, could hardly be more innocuous and he fails to get arrested. However, he is pathologically predisposed to the idea that his fellow protesters are standing up for what it means to be British, seemingly unaware that this is bollocks. They are actually standing up for something much more fundamental than the attachment to arbitrary geographical constructs, something which is impossible in the world as currently configured; that is democracy. His endless references to the spirit of old Albion and the casting of protesters as true patriots is irritating. Protesting an illegal imperialist war, which is what the above law was designed to prevent, is exactly the opposite of patriotism. Patriotism is the uncritical defence of a country that is allegedly yours (though it is very difficult to ascertain any sense in which this is true) irrespective of the illegality, immorality or inhumanity of its actions.

To back up his bizarre ideas about old Albion, under which people enjoyed boundless liberty, Kieran seeks the help of a forthright amateur expert and is told, in no uncertain terms, that there is no such thing as 'the English' and anyone who says there is a nationalist naughty swear word. But unswerving in his indispensable belief in the goodness of the apparently classless peoples of the pre-industrial past Dan Kieran is undeterred. It is undeniably true that the industrial revolution regulated ordinary people's lives in ways hitherto unimaginable, and to their great detriment, but it does not at all follow that they were previously, in any sense, free.

The fact is that we don't live in a democracy at all and when people object to government policy, as they did in very large numbers to the invasion of Iraq, they are ignored. Despite his distaste for nationalism Kieran's expert believes that standing up against tyranny is part of the British birth right; it began by standing up to the Catholic church, and continued through standing alone against Napoleon, (Churchill's) standing up alone against Hitler and (Thatcher's) standing alone against communism.

But, in obvious contradiction, the traditions of old Albion we should all be standing up for are not the ones represented by the racist Churchill or the ruthless class warrior Thatcher, but those that welcome people from all over the world and celebrate popular resistance to bullies and exploiters.

At his next picnic in defence of his right to be philosophically contradictory Dan Kieran and his friends, teddy bears included, are threatened with arrest for protesting by police officers who are unable to define what protest entails, though they admit that the exclusion zone is stupid and unjustified. The protesters leave the square when they are told to and no one is arrested.

Dan then shifts his allegiance to a woman camped on top of Derby bus station to prevent its demolition and replacement by the usual unnecessary cathedral to capitalism. And I stopped making notes.

HOW THE MIGHTY FAIL

The American War – Jonathan Neale

The US emerged from the Second World War terrified of its Soviet allies. It lost its markets in China when the communists won power and it was decided that no further loss in southeast Asia would be tolerated. Fears about a communist North Vietnamese takeover of South Vietnam coincided with anti-communist paranoia at home. The ensuing war was as much about fighting the domestic left as any principled resistance to the spread of communism abroad.

According to the 'Domino Theory' South Vietnam's fall would inevitably lead to the collapse of other pro-US states. To maintain its ideological dominance the US embarked on one of the most horrific episodes in human history, dropping seven million tons of bombs on Vietnam, Cambodia and Laos and killing millions of innocent people. The defoliant Agent Orange reduced large parts of a fertile country to barren wasteland and the flesh-burning chemical Napalm was dropped on civilians and soldiers alike. It was not unusual for three quarters of its victims to be village women.

The Vietnam War turned the US state into a brutal killing machine, as young American servicemen machine-gunned their way through villages, killing, raping and torturing. The pressure to increase the number of enemy dead was immense and representatives of the world's policeman resorted to barbarism in cutting off and handing in the ears of their victims to prove their kills. Rifleman Varnado Simpson remembered;

'... I just started killing. Old men, women, children, water buffalo, everything. We were told to leave nothing standing. We did what we were told, regardless of whether they were civilians. They was the enemy, period, kill... You didn't have to look for people to kill, they were just there. I cut their throats, cut off their hands, cut out their tongues, their hair, scalped them, I did it.'

As a deliberate terror tactic US soldiers and their allies raped and killed women and violated their corpses. This is from a novel written by a witness;

'We moved towards the corner of the forest from which the horrible odor seemed to emanate. We found six naked corpses. Women, their breasts and genitals had been cut off and strewn on the grass round them... They must have belonged to a group of volunteers or a mobile unit that lost its way. Perhaps, like us, they had come here to search for bamboo shoots or vegetables. The soldiers had raped them before killing them. Their corpses were bruised violet.'

The Vietnam War eventually cost the lives of fifty-eight thousand young Americans, the majority of them from poorer backgrounds. It was working class war; Rich Americans did not send their sons to kill and die. Early on the soldiers were disproportionately black, but the lies about a war between communism and freedom couldn't be sustained while such racism was obvious.

We are regularly befuddled with propaganda about the British blitz spirit; it was as nothing compared to spirit of the Vietnamese. The US's tactics drove the peasants and their army into implacable resistance. Their fighters dug tunnels deep into the earth and lived in them for months at a time. Fourteen year old girls fought alongside mature men, and believed no less in what they were fighting for. Villagers supported those doing the fighting and the resilience and commitment goes a long way to explain why the US lost, but it isn't the whole story.

Equally important was the anti-war movement in the US and across the west. In 1965, three weeks before the marines went in, American students started to organise. Teachers at the University of Michigan called an anti-war teach-in and three thousands students debated for nearly twenty-four hours. Teach-ins at over hundred universities followed. At Berkeley in California thirty thousand students attended. Students forced the withdrawal of the Officer Training Programs at over forty colleges and enrolment fell by two thirds; one army official said he hoped the US didn't get into another war because they wouldn't be able to fight it.

Since Korea the US had been changed by the Civil Rights movement. People had learned that American society was racist and unfair, that politicians lied to them, and that the only way to change things was to organise and protest. Leading black activist Stokely Carmichael said the Vietnam War was white people sending black people to make war on yellow people in order to defend the land they stole from red people. Greg Payton was a marine in Vietnam in 1967, he said;

'The first sergeant was telling me one day about gooks (Vietnamese)...gooks this and gooks that. That was the first time I [realised]... "A gook's just the same as a nigger," I remember telling him; then he said, "You're a smart nigger." He said that to me, just me and him.'

Martin Luther King was forced to voice his opposition to the war, despite extreme pressure from the politicians he always tried to work with. After his assassination the Black Power movement opposed the war. The Secretary of Defense's own son marched against the war, but the anti-war opposition was overwhelmingly working class; they were the ones who would have to fight and die.

In late 1966 President Johnson was told that US lives could be saved by carpet bombing Hanoi and the port of Haiphong; his advisors' computers had proved that the atomic bombs on Hiroshima and Nagasaki had saved 750,000 lives. Johnson told them to ask their computers how long it would take five hundred thousand angry Americans to climb the White House wall and lynch their president.

In October 1967 150,000 protesters met a wall of armed troops outside the Pentagon. The White House was defended by troops of the First Army. Other massive demonstrations legitimised dissent.

Ex-soldiers who hated hippies began to realise that the hippies were right. Serving soldiers knew they were being used to smash a revolt of poor peasants. They began killing gung-ho officers, refusing to advance and pretending to go out on patrol. Members of the radical left joined the army and agitated against the war from within. Over 300 anti-war newspapers were produced by soldiers. Every US base of any size had an anti-war group. Soldiers engaged in mass insubordination and dissent. At Fort Bliss reveille was cancelled because fewer than half the soldiers turned up for morning parade. In 1970 GIs picketed a talk by an army Chief of Staff and former Vietnam commander. Eight hundred serving soldiers attended an anti-war festival. Students attempted to blockade the army induction centre in Oakland, California. Between 1969 and 1970 fifty percent of draftees failed to turn up. Ten percent of those who did turn up only did so to say they were refusing the draft.

During the war 206,000 people were reported to the Federal Justice Department for refusing the draft. These were the educated young men who didn't want to fight. Working class men didn't get the chance to refuse, so they deserted. Between 1968 and 1975 93,000 people deserted from the US army alone. The rate of desertion during the conflict tripled. Seven percent of soldiers and six percent of marines deserted in 1973. In the same year 250,000 servicemen and women wrote to their congress representative opposing the war. At the beginning of the war training for possible combatants was by traditional boot camp. At the end of the war trainers had to negotiate with recruits out of fear that they would just walk away.

The protests against Vietnam started small, and the movement grew slowly. Eventually the argument against the war was won. It has been claimed that the movement was largely middle class, but the majority of those who opposed the war was greater among the working class; those who had to fight it. The unavoidable realities of war in the 1960s and the necessary resistance to it led people into asking much bigger questions. A whole generation of people horrified at what the system they lived under was capable of was radicalised and the radicalisation spread around the world.

Imperialist wars are generally naked attempts to secure markets and the supply of raw materials and the Vietnam War was no exception. But the war was also fought for deeply ideological reasons, a part of the paranoia about communism which pervaded every aspect of US foreign policy. In opposing it a sizeable part of the American population were questioning the very foundations on which their country was built.

The Vietnam War, was typically characterised by hypocritical rhetoric about freedom and the enemy was portrayed as representing an economic and political system unpalatable to the American spirit. In the twenty-first century this guff has been reinforced with cant about women's rights and the enlightenment, but nothing can alter the fact that the invasion of Afghanistan was a naked attempt to restore America's reputation as the invincible superpower.

Twenty years later the US is once more engaged in scenes reminiscent of the way it was booted out of Vietnam, its civilising mission having spectacularly failed. Three thousand Americans, numerous soldiers from its lickspittle allies and a million Afghans have died for nothing. An American official said his country couldn't carry on forever being the world's policeman. Good. The lesson from Vietnam is that we could have prevented it.

BEING AND NOTHINGNESS

Arctic Cycle – Andy Shackleton

Human beings seem to find it difficult to spend too much time on their own without embracing funny ideas; we need other people around to remind us that we are occasionally misguided. In his account of a solo cycling tour of Iceland Andy Shackleton bolsters his own view of himself as a confident explorer by promulgating the idea that the average individual is singularly incapable of understanding the motives behind his slightly less than pioneering mission. 'Why,' he imagines them saying, 'Would you want to do that?' I suspect that his friends and colleagues are perfectly able to understand why he wants to cut his ties, attach his belongings to a bicycle and ride off into the sunset, and that had they not other commitments, a good proportion of them wish they were going with him. We are empathetic creatures, each with our own preoccupations, some of them deliberately designed to prevent us facing up to our responsibilities and we recognise escape when we see it.

In this context long distance cycling is no more difficult to understand than many of the other individual activities we engage in to ward off reality, such as visiting every castle in the country, building cathedrals out of matchsticks, restoring old diesel engines, writing down train numbers or drinking lager till it makes us oblivious. Even those who have never left the Amazon rain forest have their individual peculiarities, but for the residents of a developed country, awash with leisure time and disposable income, the outlets, organised and *ad hoc*, are many and various. 'Displacement activity' used to be a psychological term denoting seemingly inappropriate animal or human behaviour, such as head-scratching, considered to arise unconsciously when a conflict between antagonistic urges cannot be resolved. The phrase has come to represent an activity engaged in as an avoidance exercise or to create purpose where there is none, often involving the setting of goals requiring consistent and dedicated input.

Evolving mysticism is a theme in solo tour literature; Andy Shackleton develops a perception that he is being looked after, presumably by a higher power of his own invention, and describes meditating and being in harmony with his equipment. But he is fully aware that he is filling time with inward nonsense like talking to his torch, and that other people would consider it strange. The mind is a complicated and marvellous thing and it has evolved through, and to be stimulated by, interaction.

Some solo travellers have even been able to convince themselves that they are gods of some kind, and I can vouch for a surreal, out of body, third-person subjectivity attached to a daily traveling and arriving, only to travel and arrive again routine. Some solo travellers will assert that a richer experience is to be obtained from being forced to seize upon every human contact, but the initiative is with the lone traveller themselves; contacts may be few and many of those she encounters will be in self-contained groups. Brief contact only highlights its general absence and alone can become lonely.

There are perhaps those who can maintain a spirit of wonder while traversing seemingly endless landscapes with only their own idle thoughts for company, but many are processing or composing literature. There is nothing intrinsically wrong with introspection, but its purpose is surely in reviewing how we have responded to personal or literary stimulus. Socrates is reputed to have said that an unexamined life is not worth living, but too much introspection risks analysis paralysis. Socrates failed to add that over-examination can only bring us swiftly to one conclusion; existence is futile and life has no meaning. Sometimes, when the answers don't come, it is better to stop asking the questions. The only alternative to facing up to this reality is to sign up for one of the many religious cults and seek comfort in illusions.

The same goes for using solo travel as a means to finding yourself. There is no true self that can be discovered by looking within. The intelligent human being is not a static entity. Any discovered self would be momentary and as such changed by that knowledge. We are changed by each single thought as a river is changed by each stream that enters it. Our constantly changing selves interact with other constantly changing selves. Who we are at any given time depends on, and develops through, interactions with other people, there is no essential and timeless self.

A few of us are lucky enough to go through life like children who don't know what we want to do when we grow up, but for many people life is stiflingly routine. They are not in a position to be able to decide what is best for them on the basis of self-analysis. The more fortunate of us can constantly recreate ourselves by breaking from who we think we are, while understanding that the world is unstable, imperfect, fragmented and sometimes downright hostile. Introspection gives us all the opportunity to recreate ourselves on a micro level, but focusing too much on the self can lead to the asinine but widespread notion that by changing ourselves we can change the world. To change the world we need collective action in which the self is both essential and irrelevant.

The search for the authenticity and individuality that capitalism promises, but only rarely delivers, drives some people to a resistance based upon a pointless 'lone wolf' mentality, even to the extent of casting doubt upon basic human relationships. Andy Shackleton insists that he wants to be 'considered as an individual in his own right, not half a couple,' saying, 'Solo travel, I guess, is a manifestation of this ethos.' Is it?

What does this insistence that he *be seen* as an individual in his own right, rather than as half a couple amount to? It isn't about what he does. It isn't about what his partner does. And it isn't about what they do as a couple. It is simply about other people's perception of him, or of them as a couple, something over which he has no control. He can cycle round Iceland on his own as much as he likes trying to prove to himself that he is an individual in his own right, but other people will continue to view him exactly as they see fit. In any case there aren't ten people in anyone's life who give enough of a shit about them to bother to categorise them. And even if there were there's no need to cycle round Iceland to prove to anyone you are an individual in your own right; why not just set yourself on fire as a protest against the banning of creosote by the European Union?

Furthermore, being half a couple does not constitute an inferior situation, any more than does admitting that you are part of a society and that you share hopes and desires common to all of humanity. It does not make a man less of a man to be seen as half a couple, which may well be what Andy Shackleton is worried about. It does not prevent either partner from pursuing their own goals, either individually or together. In reality it is the fact that people like Andy Shackleton are half a couple, no less than that they are part of a society, which gives them the springboard and support from which to launch their individual endeavour. It is not coupledom that constrains and stultifies individuals, or for that matter couples, it is property fetishism, mindless consumerism, wage slavery, constant competition, the destruction of services, attacks on wages and conditions, the prospect of insecurity and the mass media.

Actually, insisting that you be viewed as an individual in your own right, when you are *in fact* half a couple, is a denial of the support and encouragement you receive and a denigration of the other half of the couple's input to the relationship. What is actually wrong with being seen as half a couple? Other people can view my status however they like, but why would I want to deny that I am half of a couple when I am legitimately proud that someone wants to share their life with me? Sometimes we do things together. Sometimes we do things separately. The capitalist family can be a prison, but that is a problem with capitalism not human relationships *per se*.

It is claimed that Britain's most well-known and least read diarist Samuel Pepys never mentions his wife by name, though he relies on her entirely for his clean shirts, his sustenance and as a sounding board for his problems. My partner cycles thirty miles a day four days a week to sell motorcycle parts, sometimes to un-reconstituted misogynists who have yet to get beyond making sexist assumptions, in order to keep me in the style to which I have become accustomed. Given that I am a workshy artist with an aversion to full-time employment it would be ridiculous of me to claim that I am in any way independent of her; but the same applies to anyone in a relationship, whether they admit it or not, or what would be the point of them? If only more men were prepared to play the second fiddle to the dreams and projects of others we might be in a better place. In any case real independence, like freedom, for which it is a synonym, is an illusory and unattainable concept. None of us are free from physical ties, social pressures or the consequences of our actions, and mysticism, introspection and individuality, even on a bicycle, only go so far.

I SEE NO SHIPS

Cycling, Recycling and Self-delusion

A few weeks ago the twenty-sixth international COP climate conference collapsed in disarray without having done a great deal more than the other twenty-five to avert catastrophic climate change. Nevertheless, because it is now fashionable and therefore profitable, almost every commercial enterprise makes some claim to be green, carbon neutral or environmentally friendly.

You might imagine that an entirely human powered vehicle has an automatic claim to be doing no damage, certainly less damage than diesel-powered HGV trailers with sloping roofs, vegans that eat highly processed imitation meat, businesses that engage in carbon trading or pretend to plant trees to offset their emissions and the hot air from politicians' disingenuous and misleading rhetoric.

In promoting cycling as an intrinsic part of the battle to save humanity one leading cycle magazine makes on its front cover the bold claim that 'Cycling fights climate change'. Inside cycling is claimed as 'the original sustainable transport solution', central 'to reaching our goals to achieve net zero and combat the climate crisis.' It has to be acknowledged that *in use* the (non-electric) bicycle produces no emissions beyond the (CO_2) exhalations of its rider. However, as with many of the spurious claims made for other so-called green solutions, these assertions can only be sustained if the environmental costs of raw material extraction, manufacture, transportation and disposal are ignored.

The same magazine appears to be entirely dependent upon advertising revenue for its existence. Of its seventy-four pages twenty-two are direct advertisements for products (not services) and thirteen are product reviews, i.e. surreptitious advertisements. In other words over half of it is devoted to selling us things we largely don't need. The magazine is effectively a catalogue for the latest gimmicky and largely unnecessary cycling accessories. It also endlessly promotes the latest reinvention of the wheel as being incalculably better than the last one.

We can convince ourselves otherwise if we like, but the bicycle industry is not driven by environmental concerns. It is driven, like all other industries, by exploiting the market, i.e. us, by constantly creating new fashions, and 'lifestyle' magazines, such as those allegedly promoting cycling are an essential part of the process.

Hundreds of perfectly good bicycles are scrapped every day. Even a moderately sized town like Huddersfield has three charities working to save some of them being pointlessly crushed. One of them sends regular containers full of dozens of perfectly good bicycles to Africa, where I am sure they are very much appreciated. Given this situation it is disingenuous to claim cycling is green. It is just one more branch of mindless consumption, dominated by unscrupulous people out to make a quick buck. As with any possession the most environmentally friendly bicycle is the one you already have, or failing that one rescued from the voracious jaws of the dubious recycling industry. Advertiser-dependent cycle magazines cannot say this, but if you go out and buy a new bicycle, as with any other manufactured product you buy, no matter how green it claims to be, you are not helping to prevent climate change, you are contributing to it.

The parasitic publishers of cycle magazines have

also opportunistically latched onto electric bicycles, having accurately predicted the way the wind is blowing. Electric bicycles are not a sensible solution to climate change, if anything they have made existing cyclists lazy. In common with electric cars they are not a means of saving the planet but a means of maintaining capitalist profitability while pretending to do something about the problem. Nothing that involves making and selling more stuff is a sensible solution to climate change, but that's all capitalism knows how to do. What we should be doing is getting rid of cars altogether, massively investing in public transport and subsidising businesses to employ people who live nearby.

If people were buying bicycles, even electric bicycles, to replace their cars some of the claims made for cycling may be justified, but many of the people who cycle cannot afford cars, and those 'cyclists' who can tend to carry them about on the back of their cars like ornaments, to ride somewhere where it is relatively safe. For the most part there is no such thing as a cyclist, only a car driver who sometimes cycles. In the 1950s cycling was a form of transport used by people who did not own cars, today it is for many people a leisure pursuit; an add-on to our already unsustainable lifestyles.

In any case the idea that cycling is an entirely wholesome and healthy pursuit is pure fantasy. Cycling in Britain, unlike in many European countries, is inherently dangerous because there is no proper cycling infrastructure. Transport cyclists, as opposed to those who take their bicycles by car to ride circular off-road routes, have to do daily battle with forty-ton trucks, and general traffic levels are ridiculous. Drivers are increasingly frustrated, intolerant and often deliberately vindictive; both my partner and I have been hit by cars in the last year and could have been killed. The traffic fumes cyclists inhale can cause sensitive hospital breath-testing machines to identify them as smokers.

The vast majority of the bicycles sold today come from China. A large proportion of them are so poor in design, quality and construction that they are almost guaranteed to put someone off cycling for life. They are so cheap and nasty that as soon as they malfunction, even sometimes when they get a puncture, they are left outside to go rusty, prior to being thrown on the scrap man's wagon. These excuses for bicycles make up part of the thousands of container loads of worthless crap constantly crossing the world's oceans from east to west.

Almost everything we have in our homes has come from abroad because it is more profitable to make it under authoritarian dictatorships, where free trade unions are banned, activists disappear and people are denied a decent standard of living, than in a country where people have historically fought for decent working conditions. Last summer, when a massive container ship blocked the Suez Canal, four hundred and fifty container ships were held up, and the global knock-on effects are still being felt. There are currently 12,000 container ships at sea or in ports, twice as many as there were twenty-five years ago, and the largest of them are five times bigger. If this fleet were a country it would be the sixth largest polluter in the world.

Container ships run on bunker fuel, which is the sludge residue of crude oil when all other products have been extracted. This filthy and otherwise useless tar is given to shipping companies at cost in order to get rid of it. The biggest container ships burn a hundred tons of it a day and they are not subject to international pollution agreements.

No one in authority seems to have the wit or courage to suggest that this insane trans-global trade should be curtailed. Instead, like the system it is part of, its necessity is taken for granted. The shipping industry, like all other industries, is under some pressure to clean up its act, but the possibility of all these vessels being converted to electricity, using batteries that will require the very scouring of the earth, or hydrogen, produced by methods not yet invented, is just another hypothetical fantasy at the heart of the whole can-kicking shambles.

The best a leading shipping expert could do to assure us that these filth-belching behemoths would be tamed was to say that the billionaire owners of cargo fleets are parents too, and they want a better world for their children just like the rest of us. This is not very reassuring; most car dealers are parents, as are the millions of British motorists who put their own petty convenience above the future security of humanity by constantly upgrading their cars and driving absolutely everywhere.

A billion tons of coal are shipped around the world every year. This is exceeded by iron ore at 1.5 billion tons. Most of the iron ore goes to China, which makes more steel in a day than the UK makes in a year. Fifteen percent of the global cargo fleet is owned by China and the number of container ships is expected to continue to grow long into the future.

The capitalist system is predicated on endless economic growth; what Marx called 'accumulation for accumulation's sake, production for production's sake'. This in turn is dependent upon endless population growth. There are serious signs that population growth is about to peak and in some countries the birth-rate is hovering at or below population replacement. Like the cyclists on Britain's roads we are in for a rough ride.

In 2005 Katie Melua was able to sing that there were nine million bicycles in Beijing. There aren't now. The leaders of China's clearly non-communist dictatorship decreed that the bicycle was an unsuitable symbol for an advancing country and its use was discouraged. As already noted, there were many more bicycles on British roads in the 1950s than there are today. They were a form of transport not a toy and they were made here. We think we're advancing, but like the clown on the circus bike we're actually going backwards.

WET DREAMS

The sea is not a sister
A mother or a daughter
The sea is not a son-in-law
The sea is just some water

The sea is not starvation
The sea is not a war
And now and then I wonder
What the sea is for

I'll drink with any mariner
But the sea's not to my taste
The sea is just a sewer
A dustbin for our waste

The sea is just a motorway
A different kind of road
Except that on the surface
There is no highway code

The sea has many secrets
Within its swirling broth
There's lots of human flotsam
Among the dirty froth

The sea is not a court of law
It's where the rules are broke
And all the fools who cross it

Have no saviour to invoke

Philosophies and theories
Have sailed upon the tide
Because the grass is greener
On the other side

The sea has filled our bellies
And the sea has settled scores
It's not at all romantic
That it laps upon our shores

THE OFF-BEAT GENERATION

Wasting Police Time – P.C. David Copperfield

Always on the lookout for a cheap or free book I took *Wasting Police Time* from a redundant phone box-cum-library in a local 'village' while out walking, and what a revelation it is. Having previously believed in *Dixon of Dock Green*, *The Thin Blue Line* and the police as public servants I am now fully up to speed on how difficult being on the front line of our globally envied law and order system can be. David Copperfield is the pseudonym of a serving police officer who believes he cannot do his job properly due to excessive paperwork, equal opportunities, political correctness and the nanny state.

It would dishonouring the word to call James Anderton an eccentric because he was really a bigot, and the fact that P.C. Copperfield celebrates him as the kind of 'character' sadly missing from modern policing tells us a great deal. As chief constable of Greater Manchester Police (1976-91) Anderton attempted to serve two masters; an allegedly liberal/ progressive society and a vengeful Old Testament God prone to smiting people with alacrity. Anderton's dubious deity personally appointed him a moral enforcer against social non-conformists, malingerers, idlers, parasites, spongers, frauds, cheats and unrepentant criminals. He publicly pronounced that AIDS victims were swirling around in a human cesspit of their own making, that sex between men ought to be recriminalised and that thieves and burglars should be beaten until they repented and begged for mercy.

These opinions, given that they run counter to the

laws of the land, should have prevented Anderton from reaching high office, and perhaps eventually they did, but no matter. Copperfield is a clever policeman and he can hardly be unaware that Anderton was also instrumental in the sabotaging of the investigation into the alleged, and now obvious, shoot to kill policy by the Royal Ulster Constabulary and the orchestrated destruction of the career of the principled senior investigator, his own deputy. Nevertheless, he was knighted, like they all are, and is therefore a worthy hero to our literary policeman, whose lot is not an entirely happy one.

A source close to the police once told me that before the introduction of the Police and Criminal Evidence Act (PACE) in 1984 police officers did pretty much what they wanted. In fact he said they got away with murder, fitting people up at will and meting out the occasional extra-judicial chastisement. My source didn't see this as a particularly good thing, leading as it did to a bad press and a loss of public confidence, whereas P.C. Copperfield does. Getting 'scum' and 'scrotes' behind bars is his main priority, by whatever means necessary. Those of us that come under the coverall category of liberals and do-gooders aren't worthy of great deal of respect from P.C. Copperfield, due to our dangerous and misguided belief that society creates its members, and not the other way round.

Nor does P.C. Copperfield have a very high opinion of those he repeatedly refers to as the underclass, by which he means those who aren't lucky enough to be holding down some thankless employment for pitiful remuneration, and who thereby have to live largely by their wits. The fact that some of them don't live as he would have them live means they are largely written off as an irredeemable burden on society, rather than people with potential in need of proper support.

P.C. Copperfield has no respect for human rights or

diversity policies and dismisses what he calls the special claims of all minority groups, be they black, gay or itinerant. He has no problem with cops occasionally shooting alleged criminals dead, or with them getting otherwise killed, and thinks all officers should be armed with tazers so they can treat the public like cattle. Unsurprisingly he doesn't like nationalisation either, or multiculturalism, and looks forward to the day when the police become less politically correct. He is a fan of the reactionary newspaper columnist Peter Hitchens and, like him, celebrates the British Empire for the boldness it entailed.

Not unaware of the arguments of his political opponents P.C. David Copperfield despises 'liberals' 'for their belief that "offending" 'is understandable because the whole criminal justice system – indeed the whole of society – is a bourgeois creation designed to protect the rich from the poor.' Though to an objective observer this is very difficult to deny. But, while he hates 'the Stalinism of political correctness', he is himself liberal in other matters. He prefers traditional police uniforms to the ubiquitous fashion for fluorescent jackets, he does not approve of the taking and keeping of suspects' DNA and, writing at a time when they seemed a real possibility, the prospect of I.D. cards. His resentment of a hierarchical and bureaucratic police gravy train that couldn't be better designed to waste taxpayers' money leads him to say that governments are sometimes corrupt, wasteful or incompetent and often all three. He considers what he sees as harassing drivers to be a waste of his valuable time and concerted police campaigns to stop people using mobile phones while they are driving to be evidence of an increasingly Orwellian state, irrespective of the fact that it is demonstrably dangerous to others.

In matters of interpersonal relationships P.C.

Copperfield really comes into his own and he has much to say on people's domestic arrangements. His recognition that some women's groups 'made up of frothing lunatics' are claiming that rape is a far more common offence that the conviction rates suggest is inspired, especially at a time when it is widely acknowledged that rape conviction rates are abysmal and the presumption that an accusing woman should be believed is under threat. He assures us that he and the rest of the police force take allegations of rape very seriously, but says it is very hard to prove. And who can fault this logic when the police are so busy prosecuting corporate fraud, wholesale political corruption and state terrorism

The playwright Joe Orton had one of his characters say that reading isn't an occupation that should be encouraged in police officers. I suspect that many of those licensed by the state to uphold the singularly unique principles Britain is so keen to ram down the throats of foreigners are not as well read as P.C. Copperfield, and cannot gratuitously reference Proudhon's views on property or Winston Smith's hopes for the proletariat in Orwell's *1984*. But there is no doubt that many of them are equally arrogant, sarcastic, vindictive and full of their own self-importance. It takes a very special kind of public servant to tell an Iraqi man that he wouldn't get away with this or that if he was in Abu Graib, a prison now renowned for the shocking abuse of its inmates.

Occasionally, like the rabid *Daily Mail*-reading but otherwise loving grandmother we all know, P.C. Copperfield demonstrates that he is human, but he refuses to see drugs as a social problem or addiction as an illness, referring always to the criminal aspect of entirely arbitrary statutes. He'd have mandatory five year jail sentences for first time burglars when it is accepted that prison makes offenders worse, take us back to what are widely seen as the bad old days by scrapping

PACE and remove the Human Rights Act from UK law. The kind of society he wants is demonstrated in his semi-serious suggestion that Britain's streets be patrolled by ex-members of the murderous Israeli Defence Force. Swimming against the tsunami of accepted reality he comes very close to saying that police corruption is the product of an overactive imagination, and there's no reason to believe he's alone.

While having a lack of sympathy verging on contempt for those who take to the streets to resist P.C. Copperfield doesn't mind attending demonstrations, which inevitably entail generous overtime payments. His claim that police officers are genuinely innocent when faced with protesters could be taken for neutrality, did he not variously describe them as scruffy, unwashed, sandal-wearing, pony-tailed, self-satisfied, middle class crusties and anarchists who are on the dole and would be better off supporting British troops in their splendid endeavours, rather than protesting against (alleged) warmongers and multinationals.

When not reading Orwell and Proudhon Copperfield relaxes with lighter material, such as the glossy newsletter of America's National Rifle Association. Its thoughtful articles on the methods of US law enforcement agencies lead him to lament that British police forces only pretend to learn from their American cousins, and to the obvious conclusion that not only should British police officers be armed against the criminal classes, but the public too.

To reiterate, P.C. David Copperfield of Newtown nick is a jaded cynic, bogged down in paperwork, who considers himself to be hamstrung by red tape and political correctness. He spends almost his entire working life dealing with the petty concerns of the most marginalised people in society and choses to blame them for their predicament rather than the society that endlessly reproduces itself and those that live in it. And yet he thinks being a policeman is one of the best jobs in the world because it's interesting and you get to help people. Copperfield's main complaint is that he spends too much time behind a desk and behind the wheel of a car going from one waste of time crime to the next. He would rather be among the people on the mean streets wearing out boot leather in order to reassure them that everything is safe and secure in a land of obvious and intentional extremes that, for all his denials, he's doing his bit to uphold.

A DEBT STILL OUTSTANDING

William Wilberforce and the End of Slavery

In March 2007 the Blair government capitalised on the 200th anniversary of the ending of the slave trade with a nauseating ceremony in Westminster Abbey. Behind the ruling class descendants of slavery's beneficiaries were the invited descendants of slaves. No official apology was made for the vile trade and the event was described as an attempt to deify the Tory MP William Wilberforce.

Slavery was legal in British colonies for thirty years after the banning of the transatlantic trade and in the subsequent fifty years the British navy apprehended an average of one illegal slave ship a fortnight, forcibly settling 150,000 Africans in Jamaica and the Bahamas. The captives were prevented from returning to Africa. No one knows how many slave ships evaded capture or how many people were thrown into the sea to avoid fines.

Wilberforce was used by the Prime Minister to blunt calls for an outright ban on slavery. He remained the director of a company in Sierra Leone, which took intercepted African captives and kept them as effective slaves. Those transported illegally were sold on and when the Governor of Sierra Leone complained he was sacked with Wilberforce's consent. The enslavement of Africans ran in tandem with the theft and forced relocation of ordinary British people during industrialisation, a fact they did not fail to appreciate.

Wilberforce had previously reinforced the Combination Acts banning trade unions and suggested that the poor and downtrodden console themselves with the fact that life was short.

Slavery is sometimes seen as an unfortunate episode in an otherwise glorious history. The truth is that modern Britain is entirely established on the foundations of the disgusting trade in living human beings, who were packed into ships to languish on long passages in their own bodily fluids, the survivors to be brutalised and murdered on the plantations. A myth is perpetrated by those who despise all resistance to exploitation and repression that captured Africans did not fight back. In fact slaves resisted by every means possible. At the same time British Quakers, Baptists, Methodists and radical democrats all campaigned against slavery, in turn radicalising their adherents in factories and communities.

Black anti-slavery campaigners, who had demolished in print the arguments for slavery as early as the 1780s, worked with white abolitionists and predicted a terrible vengeance on slavery's perpetrators. Some black activists became leaders of the working class movement, demonstrating that the British working class has always been multicultural and has shown great solidarity. Robert Wedderburn was a black radical Christian whose congregation had passed a motion arguing that all slaves had the right to kill a master who refused to free them. He abhorred grovelling, did not believe in petitions and advised plantation owners to flee for their lives. Slavery was never legal in Britain and by the 1790s it had been largely ended by slaves absconding. Slave owners were well aware that only extreme brutality kept slaves in check and they were terrified of them having working people on their side.

The most successful slave revolt abroad started in 1791

in what is now Haiti. It signalled the end of a system allegedly ordained by nature. But slave resistance began in Africa, where attempts were made to resist imperial pillage. It continued on slave ships, where insurrection was a constant threat. One in ten ships suffered violent uprisings and some were turned back for Africa.

The resistance continued on the plantations; there were seven major rebellions in Jamaica between 1673 and 1786 and serious revolts in Antigua, Nevis and the Virgin Islands. African insurgents took over the Island of St John and held it for six months. Between 1733 and 1763 in Dutch Guiana enslaved Africans revolted *en masse* five times.

In every country where slaves were used there were large groups of escaped slaves called maroons. In many places they made common cause with indigenous peoples; such as on St Vincent, where in the 1730s and again in 1795 the British fought full scale wars against maroon armies. The Maroons fought hard, but they were defeated and re-enslaved. In the 17th century there was a Maroon republic of up to 30,000 people in Brazil. Its capital was a fortified city with 2,000 houses. It was eventually destroyed by the Portuguese in 1695. Two hundred years later, when the US fought its hardest war against the Native American Seminole people it is believed that up to a third of the Seminole fighters were runaway black Africans.

British workers and the enslaved were inspired by the ideals of the French Revolution and the government persecuted and imprisoned radical leaders. The revolution galvanised slaves in Haiti to organised revolt and the predictions of a terrible vengeance came true. Led by a man called Toussaint L'Ouverture it involved up to forty thousand slaves, two-thirds of whom had begun their lives in Africa. The French Revolution inspired the Haitian slaves to effectively abolish slavery themselves and the rebels defeated a British attempt to seize the colony and reinstate it. William Pitt dropped his opposition to slavery when he thought the British could take Haiti by collaborating with French planters.

When Napoleon took power France was determined to destroy those who had dared to resist. His general promised no return to slavery while waging a war of extermination. In one battle 1,200 blacks held off 12,000 French troops and inflicted heavy losses. French soldiers heard rebelling slaves singing the *Marseillaise* and asked why they were there oppressing people. Eventually Toussaint L'Ouverture was tricked by the French, captured and deported to France, where he was murdered on the instructions of Napoleon. The French revealed their intent to restore slavery and were swept away by the rebels and the Republic of Haiti was declared.

CLR James in *The Black Jacobins* insists that the Haitian Revolution killed the West Indian slave trade and slavery itself. Yet for a century historians ignored the revolution and refused to think the unthinkable; that the enslaved had freed themselves. The Haitian people have never been forgiven by the imperial powers for their part in the overthrow of the very profitable trade in slaves.

The British ruling class began to realise that the slave trade had had its day, recognising that it was madness to bring more African captives into such an unstable situation, and decided it would be safer to stop the slave trade than to throw fuel on the flames. Napoleon had defeated most of Britain's allies and the ruling class was in a very difficult situation. One million British soldiers needed something to fight for and the ruling class took to the moral high ground, seeing the sacrifice of the slave trade as a necessary concession. Parliament managed to head off the campaign for the abolition of slavery itself and abolitionists were angry that the government had effectively stolen their cause.

Following the rebellion in Haiti there were abolitionist revolts in Barbados and Guyana involving thousands of slaves. In December 1831 there was a great uprising in Jamaica and slaveholdings began to look increasingly unsafe. Planters were forced to compromise, particularly in pursuance of 'compensated emancipation.' The payoffs to slavers came to 40% of government expenditure and the lists of those compensated expose 5,000 British families, among them lords and bishops.

The late 18th and early 19th centuries were a period of great political ferment in Britain. People who could remember the Luddites had become Chartists. There were regular strikes and protests and a steady stream of repressive legislation. The Captain Swing revolt in rural England was suppressed in exactly the same harsh way as slave revolts in Caribbean had been. There was open class war in Britain and in the colonies.

An observer of Blair's Wilberfest might imagine that Britain had invented and prolonged slavery solely in order to demonstrate its extreme benevolence by scrapping it, and that the enslaved were docile and inactive. In fact revolt and rebellion ended slavery. If it became economically unsustainable it was because they slaves had made it so.

The fight against the slave trade was part of much wider international turmoil and people generalised from one campaign to another. The period can be compared to that surrounding the First World War and the Russian Revolution. In his *Making of the English Working Class* Eric Hobsbawn says that revolution was possible in Britain in the early 19th century. The actions of enslaved Africans meshed entirely with the actions of radicals in Britain. Whether the slaves knew it or not they were engaging in something of importance to the whole world.

The Guyanese scholar Walter Rodney says; 'In the slave trade capitalism paraded without even a loin cloth to cover its nakedness.' CLR James says; 'The negroes revolutionary history is inspiring. They revolted against the slave traders in Africa, they revolted against them on the slave ships, and they revolted against them on the plantations. The only place where they did not revolt is in the pages of capitalist historians.' It is estimated that twelve million people were taken from Africa into slavery. The best way we can honour them is by rejecting cynical and hypocritical ruling class commemorations and making their heroic resistance real again.

THAT BE BOOK LEARNING

Malcolm X: Socialism and Black Nationalism
– Kevin Ovenden

It is Black History Month, but black and white history are inextricably intertwined. The legitimate heroes of black history are invariably those who resisted white rule. The first event listed on this year's Black History Month website is a book club meeting on an autobiography of Malcolm X. It is an invitation to harmlessly discuss the literary merits of a book about a man whom the US state so hated and feared that it was in all likelihood involved in his assassination. This is what Vladimir Lenin said about people like Malcolm X;

'During the lifetime of revolutionaries, the oppressing classes constantly hounded them, received their theories with the most savage malice, the most furious hatred and the most unscrupulous campaigns of lies and slander. After their death, attempts are made to convert them into harmless icons, to canonise them...while at the same time robbing the revolutionary theory of its substance, blunting its revolutionary edge and vulgarising it.'

During the First World War black people entered the American industrial workforce. There was rising working class militancy and the bosses played the race card to undermine it. The trade unions went along by banning black members. Black people began to resist. In 1919 there were 26 race riots. The Universal Negro Improvement Association (UNIA) became a big organisation and moved leftward in response to general discontent, but when the industrial militancy subsided it fell apart.

Malcolm Little was born in 1925 into a world of racism and violence. His parents were members of UNIA, which accepted racism and wanted a separate black state. Four of his uncles died violently; three were killed by white men and one was lynched. When he was five the family moved to Michigan, where their home was set on fire by racists. The police watched it burn down before arresting Malcolm's father for arson. All this was normal.

After his father had been murdered by racists Malcolm went to Boston and became involved in crime. While serving time in jail he joined the Nation of Islam, a religion that encouraged action rather than meekness and passivity.

By the mid-1950s segregated education had been declared unconstitutional and the first buses had been desegregated, the latter by the mass action of ordinary black people. It was the beginning of the civil rights movement under Martin Luther King. As the Nation of Islam grew Malcolm became a prominent spokesmen. In 1959 he said on TV that white anti-racists thought they were doing black people a favour after enslaving them for 300 years and he became instantly notorious. The media called him a black supremacist and a racist in reverse. The civil rights movement stuck to its strategy of non-violence and Malcolm defied the Nation of Islam leadership by becoming the first leader to express doubts about it, asserting that self-defence was no offence;

'If we react to white racism with a violent reaction, to me that's not black racism. If you come to me and put a rope round my neck and I hang you for it, to me that's not racism. Yours is the racism, but my reaction has nothing to do with racism.'

This allowed black people to move beyond passive

appeals to white society and confront racism properly. At the same time civil rights moderates wanted to end street protests in favour of lobbying liberal politicians for civil rights legislation and King struggled to hold together a polarising movement. Echoing Malcolm X he said the biggest enemy was not the Ku Klux Klan, but white liberals who tried to set a timetable for other people's liberation. However, his famous 'I have a dream...' speech was toned down in case it upset the Democratic Party and Malcolm dismissed the march at which it was made as 'a one day integrated picnic.'

Malcolm's opinions began to influence the movement. He mixed increasingly with non-Muslims and became more political. He urged the Nation of Islam's leadership to action, but was ignored. In 1962 their separatist policies came to a logical conclusion when they invited the leader of the US Nazi party to discuss the possibility of separating the US into white and black areas.

Later, after Malcolm X had been expelled from the Nation of Islam, he wrote to the Nazi leader;

'This is to warn you that I am no longer held in check from fighting the white supremacists by... the Black Muslim movement, and that if your present racist agitation against our people...causes physical harm to Reverend King or any other black Americans... that you and your Ku Klux Klan friends will be met with maximum physical retaliation from those of us who are not handcuffed by the disarming philosophy of non-violence, and who believe in asserting our right of self-defence – by any means necessary.'

Even before his break with the Nation of Islam Malcolm told one reporter;

'But I will tell you this. The messenger has seen god. He was with Allah and was given divine patience with the devil. He is willing to wait for Allah to deal with this devil. Well, sir,

429

the rest of the Black Muslims have not seen God, we don't have this divine patience with the devil. The younger Black Muslims want to see some action.'

When President Kennedy was assassinated Nation of Islam members were told not to comment. Malcolm said the chickens had come home to roost and was expelled. Kennedy said there'd been a Negro revolution and had tried to divert the struggle into endless debate and weak legislation. In 1964 Malcolm said there could be no revolution without bloodshed and that it was nonsense to describe the civil rights movement as a revolution. The internal tensions within the movement continued and the state murders of activists led many to accept that some form of armed self-defence was required.

Under pressure from moderates King backed the former segregationist Lyndon B Johnson for US president in return for the possibility of a pathetic civil rights bill. Worse still he promised the attorney general that a march in Selma would not confront state troops and kept to his word by turning it around. Eventually King did move to the left; opposing the Vietnam War and supporting working class struggle. In doing so he had become dangerous, so they shot him.

Malcolm X was assassinated less than a year after leaving the Nation of Islam. In that time he began to see that oppression and exploitation were fundamental to capitalist society and that it could not be reformed. It is pointless to predict the possible trajectory of one whose life was cut so short, but he distrusted mainstream politics and the Democratic Party in particular. He didn't entirely rule out the possibility of elections bringing change, but he was dismissive of black voter registration campaigns, saying black people should register themselves for action. For most of his political life Malcolm believed that the struggle against racism was a struggle of all blacks against all whites, but his attitude changed when in Mecca he saw Muslims of all races and colours. He also began to separate religion and politics, saying;

'It's true we are Muslims and our religion is Islam, but we don't mix our religion with our politics and our economics and our social and civic activities – not any more. After our religious services are over, then as Muslims we become involved in political action. We become involved with anybody, anywhere, anytime, and in any manner that's designed to eliminate the evils, the political, economic and social evils that are afflicting the people in our community.'

In the months before his death Malcolm's attitude to white people changed dramatically. At first he accepted that there were good white people and that not all whites were racists. Later he said that the sincere anti-racist whites tended to be socialists. He went from saying that there could be no black and white unity until there had been some black unity, to accepting at the end of his life that while black and white unity was desirable it was difficult to achieve. He was still searching for black unity when he was assassinated. What we can say is that he would have run into problems. Black people, like everyone else, are divided by class. Those who benefit from a system do not generally want to overthrow it.

Malcolm X visited several African countries and celebrated the socialism that some of their leaders claimed to represent, but they weren't socialist, they were only aligned with the Soviet Union and believed in central planning. Malcolm X hated the system and both capitalist parties. His uncompromising challenge to racism and his defence of violence when necessary put him way to the left of the other leading figures of the black movement, but he was not a socialist. He was dismissive of black and white unity and said there could be no worker solidarity until there was black solidarity. He said black people needed to sort out their own problems before addressing the white man's problems. His strategy for getting rid of racism was wrong. We do not have to spend a lifetime learning what Malcolm X was probably beginning to learn before his life was cut short by an assassin's bullet. Studying the life and thought of Malcolm X isn't just a literary exercise.

DULCE ET DECORUM EST...

The Armistice, Remembrance and Resistance (2018)

Last month the *Telegraph* said the First World War should not be celebrated as a British military triumph lest it upset the French, who apparently regard it as futile waste of twenty million lives. This was once the case in Britain; the poppy seemed to signify regret and a desire for peace, though it was actually inspired by a propaganda poem urging the reader to resist the nation's foe. In 1957 enough poppies were manufactured for one percent of the population. Today enough are made for every single adult in the country and it has become a blatant symbol of patriotism and racism. What began as a commemoration of the armistice has become a conscious and concerted attempt to rehabilitate militarism.

It is worth reminding ourselves what we are celebrating. Richard Holmes has written of the Great War: 'Men might be killed instantly, but without apparent damage... blown to tatters by direct hits; cut up as if by some malicious butcher; crippled by flying fragments of their comrades' bodies or shocked into babbling incoherence... unscathed among the remnants of their friends...splintered trees [were] heavy with dismembered limbs and glistening ropes of entrails.' It was impossible to distinguish mud from flesh and flesh from mud. After futile charges men had to helplessly endure the death throes of their friends as they expired moaning and screaming in flooded shell holes.

Ordinary soldiers who broke down in the face of this nightmare were deemed to lack moral fibre, or suffer from 'hysteria', a condition seen as primarily affecting women and inferior races, which proved the physical and mental degeneracy of the working class. The obvious answer was increased discipline and three thousand British soldiers, routinely denigrated in official documents, were sentenced to death for cowardice or desertion by public school officers. Half of the war's survivors were deafened, blinded, limbless or badly disfigured. Tens of thousands were destroyed by 'shell shock.' Others sobbed, screamed, lost their memories, hallucinated, were rendered sleepless, hopeless and incapable. Their subsequent treatment was entirely in keeping with the British class system.

In this context we should regard the centrally orchestrated and entirely novel campaign to carve the names of working class cannon fodder on stone for the utter hypocrisy it is. It is no coincidence that it took place during one of the greatest periods of working class militancy the world has ever seen and early Armistice Day events were repeatedly disrupted by groups of veterans, often with local support, who were contemptuous of the political opportunism.

The culmination of today's remembrance jamboree is the 11th November, when in 1918 the guns are said to have fallen silent. Hostilities didn't actually end until August 1921 because the principled British state sent troops to aid rampaging, anti-Semitic counter-revolutionaries in Russia. The combined powers were bent on destroying the revolution and even after the Red Army's pyric victory the British government was only prevented by the labour movement from sending troops to continue the war.

At a series of post-war peace conferences the spoils were divided among the victors. Everyone knew the participants had made a bad peace and Field Marshall Foch of

France said it wasn't a peace but a twenty-one year armistice. Nevertheless, Lloyd George declared himself satisfied with the outcome, Britain having obtained Palestine, the German colonies in South Africa, mineral rich islands in the Pacific and Iraq, which contained some of the richest oil fields in the world.

Prior to 1914 there was much anti-war activity across the contending countries. In Germany the Social Democrats betrayed the working class and backed the war. In Britain the Labour Party joined Lloyd George's government and fronted the recruiting campaign that sent tens of thousands of its supporters to their deaths. Lloyd George was very grateful, admitting that had Labour taken a principled stance against the war it could not have been effectively fought.

Pre-war working class militancy was carried into the army, where wholesale abuses provoked numerous uprisings and mutinies, particularly following the Russian Revolution. Protest and dissent were commonplace and General Haigh expressed concern that socialist and anarchist views were rife among the ranks. Widespread unrest erupted again in 1918 and soon became endemic, with full scale rebellions at numerous army bases, causing the *Daily Herald* to report 'sheer, flat, brazen, open and successful mutiny.' British soldiers fighting the Bolsheviks in Russia also revolted and they were eventually withdrawn having achieved nothing.

Soldiers were discharged into an atmosphere of general resistance, joining activists who had previously been silenced by nationalist hysteria and state intimidation. There followed eight years of international resistance that only ended in Britain when Labour and the trade union leaders sold out the 1926 General Strike. The twin products of this momentous global defeat were Stalinism and Fascism.

This is not the story our rulers would have us discover.

They would rather we celebrate patriotic heroes charging selflessly into machine gun fire. The First World War was a revolting trashing of human life and the veterans would be horrified at what Armistice Day has become. They would be disgusted to see the ostentatious wearing of poppies by cynical politicians who have turned their sacrifice into a patriotic fashion appendage and have no idea and no interest in what the trenches were like, what it felt like to have your friends die beside you and then to confront their wives, lovers and parents.

Remembrance celebrations are never about the past, they are about the present. For a long time it was accepted that no cause was worth the suffering that had taken place. Today establishment historians like Max Hastings are attempting to revise our understanding of the war, to transform it from the Futile War into the Necessary War; a view enthusiastically supported by third generation millionaire David Cameron, the despicable Michael Gove and all-round arse Boris Johnson, who said his Labour shadow should be sacked if he was not prepared to blame the Germans.

They want us to forget that the road to the concentration camps began in 1919 and 1920 when they smashed the international attempt to take humanity beyond the barbarity of aggressive imperialist competition. They want us to forget that between 1918 and 1924 empires tumbled and workers councils ruled in Moscow, Petrograd, Berlin, Vienna and Budapest. They want us to forget the civil war in Ireland, the national liberation movements in India and China, the factory occupations in Italy, the bitter industrial struggles in Barcelona and some of the biggest strikes in British history.

The soldiers of the First World War did not lay down their lives for their friends; they surrendered them for their class enemies. But the armistice celebrations are not about men who died a century ago; we can do nothing for them. They are a patriotic circus designed to obscure reality. Our rulers want us to forget the resistance to war and the revolution that ended it. They want us to forget that our side made them afraid. As Lloyd George said 'The whole existing order, in its political, social and economic aspects, is questioned by the masses from one end of Europe to the other.' The October Revolution of 1917 was the most successful anti-war movement in history. If we support 'our' country in war we end up denouncing every protest and strike. Better to take advantage of the struggle between the robbers to overthrow them all.

Attempts are being made to project a false memory of the First World War as a conflict between civilisation and barbarism, a fight to defend our homes and our way of life, from an enemy who attacked without provocation because it was their nature, an enemy that had to be defeated because our very existence depended upon it. It was actually a war to re-divide the globe between rival capitalist states, of which Britain was the most rapacious, having destroyed the independence of more countries than the rest of the great powers put together; a mission that was carried out with unspeakable savagery and officially sanctioned looting.

One hour of anti-war activity is worth all the sentimental state-sponsored hypocrisy at cenotaphs and memorials. We should be angry at those who wasted countless human lives in search of profits and do the same today. The privileged dignitaries and politicians who wear the poppy as a badge of honour and patriotism are a disgrace. The First World War was neither a futile war nor a necessary war; it was a criminal war. The criminals who prosecuted it are still in charge; they compound their crimes by cynically manipulating history and we should despise them.

None of this means we don't empathise with those who were conscripted to fight the rich man's war in 1914-18 or those who fight the rich men's wars today. But the way to support 'our' soldiers is not to join in with the cynical, on-demand sympathy of the hypocritical state and warmongering politicians. It is to resist the endless drive to war and to resist the profit at all costs system that even now makes war inevitable.

AND DID THOSE FEET

The English – Jeremy Paxman

It ought to be made clear at the outset that when Jeremy Paxman speaks of 'the English', though he does not dismiss or ignore those of inferior station, he is largely referring to the English elite, that timeless band of self-congratulating gentlemen at whose gracious pleasure the rest of us exist.

It seems that the origin of William Blake's *Jerusalem* was a bizarre notion that Jesus had visited Britain as a boy and that part of the crown of thorns had been brought here, along with the body parts of other martyrs, to be venerated by pilgrims. This inspired the belief that the English had been selected as God's chosen people, an opinion confirmed when He allowed them to occupy half the globe.

Along the way legitimate heirs were bypassed to avoid a Catholic monarch. Rather than being the product of a thousand year reign, Elizabeth II is the descendent of those appointed by religious bigots. The urban Church over which she presides is an irrelevance and its clergy are reduced to impoverished social workers. The grand churches built by pious philanthropists were never full and the mission to impose religion on the urban proletariat largely failed. Blake's paean to Englishness, with which some would replace the present sycophantic dirge, irritates the metropolitan clergy because its elevation of the green and pleasant land practically institutionalises the secondary status of city dwellers.

For Paxman protestant individualism led to the English tendency toward utopian romanticism, evident in formations as diverse as the Diggers and the Labour Party, and a belief in the perfectibility of mankind. Leaving aside assumptions about the current status quo; no advocate of social progress is under any illusion that humanity can be made perfect, only that things can be a whole lot better. As for the Labour Party; its leaders have never sought nirvana, only to curb the very worst excesses of capitalism, a failed and now largely abandoned project. In any case such 'romantics' as there have been have tended to focus on the community, not the individual, collective improvement being implicit in human progress.

Margaret Thatcher allegedly better understood the English, particularly their desire to own property, forcing local councils to sell their housing stock. But what Thatcher recognised was much cruder; the tendency of homeowners to vote Tory. Paxman's romantic portrayal of the British police as the citizen's friend is also undermined by her concerted class war and is preposterous today, when armed paramilitaries speed about in unmarked cars, numerous people have been shot dead with impunity and 'ACAB' and 'fuck the police' decorate many an urban underpass.

A timeless villagey Britain was central to First World War propaganda; soldiers were meant to be defending the kind of idyllic rural existence they hadn't lived for the best part of a century. But wherever this rustic unreality was, it wasn't in the north. The northern industrial revolution was obscured by a contrived counter-revolutionary alternative in the south. It was where the real and elusive Englishman lived, uncorrupted by filthy cities.

It has been seriously argued that people who live in flats have a propensity to riot. Considering much of continental Europe lives in flats it is possible that in the land of timeless delusions something else is at play. Perpetuating the myth of

England as a green and pleasant land, in which anyone can theoretically live, is a denial of reality guaranteed to turn the countryside into a vast suburb. Giving great swathes of the countryside to developers and party donors to influence voting patterns is a crime that does nothing to address the poor housing many people inhabit.

At the beginning of the twentieth century the ideal Englishman had a conceited belief in his country's supremacy. He was a repressed, Eton educated cultural philistine with a private income and a world view that divided people into good chaps and lazy agitators. He represented a class not a nation, was bred for empire and floundered when it faded, but not all his traits have disappeared. Conversely John Bull, the iconic symbol of Englishness, is a fat, red-faced tradesman invented by a Scot, who saw the Englishman as a dozy, conservative and temperamental drunk, prone to endlessly expressing his brand of the truth. It was never claimed that John Bull was anything but belligerent and stupid and he had transmogrified into a moronic bulldog long before Churchill came along. Indeed stupidity was endemic among the country gentry, who only saw any importance in education when they realised their children needed it to maintain their lavish lifestyles.

The English, unlike foreigners, do not need intellectuals to tell them who they are. The cerebral citizen is distrusted and mocked, and the mistrust of ideas is alleged to have saved them from communism and fascism. Nor are the English very good at honouring cultural figures, preferring to celebrate soldiers and statesmen. This is because the intellectual exists largely in a world where social progress is possible, not in one whose leaders pretend to hold no ideology, while knowing the price of everything and the value of nothing.

Instead of exercising their minds the English have

exercised their bodies, creating and codifying many of the world's sports. Prior to 1914 life itself seemed like a game; the English pretended to play by the rules and the opposition generally lost. The English, or at least those who mattered, deluded themselves that a healthy nation could be created via the metaphor of cricket, and yet of every nine men who underwent an army medical in 1917-18 only three were fit for service. The leading newspapers preached that sport had taught the English individuality and that this would be crucial to military victory. It had rather inculcated in ordinary men the kind of discipline they required to willingly charge to their certain deaths.

It is believed the widespread English fetish for being spanked and caned originated in public schools as a substitute for affection. When Victorian double standards were at their zenith London had up to six thousand brothels and 80,000 street prostitutes, with some as young as twelve ready to meet the demand for the deflowering of virgins. What one Frenchman described as 'a festering sore on the body of English society' the English pretended did not exist. When men went astray the fault was with their temptresses, the clergy regularly preached against women and it was not unknown for men to sell their wives (in 1884 one paper detailed twenty cases), which done properly was as legally valid as marriage. It wasn't that Victorian England had no place for women, it knew their place very well.

The English tradition of women withdrawing after dinner so men could discuss serious matters stemmed from the common belief that women had nothing of any merit to say. Influential women argued that independence was unfeminine, unnatural and offensive and the new middle class tended to view working women as the mark of a barbarous society. Electoral reformers did not even consider enfranchising women, and nice women did not trouble themselves with such things.

The advocates of female education were mocked and patronised by a male elite that judged everything by the standards of martial prowess, and women knew that only Englishmen treated them with such contempt. Some were so angry that they were prepared, even on the eve of the Second World War, to repudiate the country that had treated them as slaves. The ideal Englishman *entailed* the subservient woman, undesirous of sexual gratification and content to submit when required.

Since the 1950s things have changed a great deal. In 1998 Paxman felt able to say that advancement in England was now by ability and that women had greater parity with men in public life (It was another two decades before anyone noticed that his female colleagues at the BBC were paid much less than him). It is more accurate to say that well-placed women are now able to pull the same strings as well-placed men and that this is of little consequence to the ordinary women who do most of the menial and low-paid jobs.

The ideal Englishman was invented for empire; he could not survive England's decline and he has no place in the new global village. The English have entered the future trying to relive a selective and sanitised version of the past. The fact that Paxman can write a whole book about the pre-eminence of the English without a single reference to the vile trade upon which it was all predicated, one of the most shameful episodes in human history, the repercussions of which are far from exhausted, is indicative of a deep-seated national amnesia.

The English ruling class could maintain their arrogant aloofness only because they were inured to human suffering. The English gentleman only ever seemed tall because he was stood on the bodies of women, black people and the working class. As Paxman says, the oppressed tend to remember their history, the oppressors forget it. With the layers of lies and self-deception peeled away the Englishman's appeals to honour and a sense of fair play are entirely vacuous.

Ordinary people need not mourn the passing of a certain type of Englishman, only be aware that shrouded in democratic rhetoric his hypocrisy has taken on different forms. Paxman may wish to withdraw his concluding assertion that any new nationalism won't be based on flags and anthems. He perhaps forgot to allow for terminal recession and the renewal of imperialist war, albeit with the English as very junior partners.

A MAN FOR ALL SEASONS

The Worm Forgives the Plough – John Stewart Collis

Ostensibly, *The Worm Forgives the Plough* is an account of the author's time as an agricultural worker during and after the Second World War. In reflecting upon his experiences John Stewart Collis says 'I have spent some time in the company of the philosophers and the priests, and have undertaken long journeys with them in search of the Absolute. It was all necessary. For only then could I understand that it was not necessary, and that if we will but look out of the window the answer is there. It is clear to me now that if we take the trouble to regard phenomena, with the eye, *not* of a child, but of an adult who weds intelligence with wonder, we shall soon find ourselves at ease with the Problem of Purpose and all the rest of it.'

During the 1960s we were told that in the future filling our leisure time would be the primary problem. By 1947 John Stewart Collis had already written; 'We have reached the Leisure State. But the moment we say that, we know that it is purely theoretical... for we have done nothing to increase leisure while increasing the saving of labour. Some of the workers are simply exchanged for metal, while those who are not exchanged continue to work... for exactly the same hours as before... [It is] unfortunate... that no one wants the Leisure State. All we want is work that suits us... the idea of much leisure is something from which everyone turns in dismay. You can never make *that* a goal! We are quite unfit for it mentally... We cannot bear idleness, we cannot fill that empty cup with happiness. Owing to the failure of intellectual leadership, the breakdown of religion, and the short-cuts to culture, our minds are now for the most part demoralised; in any true sense we know nothing, we understand nothing, we study nothing, we see nothing, we listen to nothing, we are incapable of reflection. Hence the hardest toil is a welcome refuge from the horror and tedium of leisure. We loath a long holiday. We cannot endure pleasure for more than half an hour. Even picnics drive us mad. Agricultural labourers die six months after retiring. Unemployed middle-class people die slowly all their lives. Thus conditioned, where shall we find the *will* to create the Leisure State?'

From this flow Collis's opinions on technology; 'My own view of machinery is not notable for consistency; but I welcome a machine which is in the right place, when it is in full use, *useful*; and not when we should use much less of it, when it is *useless*. It is unnecessary to go to extremes. Not so long ago I saw a photograph of an interesting gentleman called Captain Roberts who had invented a motor car which came to him when he whistled for it, and of a man who had invented the means by which he could drive a tractor while he stood at the corner of the field simply pressing a button. Such men have their place in our comedy and add to the gaiety of nations. But in practice they go too far.'

Collis asks what the point is of ploughing a straight furrow and concludes; 'I think the real reason is aesthetic. It is the tribute that agriculture pays to art. It is felt that there is virtue in a straight line, not to be found in one that wobbles even slightly. This calls for concentration and skill. Where there is skill there is art. Where there is art there is passion for the absolute. The straight furrow is the labourer's acknowledgement in the validity of art for art's sake.' In recognising the efforts of the farmer he pleads for art as an equally valid enterprise.

But while haymaking Collis witnesses a passing military convoy. He decides that on their side of the fence is history and on his side eternity, with the hedge a barrier. This romantic fantasy is contradicted by reality; the first armoured vehicle was a tractor with steel sheets bolted to it and the modern mechanised minelayer is a development of the ancient plough. In the First World War men injured on the battlefield had a good chance of dying from blood poisoning. In the ancient world they did not. This is because ancient Greeks and Romans fought on uncultivated ground, whereas the fields of France and Belgium had been fertilised with animal waste. Any attempt to separate different areas of human activity is artificial; everything is connected to everything else. In fact Collis himself says 'Life is incredibly departmentalised, and we deceive ourselves if we think that others outside our department see us in the smallest degree as we see ourselves.' Perhaps this is the problem.

In refusing a military commission in favour of farm work Collis effectively turned his back on the world. An unkind reviewer might dismiss the pastoral idyll he depicts as his own creation, and the book as proto-postmodern nothing-outside-the-text nonsense by a conservative-minded man, in which the farm gate forms a physical barrier against the horrors of war. But Collis has other insights. He says that on arrival at his first farm, filled with apprehension, he gave up shyness as 'a kind of self-consciousness and conceit' as well as being, like bad manners, 'a sign of ignorance of human nature.' He presumably means that shyness is misplaced because people are naturally welcoming and good. But perhaps pretending to be exempt from human emotions is an equal conceit.

On his very first day Collis is set to work on his own and

experiences loneliness for the first time, but aboard a horse cart he starts to feel part of something he has only previously seen from the outside. He soon finds out the meaning of 'quality toil' and enjoys his cheese and bread all the more for it. He knows there's nothing romantic about planting by hand, but he's doing the oldest and most necessary work done by man and knows that without machines it could still be done. He pokes fun at those who suggest country folk 'live out in the wilds' and that Mother Earth keeps men sane, considering all farmers to be slightly mad. Witnessing the germination of seeds he has spread Collis is delighted, but while treating fruit trees for blight and bugs he wonders at the amount of chemicals used.

Collis saw getting his hands dirty and his back ached with food production and his relationship to the land as un-alienated labour, but he was well aware that those who actually needed the money saw things quite differently. He believed only good conversation could make a monotonous task bearable and is dismissive of the suggestion that mundane work gives you time to think, saying it only gives you more time to hate it and those who make you do it. He is equally dismissive of the idea that hard work never hurt anyone. Hard work destroys men and women just like it destroys drills and donkeys, or the idle rich would not live longer.

Collis comes to realise what 'the cost of living' means: it means the price we have to pay to stay alive. Ordinary people aren't allowed to make a life for themselves, they are too busy making a living, and despite outward impressions there is nothing gentle about doing it on a farm. And yet he feels freer than someone given the freedom of a city. He felt he had extricated himself from the fetters of modern civilisation, 'which is a good working definition of hell.' He speaks of bosses being angry at the rain or at having to give some labourer an easy job because they can't see wages in the round. They only resent the fact that they aren't endlessly earning their pay. He speaks of bosses who take 'being in a hurry' as far as it will go and it took him a while to realise that the labourer is *owned*, not merely employed.

As an academic Collis doubts that his observations from outside have validity, and is delighted to hear himself described as 'nobody, just a worker', and all the more so because neither did he feel fully accepted by his colleagues. He describes agriculture as the manliest of the necessary professions, but not one for those with ambition or for the intellectually inclined. He expects men who are good at their jobs to be happy and is surprised to hear an expert horseman say he has hated farming from the day he started and wanted be a musician.

The seasonal fruit pickers are of low station and the scene is pitiful. Collis acknowledges that Marx was mostly right in asserting that people are for the most part what circumstances have made them. It was an object lesson in inequality at a time when people were supposed to be all in it together. When extra workers are sent from the Labour Exchange to help with the potato harvest Collis is critical of the dehumanising words used to describe them, such as 'hands' and 'casual labour'.

After speaking with a 'resting' actor Collis notes how 'companionship depends upon what we have in our heads not what we have in our pockets.' He daydreams of a time when all kinds of people come into the fields for the love of it and enjoy stimulating conversation while they work and says it would be a sad reflection on life if dreaming of a better world was futile. His vision is the antithesis of 'human resources' and production line boredom. Collis is well aware that when working by the hour the time drags, but when he is on piece work it flies by and he can hardly make his pay in the hours available.

'Of course,' writes Robert MacFarlane in the introduction to this most human of books, 'several of these work-worshippers developed thoroughly repellent politics. It has often been the case – and especially among English land-lovers – that writers about "connection" with place entangle themselves in dubious thought.' What he means is that love of the land can easily descend into myths about blood and soil, and hence to the European convulsions Collis chose to ignore.

Collis does not, in this work at least, exhibit these undesirable traits, but nor does he speak, as his equally privileged contemporary George Orwell did, for political progress. Despite its extensive and valuable insights on nature and human relationships this delightful book is as much escapism for the reader as it was for the writer, and is all the better for it.

DEEDS NOT WORDS

Class Struggle and Women's Liberation – Tony Cliff

Prior to the Great 1832 Reform Act women were not explicitly barred from voting, they were simply ignored. Women had been active in the Chartist movement and in the early illegal trade unions, but when trade unions became legal they accepted only skilled men. Women-only unions tended to be run by rich women patronising the poor. The Labour Party was founded by largely sexist trade unions, and there has always been a division between female workers and middle class feminists.

The early twentieth century was a high point in British working class struggle, but it was half a century before some craft unions accepted unskilled workers, let alone women. In contrast, the German metal workers' union had a large female membership and all progressive parties demanded general adult suffrage. In Britain the trade unions collaborated with the state and the left was divided. Some believed women should be subject to the same property qualifications as men, some wanted total adult enfranchisement and some opposed votes for women entirely.

When in 1903 Emmeline Pankhurst founded the Women's Social and Political Union (WSPU), which the *Daily Mail* nicknamed the Suffragettes, it saw obtaining the vote as a means to improve the lives of working women. It acted for the unemployed, supported strikes and empathised with the victims of British colonialism. In 1905 several big marches demanded employment, food for the hungry and

even global working class unity, but under the influence of
Christabel Pankhurst the WSPU dropped its focus on working
women, narrowed its aims to securing the vote for wealthy
women and moved from Manchester to London in pursuit
of a more influential membership. Generous donations from
dubious sources and dictatorial rule by the Pankhursts further
compromised the organisation and it was dismissed by female
trade unionists as 'Votes for the Ladies.'

A series of big demonstrations, culminating in Hyde
Park in 1908, failed to overcome the Liberal government's
intransigence and a retreat from mass action led ineluctably
to self-immolation and martyrdom. After a window breaking
and meeting disruption campaign the WSPU decided in 1909
that its imprisoned members would go on hunger strike.
The government responded with brutal force-feeding and the
release and re-arrest of those who became ill. The WSPU
became actively anti-working class, denounced strikers and
called for those who urged soldiers not to shoot them to
be charged with treason. Christabel Pankhurst opposed home
rule for Ireland and when King Edward died in 1910 she was
effusive in her support for the monarchy.

The WSPU ignored a series of crucial strikes prior to
the First World War and began a campaign of arson against
public figures. It adopted an extreme anti-man outlook and
launched a moral crusade blaming men for the spread of
venereal disease. At the outbreak of war the WSPU defended
the empire and became one of the most patriotic organisations
in Britain. It fronted a campaign to recruit women for
munitions work and renamed its newspaper *Britannia*. In
1915 it began attacking strikes, outing radical shop stewards
and repudiating socialism. It said men's patriotic duty was
to enlist and began the disgusting practice of giving white
feathers to those it regarded as cowards. It opposed the 1917

Russian Revolution and Mrs Pankhurst travelled to Russia to encourage the reactionaries.

Only Sylvia Pankhurst remained loyal to working class women. She opposed the vandalism and arson campaign in favour of collective mass protest and votes for women only on the same terms as men, but kept quiet for the sake of unity. Nevertheless, in 1914 she was expelled from the WSPU by her mother and sister after speaking at a meeting of striking workers. While they moved in society circles Sylvia worked in the east end, founding the East London Federation of Suffragettes.

Until the Russian Revolution Sylvia Pankhurst's paper, the *Women's Dreadnought* concentrated only on securing the vote for women, but she also provided vital social services for the poor, many of which were funded by wealthy patrons. In 1915 and 1916 she supported striking Welsh miners and her paper provided the best coverage of the dispute. The Russian Revolution had a profound impact on Sylvia Pankhurst. She supported it wholeheartedly, recognising that equality could be obtained only as part of a general advancement, and the *Women's Dreadnought* became *The Workers' Dreadnought*. At its 1918 conference her organisation voted to change its name to the Workers' Socialist Federation. It recognised the Soviet government, opposed all war, supported self-determination for India and Ireland and advocated the abolition of the capitalist system. Unfortunately Silvia Pankhurst later lost her way politically. Her newspaper disappeared down a cultural dead end and, somewhat bizarrely, she became a reactionary apologist for the brutal and tyrannical dictator of Ethiopia Haile Selassie.

In 1918 all men over twenty-one were granted the vote, as were all women over thirty *with property*. Ten years later the franchise was extended to women on the same terms as men.

The question is of how much these reforms were obtained on the basis of actions by the Suffragettes and of women such as Emmeline, Christable and Sylvia Pankhurst and how much the hard fought for concessions were granted on the basis of objective global factors.

It does not detract from the courage and self-sacrifice of Suffragettes of all classes who were bullied, beaten, ridiculed, jailed and force-fed by a brutal system that has from time immemorial resisted reform of any kind, to point out that in the years succeeding the First World War and the Russian Revolution the international ruling class was extremely exercised about the spread of progressive and socialist ideas which, if allowed to take hold, could threaten the entire capitalist system and its advocates' parasitic existence. As well as insurrections and near revolutions across Europe there had been mutinies in the British Army and tanks had been used to crush a strike in Glasgow.

Our rulers are well aware that repression can lead to escalation and that, though concessions can also lead to increased demands, they sometimes have to take a gamble. Governments across Europe came to the conclusion that the best way to dissipate wholesale resistance was to divert it down the well-tested parliamentary cul-de-sac. To stave off revolution the right to participate in the bogus electoral process was granted to the citizens of Germany, Austria, Hungary, Poland, Latvia, Lithuania and Estonia as well as Britain. It is likely that but for the cataclysmic events in Russia, ruling classes would have been able to withhold the franchise for longer. In New Zealand women could vote from 1893. Swiss women were not granted the vote until 1971, women in Liechtenstein not until 1984.

Mainstream historians would have us believe that reform occurs when parliamentarians are convinced of the need for it by reasoned argument, sometimes accompanied by pathetic, good-natured protests that do not disrupt the everyday making of money. Unfortunately this is nonsense; what generally drives ruling classes to grant reform is fear. For all the bizarre assertions made by conspiracy theorists and coronavirus deniers during the pandemic their latest sticker says, 'People shouldn't be afraid of their government. Governments should be afraid of the people.'

The ruling class is not currently afraid of us. Consequently they have been able to engage in the wholesale theft of our services, the driving down of wages, the emasculation of the trade unions and endless aggressive wars, while enriching themselves to the tune of billions. Their lack of fear means that a century after women were granted the vote they still lack true equality. Indeed in some countries key legislation allowing women to control their own bodies has been overturned.

Listening to social pundits we might assume that all we have to do is get more women into positions of power and influence and everything will be fine. This palpable nonsense is everyday disproved, as token women are incorporated into the barbarous global system we endure, only to become as sociopathic and belligerent as their male counterparts. The Suffragettes may have gained an earlier victory had they remained part of, and encouraged, the general working class movement, rather than resorting to rich backers, at whose behest they turned on other progressive forces and supported the slaughter of thousands of men on the western front. The mass participation of women in the prosecution of the first total war, particularly as workers in the armaments industry, had as much to do with their securing the vote as did the actions of leading Suffragettes. Women simply were not prepared to be driven back into the home in reward.

Attempts to boost the number of women on the boards of FTSE 100 companies are absolutely irrelevant to the majority of women. Unless class is at the centre of the campaign for equality it will inevitably be dominated by those who are comfortable with the present exploitive system. It is only the power of women in the workplace, combined with the power of their male colleagues, who can bring real change. For the majority of Suffragettes the campaign was about much more than simply getting the vote. If we could do anything with a vote they would never have given us one. For all her radicalism Emmeline Pankhurst eventually joined and stood in a general election for the Tory Party.

METALLIC SILVER SUV

At first there was the word of God
Then Otto set us free
We could leave a trail of diesel
As far as we could see

When God had made the animals
The flowers and the trees
Out of a giant phlegm ball
He made silver SUVs

He granted every one of us
The automatic right
To the latest shiny minibus
For mass suburban flight

No more do we require our legs
To get from A to B
We're one collective Davros
In a silver SUV

Moses brought the Ten Commandments
Then he brought the Highway Code
He decreed there'd be an SUV
Outside each snug abode

And it's only democratic
To keep the dream alive
With a shiny silver SUV
On every block-paved drive

We disdain public transport
When we travel aimlessly
And take our personal charabanc
From sea to shining sea

Our children need their safety
In the climate credit crunch
You can put your mum and dad in it
And take them for their lunch

Now ever-growing families
Take to the open road
Shoehorning into SUVs
Their diabetic load

So go for the nuclear option
And let your family sit
In a shiny silver handcart
And ride to hell in it

Problems aren't so pressing
In climate controlled air
So keep the motor running
When not going anywhere

Those who seek election
Don't want to disappoint
The flock is feigning deafness
And the priests with oil anoint

So until the flames consume us
Prisoners we will be
Gawping through the tinted windows
Of a silver SUV

We cannot see nirvana

Or the sacred sylvan groves
Just a hundred thousand grockles
Debussing in their droves

The free will we were given
Is coming under stress
And our collective will to power
Has got us in a mess

We are not flocks of woolly sheep
Despite what Nietzsche said
We'll know were at the sea-side
When the four-wheeled god is dead

HELL, HULL AND HARTLEPOOL

You are Awful – Tim Moore

In his tour of shitty Britain Tim Moore is so hard on Hull that as a fairly frequent visitor I feel obliged to defend it. The city may have been on its knees for years but, as well as endless acres of post-industrial wasteland, it has museums brimming with Britain's glorious industrial, maritime and slave-owning past, as well as two of Tim Martin's delightful budget hostelries; one near the railway station for the marginalised products of institutional neglect, and one among the faded imperial-age splendour for the semi-affluent samplers of the city's repurposed delights.

While touring Hull's hinterland Tim Moore asserts that an understanding of animal behaviour shows us it is difficult for a rational entity to commit a deliberate and foreseeable wrong. Obviously, given Britain's past, he doesn't mean morally wrong, just actions that come under the broad category of shitting on your own doorstep, but maybe Hull's civic leaders brought it upon themselves.

It was different in Gateshead, where urban planners saw a future cast largely in concrete. It should no longer surprise us that any town is entirely dominated by a multi-story temple to our childish fixation with the motor car, or that whole cities have been built around it. Sadly we are in no more imminent danger of confronting our Jeremy Clarkson complex than we are the morbidly sick economic system the private car so aptly represents.

It seems that the people of Hartlepool are entirely innocent of executing Gallic primates, but that hasn't stopped a man in a gorilla suit being elected three times mayor. The desperation is perhaps understandable, given that the MP was once Peter (later Baron) Mandelson (Oxford), willing adjutant to Sedgefield's resident war criminal. Nevertheless, it is probably unwise to generalise from Tim Moore's single eyewitness observation of Hartlepool men so bored and alienated that they make sport of smiting each other in the street with home-made maces.

In the 1950s the annual death rate for British miners was one in a thousand and Easington's graveyard is full of the sacrificed. The town's life expectancy is still low as being out of work is even unhealthier than working down a coalmine. And if Scotland wants to maintain its reputation as a socialist paradise it needs to pull its socks up. The country has one of the worst alcohol and drug death rates in Europe, as well as the worst diet, one of the highest smoking rates and the highest incidence of heart disease. It also has the highest number of tanning salons and a skin cancer rate higher than Australia. Scots also share with Australians an often profane vernacular, in which the word 'fuck' and its derivatives operate as mild linguistic intensifiers.

In the 1950s Cumbernauld was claimed to be taking civilisation toward a modernist utopia and Glasgow's former tenement dwellers were guaranteed a happy and gracious way of life. In reality a perverted assumption that the entire population would become unquestioning car-based consumers led to the erection of an ugly monstrosity alleged to contain the essence of the high street, surrounded by ugly houses that contain the debilitated product of a singularly crap idea, and the town barely achieved a third of its intended capacity.

Barrow has been called the most working class town in Britain. It was a fishing village when Victoria ascended the throne and just about Britain's' biggest shipyard when she shuffled off in 1901. It still manufactures life's little essentials, such as bog paper and nuclear submarines.

Considering that no UK tour could be complete without at least one night in a Pontins' holiday camp Tim Moore finds working class people ignoring Keith Harris and his stupid toy duck, while getting down to the important business of dangerous drinking. Keith doesn't care; his pathetic act got him a nice house in Portugal, and he tells the audience so.

More people in St Helens tick 'white' and 'Christian' on official forms than in any other British town, but the place is still full of pawnbrokers, tanning shops and takeaways and Tim Moore worries for the future of his children now the country has so little to offer the world. The lack of manufacturing jobs seems to have led a generation of young people to seek fame for its own sake and at any personal cost; willing even to humiliate themselves on limitless, low budget self-flagellating TV shows.

Croxteth and Norris Green in Liverpool are notorious for inter-estate feuding, but Tim Moore finds streets of well-kept council houses and welcoming parks, and realises he's been suffering from Scousophobia. Despite the boarded up municipal buildings he also likes Birkenhead. Less so Pontins Southport, where the clientele ignore a Barry Manilow tribute in favour of binge drinking and texting. A second night in a freezing room forces him to leave a day in credit and the following year it went bust.

Lamenting the British public's unwillingness to amuse themselves with what nature provides is not original, and it surely cannot be true that the majority are attracted only to packaged and processed experiences featuring juvenile cartoon mascots, en-suite refreshments and hateful gift shops full of tenuously relevant rubbish, usually featuring whatever is trendy on children's TV. Nor am I convinced that Sheffield has recently become immeasurably better. This kind of claim always requires a caveat; better for whom. To me it looks like they've largely pulled it down and built an ugly, sprawling university campus.

At the time of Moore's visit Nottingham was making much of Maid Marion, even naming its most horrible street after her, and being the country's leading gunshot wound capital. Maid Marion Street actually slices the city in half at the cost of important parts of the city's heritage, for the sake of cars. Maid Marion is in any case a made up person who wasn't even associated with Robin Hood's merry men until three hundred years after neither of them were born.

Walsall has been described as Ceausescu's Romania with fast food outlets and a survey revealed that only 49% of its residents were happy with their existence. During Victoria's reign there were millions of horses in Britain and Walsall made many of their saddles. One firm alone made a hundred thousand military saddles in a single year of the First World War. The demise of the horse should have signalled the end of Walsall, but for the fact that a very large number of its petrol-engined successors were built at Longbridge. At its height the largest manufacturing plant in the world employed 30,000 people and made 200,000 cars a year. What all these people and their offspring do now is anyone's guess.

Merthyr Tydfil was for many years the world's primary producer of iron and the largest town in Wales. In June 1831 ten thousand ironworkers protested against the truck system, which required them to spend the wages in their employers' overpriced shops. During the subsequent siege the army killed twenty-four people. The prime minister demanded the execution of at least one leader and thanks to state perjury two were eventually despatched. It was the first time the red flag was flown over a British protest and a key moment in the development of the trade union movement. For the past century the town has been engaged in its own slow death, the only hiatus being a Hoover factory destroyed by stupid management. In 2011 Merthyr was home to the UK's biggest abattoir, three landfill sites taking most of South Wales' rubbish, Britain's largest open-cast coal mine, one of the dirtiest power stations in Europe, a new prison, a massive incinerator and a very large rate of unemployment. It also held the UK record for those claiming incapacity benefit, had a significant and growing obesity problem and one in ten of its population was on anti-depressants.

At least Coventry had an excuse for replacing all its fine buildings with concrete monstrosities. Most of the cement for the city's regeneration came from the massive works in nearby Rugby, a still very much thriving enterprise. But this is hardly something to celebrate, given that cement production is so ridiculously energy intensive.

While staying in one last grubby and rundown hotel in want of a competent inspector, Tim Moore consoles himself that half of the shit he's seen will soon be demolished as part of 'Britain's relentless drive towards the competent, blandly inoffensive, ruthlessly focus-grouped middle ground, just another globalised consumer nation that [shops] in the same vast retail parks and [drives] the same metallic-grey people carrier [while] conversing in the same droning upspeak.' He's glad to have seen the country at its grubby nadir.

I'm not sure we've reached the bottom yet. It is over three decades since Tony Blair's wild-eyed spin doctors coined their crass slogan; 'Things can only get better.'

Actually things could get much worse. They did get worse, and there is no reason to believe they won't continue to get worse, largely due to deliberate government policy. This book is very funny, but what's happened to Britain is very sad.

MORE OR LESS BUNK

The Invention of Tradition
– Eric Hobsbawm and Terence Ranger (Eds.)

Novelty often arrives in the garb of antiquity. Invented 'traditions' invariably infer continuity with a timeless past and occur most readily in periods of social and technological upheaval. A tradition only requires defending once it has ceased to be common practice and in this sense they are all invented. Where ancient practice actually survives reference to 'tradition' is unnecessary.

Since the industrial revolution invented traditions have been used to create social cohesion, legitimise institutions and influence behaviour. They are a form of social engineering that has allowed the imposition of social contracts and the continuance of inequality, but they always remain secondary to economic, technological, political and bureaucratic priorities. The invented traditions of the British military, the law, parliamentary democracy and patriotism currently seem secure, but what goes for the language goes for the nation. English is not the language of our ancestors; it is an invention.

The Scottish Highland traditions of the kilt, the clan and the bagpipes are believed almost to predate written history. In fact they hardly existed prior to the union with England, in no way represented highland society and were regarded by most scots as representing predatory, blackmailing highland rogues and barbarians. There was no specific highland culture and highlanders were never a distinct people, only an overspill from Ireland. Racially and culturally the west of Scotland was a colony of Ireland. The culture was Irish, the language was Irish and the musical instrument was the harp. The highlands and islands had no independent non-Irish culture.

The highland tradition, and its subsequent imposition on the whole of Scotland, came about by stages. In the eighteenth century, Ireland's cultural history was stolen and, through a process of forgery, theft and blatant revisionism, rewritten as Scottish history. This calculated misappropriation eventually resulted in claims that Celtic Scotland was the 'mother nation' and Ireland its cultural outpost. The ancient highland traditions were then artificially created, to be subsequently adopted by the rest of Scotland. Even eminent historians such as Edward Gibbon were fooled by this fiction, which elevated the despised savages of the highlands to internationally celebrated representatives of an ancient culture. All that has since been necessary is to continually bolster that tradition with the visible symbols of a strange national dress. The man initially responsible for this was Walter Scott. He did not subscribe to the fabricated cultural history, but claimed, without a shred of evidence, that the highlanders as long ago as the fifth century had worn a short tartan kilt.

Tartan cloth actually came from Flanders in the sixteenth century and entered the highlands via the Scottish lowlands. Originally 'kilt' signified only a particular way of wearing this cloth, a single length being wrapped round the body and thrown over the shoulder. The kilt in the form we know it today, a separate skirt with sewn in pleats, was invented by an English Quaker from Lancashire who set up an iron smelting plant at Invergarry and sought a more suitable and convenient dress for his workmen. The ironmaster himself wore the new garment; it was taken up by his influential friends and soon spread further afield.

This history of the kilt was first published in 1785. It was not challenged for nearly half a century and has yet to be disproved. The kilt was invented by an English industrialist, as a workman's garment. Its invention was the very antithesis of preserving a way of life, consisting as it did in the active discarding of unsuitable apparel and its replacement in the interest of heavy industry. It was first a symbol of the simple workman, not the strutting lord and his aping acolytes. The first kilts did not need to be flamboyant and were largely brown, bolder colours were introduced, at random, only to reflect an elevated status.

When the Scots rebelled in 1745 the kilt was a recent English invention and the clan tartans had yet to be dreamed up. After the victory at Culloden the outward signs of highland culture were proscribed and an alleged way of life systematically erased. By 1780 highland dress was extinct and the bagpipe forgotten. The working class of the highlands had no reason to return to either the cumbersome plaid or the slightly more convenient modern kilt, but when the ban was lifted the affluent classes in Edinburgh and Aberdeen, who until then had despised the dress of their inferiors, began to display themselves like cocks in a very expensive version of a recent invention. The fashion was encouraged by the elevation of the uncultured highland savages to the noble representatives of an endangered species and the formation, by the British government under the English imperialist Pitt the Elder, of the highland regiments, a calculated means of redirecting the independent spirit of highland Scots into British imperial conquest. The military alone kept alive the great Scottish tradition of the Lancashire kilt and eventually, through them, it became associated with a spurious clan system.

In 1778, as influential Scots made their way up the British imperial bureaucracy, they founded a highland society in London. Its aim was to promote the fake values of an entirely fabricated tradition, which was backed up by an extensive library of contrived cultural history. The society eventually secured the repeal of the ban, but before it was lifted they could legally meet in London in highland dress. This dress did not include the kilt; the society's rules described highland dress as tartan trousers or the plaid worn in one piece. When the ban was lifted in 1782 the artificiality redefined version of an allegedly ancient highland dress superseded all others.

The unjustified claims by the descendants of highland barbarians to be the sole source of Scottish history and culture did not meet with universal approval. When more honest historians pointed out that the country's early inhabitants had worn bifurcated garments, not belted plaid and certainly not tartan kilts, it led one military leader to kit out his soldiers in tartan trousers. The vociferous opponents of the kilt considered it indecent, ugly, absurd and effeminate, but they protested in vain as other Scottish regiments accepted the kilt as the reintroduction of a timeless national dress. When in 1804 the war office proposed the alternative of tartan trousers the commanders of Scottish regiments were infuriated at the threat to their ancient and traditional garb.

The kilt's advocates refused to believe that it, and the clan tartans, had not existed forever. As the highland takeover of Scottish culture got underway in the nineteenth century more societies were founded to promote their wearing. The discovery of clan tartans, by highlanders and lowlanders alike, greatly invigorated kilt makers, who naturally rubbed their hands in glee, even though there is evidence of proud clan members being sold a family tartan that had previously been sold in bulk for the clothing of West Indian slaves.

The conflation of the previously unimportant west of Scotland with the entire nation was described by one critic as a collective hallucination, but the 'tradition' was further boosted by a royal visit in 1822. The great and the good turned out in their highland finery and, similarly adorned, the monarch proposed a toast to the chieftains and clans of Scotland, only to be accused of attempting to ingratiate himself by wearing what ninety percent of Scots regarded as the uniform of a thief.

Much of the rest was done by two English brothers with delusions of grandeur. They pretended Scottish ancestry, took on various Scottish names and wormed their way into Scottish high society, wearing 'every extravagance of which the Scottish tradition is capable, every kind of tag and rag, false orders and tinsel ornaments.' They produced an entirely fake history of the clans and their tartans, which they claimed had even been worn in the south of Scotland. Their colour catalogues of the various tartans came with an entirely made up history, including claims that highland dress was a fossil-relic from the middle ages, when highland Scotland had been 'a flourishing part of cosmopolitan Europe... a rich and polished society in which the splendid courts of the tribal chiefs shared the luxuries and enlightenment of the continent.'

Far more than revive a dress alone, the brothers created a whole imaginary highland civilisation through outrageous fiction. Their claims to royal blood were exposed just as Queen Victoria bought Balmoral, but their spurious clan catalogues were taken up by the Highland Society of London and the Scottish tartan industry prospered. And so it went on, with the publication in 1843 of the lavishly illustrated *Clans of the Scottish Highlands*; seventy-two paintings of clansmen in their distinctive tartans. Queen Victoria's praise of the highlands provided another boost and works on the clan tartans followed one upon the other, all of them based on the same completely fabricated source. All the exponents of the timeless highland tradition have been unmasked, but it makes no difference. Nowadays the cult of Caledonia has a following to rival some religions and highland 'clan tartans' are worn, with tribal enthusiasm by Scots and pseudo-scots, marching bands, princes, kings and bridegrooms around the world, which is quite an achievement for fairy story.

GOING OFF THE RAILS

The Road to Little Dribbling – Bill Bryson

Railways began in Britain and the country embraced rail travel with such enthusiasm that lines once covered a map of the country like a spider's web. But when the network was nationalised in 1948, it was poorly structured, old fashioned and in danger of going bust. No one knew exactly how many people British Rail employed, and it assumed responsibility for thousands of stations, hundreds of repair depots, fifty-four hotels, seven thousand horses, a fleet of buses, canals and docks, a film company and the Thomas Cook travel agency.

In 1961 Harold MacMillan's transport minister, the oily Ernest Marples, was assigned the task of bringing order. Marples had a clear conflict of interest, having been the boss of a construction company that had made a fortune from road building contracts, so to ensure his neutrality he sold his shares to a company controlled by his wife. He then appointed Richard Beeching, on a salary double that of the prime minister, to sort out the railways. Beeching was the director of a chemical firm and had less knowledge of the railways than the average train spotter. Nevertheless, his 1963 report, two years in the making, proposed the closure of 2,636 stations, two hundred branch lines and five thousand miles of track.

Beeching wanted the closure of several very prominent stations. Mostly these stations did not close; in fact many of the subsequent cuts had very little to do with Beeching, and Harold Wilson's Labour government closed 1,400 stations he hadn't even mentioned. The cuts were devastating for some fairly major towns, especially in the West Country and several never recovered. There was once an Atlantic Coast Express; today the fastest London-Penzance train takes five hours at an average speed of fifty miles an hour. Beeching was given a peerage for decimating the public transport system of Britain on the basis of unreliable and dishonest passenger figures. Ernest Marples was likewise elevated, he then fled the country to escape arrest for tax fraud and never came back.

Thanks to Beeching, Marples and the Wilson government large areas of the Britain are practically cut off except by road and you can't visit any place of interest that isn't blighted by hundreds of parked cars. Motor vehicle use has reached such insane levels that an objective alien would be forced to ask what we imagine we are doing to ourselves, the planet and our self-respect. Our cities are filthy hell-holes that stink of diesel fumes, our children are blighted by astronomic asthma levels and our much-celebrated wealth creators are forced to fly up and down an island that isn't even a thousand miles long. The current government proposes to address the desperate national public transport situation with a multi-billion pound vanity project white elephant that will shave twenty minutes off the unnecessary journeys of Birmingham businessmen, at a phenomenal social and environmental cost. The most frightening thing is that the self-aggrandising thieves who systematically dismantled the country's once enviable rail infrastructure are also in charge of education and the NHS.

It isn't bent Tory politicians or grossly overpaid bean counters that we ultimately have to thank for the fact that the Lake District is today clogged with cars, but poets. Wordsworth and his fellow romantics objected to the noise and smoke of the railways, as well as to the unappreciative lower class visitors they might have carried. The only upside is that because the Lake District was never penetrated by the railways it never got the filthy factories and the slum towns that went with them.

Having spared the Lake District a decent public transport system the British government decided to despoil it with a nuclear power station instead. During the Second World War Churchill and Roosevelt agreed to share research on nuclear weapons and energy production, but the US reneged on the deal and made disclosure of any such information punishable by death. Britain's descent from industrial world power to glorified money-laundering spiv has been a long one, and it was still doing relatively well in the 1950s. It demonstrated just how great it was by making its very own nuclear bomb and building the world's first working nuclear power station on the Cumbrian coast. The wisdom of siting a dangerous nuclear plant in the Lake District soon became apparent. In October 1957 one of Sellafield's reactors caught fire and the boffins had no idea what to do. They feared squirting water on the fire would cause a nuclear explosion that would make much of Cumbria uninhabitable for centuries. Luckily for us all, it didn't, but for some reason the British public have ever since been suspicious of nuclear power.

It is probly pointless to try to establish a league table of which ruling class cares least for its own population, because none of them really do, but the United States often comes up trumps, between the 1940s and the 1980s the Hanford nuclear facility in Washington State, mostly intentionally, discharged millions of litres of highly radioactive waste directly into the Columbia river basin, while at the same time claiming that the river water was fine for human consumption. In evidence they said salmon caught in the river showed no signs of having consumed radioactive matter. What they failed to disclose was that salmon only enter the Columbia River to spawn and they don't eat while they are there. Any other river-dwelling animal they'd tested would have showed concentrations of radioactivity one hundred thousand times greater than normal.

In 1972 Britain signed up to the London Convention, which forbade the dumping of high-level radioactive waste at sea from ships. It didn't mention pipelines, so Britain exploited the loophole and pumped thousands of tons of dangerous nuclear waste straight into the Irish Sea. By the late 1980s Sellafield had exposed Europe to more radiation than that from all other nuclear sites put together, as well as from weapons testing, the Chernobyl accident and 'packaged solid waste' (whatever that is), all the while claiming it was adhering to the London Convention.

Sellafield used to have a kiddified visitor's centre full of cartoony pro-nuclear propaganda that received 200,000 visitors a year. It closed in 2012, but the rest of the site didn't, and couldn't. By 2015 Sellafield was home to the most hazardous building in Europe, as well as the second most hazardous building in Europe, both of them filled with decaying nuclear fuel rods and contaminated machinery. It also housed the world's largest stock of radioactive plutonium and, given that record keeping ranged from abysmal to non-existent, who knows what else.

In 2014 John Clarke, the man entrusted with the £79.1 billion plan to clean up Sellafield described it as 'a voyage of discovery', which was another way of saying he had no idea what was on the site. The cost of cleaning up Sellafield far outweighs any benefit it provided and it still contains tons of materials that will be lethal for millions of years. All of which makes current (as yet largely hypothetical) plans for nuclear power stations the size of football fields dotted around the coast rather worrying.

Nuclear power has long been a cover for nuclear weapons and it may surprise those who think we live in a democracy to discover that Britain's decision to join the nuclear arms race was taken entirely in secret, even from most of the cabinet, and that during the period of the 1945-51 Labour government there wasn't a single commons debate on atomic energy. Our elected representatives were apparently unaware that research facilities were being built, uranium was being accumulated and separated and an atomic bomb was being built until the first one was tested in the pacific in 1952.

Between 1965 and 1980 parliament did not once discuss nuclear weapons or the arms race and a conspiracy of silence existed within the media. In 1965 the BBC banned a film about the possible effects of a nuclear attack on the grounds that it might upset the faint-hearted. The corporation said that it had reached the decision to ban the program itself, without any external pressure. This was a lie. The real reason was a fear that the public might be persuaded to withdraw their support for Britain's nuclear program, and the BBC surrendered its editorial control to the government. The film was still banned in 1985, on the grounds that it might upset elderly people living alone and those of limited intelligence, the intelligent people being those who consider stockpiling weapons capable of destroying the entire planet and accumulating dangerous waste we don't know what to do with to be rational and sensible.

The line that connects the railways to radiation and public transport to plutonium is the profit system itself. Britain's post-war boom was sustained by the arms race and in helping to destroy the Soviet Union the west undermined its own productive profitability. The systematic destruction of the railways meant more private and commercial traffic on the roads and more car sales. Car sales remain the key indicator of the strength of the capitalist economy, hence the preoccupation with electric vehicles, and the road haulage industry remains one of the country's most powerful political lobbies. For health and environmental reasons it makes perfect sense to suppress car use and force freight back onto the railways. Economically it would be suicidal; damaging our children's health, building ever more roads, telling lies about the sustainability of the system, making ever more weapons and endangering the future of humanity is simply more profitable.

THE FIRST CASUALTY

Unreliable Sources – John Simpson

The media's manipulation of the public mind long precedes the transparent jingoism of today's tabloids. The Victorian press faithfully backed national causes and reported only Britain's version of events. The *Manchester Guardian* revealed that imperialist theft was behind the Boer War, but the *Times* did its best to popularise the conflict and the *Daily Mail* considered any criticism as a betrayal of British soldiers. Cruelty, wholesale looting and concentration camps were ignored.

Prior to the First World War the gutter press fed a national paranoia about the ruination of the white race and nurtured public fears until politicians were infected. The *Daily Mail* wanted war and the *Times* threatened to bring down the government. Once hostilities began the *Mail's* distorted coverage meant the few survivors of insane assaults didn't recognise their own gallantry and any reporter stupid enough to go near the front risked being lynched. As their menfolk were uselessly blown apart the public were fed lies and rumours the authorities chose not to deny. After the Russian Revolution the *Daily Mail* turned its hatred from conscientious objectors to socialists, conflating them with German spies in coverage suffused with anti-Semitism. By 1918 the noble cause was in tatters and sensible commentators worried what thousands of resentful veterans would do when they returned to the same old shit. The *Manchester Guardian* wanted the defeated Germans treated humanely, but right-wing press vindictiveness contributed to the disastrous reprisals taken at Versailles.

During the 1916 Dublin Easter Rising some sceptical journalists favoured the IRA's version of events over the army's, but the pro-union press only saw mindless criminality. The *Daily Mail* resorted to racism and celebrated the execution of the rebel leaders. The *Manchester Guardian* said the army had made things worse. When the government sent in 10,000 'Black and Tans' their reign of terror was universally condemned, but military excuses for massacres were still accepted. The government lost all trust, the press predicted a backlash and the untenable situation forced the granting of a Free State.

In the 1920s the left-leaning press began reporting Hitler's hate-filled speeches. Lord Rothermere saw in the fascists the restoration of European manhood and his *Daily Mail* parroted their propaganda. In response the *Daily Mirror* was equally flattering. The *Times* condemned Hitler's excesses, but said the parliamentary system would tame him. On both sides of the Atlantic he was regarded as a useful bulwark against Marxism. The *Manchester Guardian* reported the wholesale repression and the *Express* campaigned tirelessly for Germany's Jews.

After a failed right-wing coup against the Spanish government in 1936 General Franco's army carried out arbitrary executions and mass rape, but the British press reported it as the reasonable suppression of leftist terror. The *Daily Express* titillated its middle class readership with wild exaggeration and the rest competed in stories of crazed left-wing bloodletting. Lord Rothermere's *Mail* allowed Franco to claim leniency for his enemies while he perpetrated atrocities that were a model for the Nazis. When others objected the *Mail* claimed left-wing bias, particularly by the BBC. The *Times* accurately reported the destruction of Guernica by German warplanes.

As Edward VIII's dalliance with Wallis Simpson developed it was widely reported in the United States, but the British media maintained a conspiracy of silence. WH Smith first censored American publications, then removed them from sale. When the story finally broke the *Mirror*, the *Mail* and the *Express* backed the king and the *Times* opposed him, but the British press had shown that it was willing to supress a constitutionally vital story in the greater interests of the establishment.

Neville Chamberlain flattered the *Times* and *Telegraph* into supporting appeasement. The BBC stopped criticising Hitler, Churchill was denied airtime and the fascist-supporting Lord Beaverbrook sacked him from the *Evening Standard*. The *Daily Mail* allowed Hitler a sympathetic interview, downplayed Nazi violence and praised British fascists, while Lord Rothermere encouraged Hitler in his conquests. The *Times* gave Hitler confidence by calling for the sacrifice of Czechoslovakia. Following the Munich meeting the *Express* proclaimed peace, the *Mirror* fantasised that Hitler had been tamed and the *Mail* reported a jubilant Wall Street.

At the outbreak of war the BBC vowed to tell the truth and the *Daily Mail* tried to obscure its former fascist sympathies by exaggerating French successes and belittling Hitler and his army. The *Manchester Guardian* exposed Churchill's inflated U-boat sinking figures. The BBC was absurdly optimistic about the disastrous invasion of Norway; the *Daily Herald* complained of being misled. The press ignored military incompetence, the attempt to oust Chamberlain and his use of the German invasion of the Low Countries to cling onto power. The Norway debacle could have brought Churchill down, but the *Daily Mail* and the *Mirror* shelved their intense criticism of him while the *Manchester Guardian* and the *Herald* called for a national government.

The German blitzkrieg began as Churchill took over. The press had no idea what it entailed and the *Mail* and the *Herald* remained positive as British troops were driven back to Dunkirk. There was no hint that they were being desperately evacuated, that a thousand pieces of heavy artillery had been sacrificed or that among the bravery there was drunkenness, robbery, murder and cowardice. The whole British media sought refuge in patriotic nonsense about undefeated British forces desperate for a proper crack at Jerry. The *Daily Mail* ignored the massacre of the British rear-guard and reported the same heroics that made soldiers despise it in the first war. Defeated soldiers were only glad they weren't spat at and joined in with the banter as if they'd come off for squash and sandwiches. It took Churchill to remind the public that it had been a colossal military defeat.

After Dunkirk Churchill said JB Priestley's popular radio talks were too left-wing and the BBC dropped him. The public were unaware that the 'Battle of Britain' was a decisive contest or that the RAF was seriously stretched. The papers printed distorted figures about British and German losses, but when they discovered the names of Douglas Bader and two other airmen they had their heroes.

When the Germans began bombing British cities the public were systematically manipulated and the Blitz Spirit became self-perpetuating propaganda. The *Daily Herald* highlighted any lack of care for the population and tried to hold the authorities to account, but George Orwell argued in Labour's *Tribune* that it was better to lose innocent civilians than fighting men. All the press except the *Daily Worker* supported the carpet bombing of Germany. It said workers were the victims of a war between rival capitalists. It castigated the jingoistic press and when it told the homeless to occupy the property of the rich the government shut it down. When Hitler invaded the Soviet Union it was allowed to publish again, but never sank to flattering Churchill.

When Rudolf Hess landed in Scotland with peace terms the press allowed the public to believe Germany was losing. It accepted the significance of Churchill's North Africa campaign and when Tobruk fell and panic gripped Cairo and Alexandria no hint of it reached home. The *Express* and the *Mirror* manufactured in Montgomery a people's hero fighting a people's war, exaggerating his contrived humanity out of all proportion.

Unprecedented censorship preceded the D-Day invasion. The press dutifully provided heroes and ignored soldiers drowning in deep water and being cut to ribbons by enemy fire. When reporting on the devastating V1 rocket attacks on London was banned the public began to distrust official pronouncements, rumours circulated and media's credibility was damaged. The horrific scenes at liberated concentration camps were reported in all their gory detail. No newspaper covered the devastation of the bombs on Hiroshima and Nagasaki until an *Express* reporter got through the American cordon a month later and saw countless victims in their death throes. The US called his report Japanese propaganda and said radiation sickness didn't exist.

The press effectively destroyed the Attlee government by lying about the effects of its policies. It ignored a series of decisions regarding a British nuclear bomb and that loan repayments to the US were crippling the economy. In the run up to the 1951 general election the *Daily Mirror* called Churchill a dangerous warmonger, but the *Manchester Guardian* said he was the better of two evils. When he was re-elected aged seventy-seven they all politely ignored his unfitness for office. The BBC went along with the deception and much important cabinet business went unreported. When Churchill had a stroke the public was deliberately misled and he clung to power for two more years.

His successor Anthony Eden was in even worse health, as well as being weak and arrogant, and saw President Nasser's nationalisation of the Suez Canal as an opportunity to prove his strength. The *Mail* compared Nasser to Hitler and the *Express* said that if Britain didn't make a stand it was finished. Eden's friends at the *Times* supported intervention, the *Mirror* wanted UN backing. The BBC reported that opinion was divided and the government discussed taking it over. Anti-communist journalists in the Middle East posed as the BBC to broadcast black propaganda. When Britain and France encouraged Israel to invade Egypt the press ignored it. The *Mail* glorified British forces, which it said were only engaged in a police operation. The *Mirror* made the most of the British invasion and its gung-ho journalist parachuted in, breaking both ankles. The *News Chronicle's* reporter witnessed the reality and the military held up his despatches until the action was over. Britain was humiliated, parliament was deceived and the public was lied to. The *Guardian* said Eden should go and he went.

Harold Wilson's white heat of technology speech was celebrated by the press, but they soon noticed his dubious friends and his coterie of unelected advisers. As economic crisis loomed the *Express* turned on him. The *Mirror*, the *Sun* and the *Guardian* all backed him over Ian Smith's Rhodesia; the *Express*, the *Mail* and the *Daily Sketch* supported white rule. The *Telegraph* and the *Times* sat on the fence.

The entire British press chose not to notice the elected dictatorship that ruled by violence and intimidation in Northern Ireland until protests began in the late sixties. Many younger reporters were disinclined to accept what the RUC and the army told them and in 1971 a BBC reporter discovered that the army was torturing often innocent young men; the army denied the story and BBC bosses shelved it. Another BBC reporter witnessed mass murder by British paratroopers on Bloody Sunday and from the main evening news it was obvious that the army's claims of being fired on first were lies, though the *Times* stuck to the story of a gun battle. Subsequently the *Telegraph*, the *Mail* and the *Times* blamed the Civil Rights movement, the IRA and the organisers of the march, as did the *Guardian*, the famous defender of human rights abroad. Only the *Mirror* suggested soldiers shouldn't be there at all. The *Times* revealed that undercover soldiers were posing as journalists on both sides of the border and it became clear that the army had a great deal to hide.

Edward Heath initially disregarded the press, but soon began trying to manipulate it, even asking a *Daily Mirror* boss if he should call an election. His defeat allowed back in the lethargic, heavy drinking amnesiac Harold Wilson. His handlers tried to keep him off television and the papers reported that Wilson was a drug-taking Soviet agent who attended sex orgies and was having an affair with his secretary, rather than that he was entirely unfit for office. The *Mail* discovered a dodgy land deal and the *Evening News* and the *Sun* continued to libel him after writs had been issued against them, discovering that it was worth ignoring the law for a good story.

After 1969 Rupert Murdock turned the *Sun*, a quality Labour-supporting paper, into a cynical sex-obsessed, aggressively amoral scandal sheet. The *Times* parodied its masthead and within a year he owned that too. By the mid-seventies the *Sun* was purveying nasty political invective and Murdoch cast himself the political kingmaker many politicians came to believe in.

Margaret Thatcher overcame her dislike of television and projected herself to the politically uncommitted, eventually making the calculated claim on *World in Action* that Britain was being swamped with immigrants. The *Sun's* success led the *Mirror* to ditch in-depth political reporting. Between them they fostered a short attention span which spread to TV, as politicians became ever more image conscious and politics was cynically marketised.

Northern Ireland was a constant through Thatcher's reign and she bullied the BBC into reporting her version of events. When she libelled Roger Bolton and *Panorama* the *Telegraph* joined in and the Tory-supporting tabloids learned that attacking the BBC pleased her. The BBC would have sacrificed Bolton but for the solidarity of his colleagues in the National Union of Journalists. The corporation's supine management once more demonstrated its enduring timidity, betraying program makers who only wanted to tell the truth.

Despite her strong moral streak Thatcher managed to ignore the *Sun's* soft porn, its nasty politics and its celebrity tittle-tattle and knighted its editor, along with the obsequious editors of the *Daily Mail*, the *Daily Express* and the *Sunday Express*. She couldn't knight Rupert Murdoch and instead made sure his takeover of the British media went unquestioned. In the last months of her reign Murdoch was given control of British satellite broadcasting. In reward he dumped his apparent friend to focus on the next protector of his media fiefdom.

When General Galtieri of Argentina invaded the Malvinas the *Daily Mirror* said 'Might isn't Right' and lost tens of thousands of readers to its jingoistic rivals. The *Sun* saw an opportunity to secure its dominance and decided it meant war. It criticised the foreign office for previous weakness, accused the *Mirror* of appeasement and called the opponents of war termites. The *Mail* said a defeat would sink the government and the Tory Party. Once fighting began the BBC's Peter Snow doubted the official casualty figures. This incensed Thatcher and the *Sun* called him a traitor who had abused his right to free speech. It reached rock bottom with the crass 'GOTCHA' when a British nuclear submarine sank the retreating *General Belgrano* and hundreds of Argentine sailors drowned.

After the Falklands War Murdoch ensured that the *Sun*, the *News of the World* the *Times* took a hard Thatcherite line. The *Sunday Times* provided propaganda for Thatcher during the 1984-5 miners' strike and Murdoch used the *Times* to break the power of the print unions. In 1990 the *Daily Mail* couldn't decide whether Thatcher would win the leadership contest forced upon her or be stabbed in the back. When the Tories dumped her the press lined up to pay their respects. The *Mail* said John Major had a world to conquer and a great adventure was beginning.

The first place to be conquered was Iraq and only Robert Fisk of the *Independent* resisted the rush to war. The rest built Saddam's army up into a worthy opponent, portraying as a glorious victory a typical imperial massacre of a badly-trained, weak and demoralised third world army of conscripted cannon fodder who couldn't wait to surrender. In February 1991 the US dropped a 2,000 pound bomb on a Baghdad shelter containing three hundred women and children, killing most of them. The BBC's Jeremy Bowen described wading in liquid fat from incinerated bodies. The *Mail* accused Bowen and the BBC of treason, saying its witnesses were Saddam's stooges.

Having annihilated Neil Kinnock the *Sun* claimed credit for the 1992 Tory victory. Along with the *Mail* and the

Star it then systematically destroyed John Major. By 1997 Murdoch had chosen Blair to do his bidding and the *Sun's* announcement that it was backing him was accompanied by a big picture of the future war criminal's grinning face. Before the election Blair flew 12,000 miles to reassure Murdoch Group executives that he would complete Thatcher's economic revolution and protect the interests of his global media empire. Peter Mandelson thought he was using the media, but Murdoch used Blair's criticism of the BBC to undermine its influence in America in favour of his Fox News channel and George Bush.

The *Sun* simplified Balkan politics to Blair's advantage and he used 'humanitarian' intervention to reinforce his position. Amid vague press reports of Serbian atrocities the BBC infuriated Blair by featuring Belgrade citizens who said Britain was a slave of the US and they had been driven toward Milosevic. Their hatred, and reports of high civilian casualties of NATO's bombing, were dismissed as Serbian propaganda and in the *Times* Martin Bell defended telling the truth over government inconvenience.

When it became clear that Blair was going to back George Bush's invasion of Iraq the *Times* said the public needed to be made afraid and the *Sun* reproduced Alastair Campbell's ridiculous claim that Saddam could launch chemical weapons in forty-five minutes. The *Mirror* said war was insane and John Pilger slated it as cruel, low-risk, macho opportunism. Murdoch instructed his whole empire to back the invasion and from hundreds of miles away the *Sun's* reporter gloried in British actions against a pitiful opponent, saying predictions of heavy civilian casualties were wrong and it would not become another Vietnam. The *Telegraph* cast Blair as a second Churchill and his opponents as appeasers, doubting the figures for civilian casualties and repeating nonsense about smart bombing. The *Express* impugned France and Germany for their refusal to join in and said Saddam's entire family should burn in hell. The *Independent's* reporter in Iraq revealed the despicable barbarism of the invading forces. Blair's abusive bully Alastair Campbell began a vendetta against the BBC, causing even the *Daily Mail* to defend it, and when the corporation was forced to apologise for telling the truth its staff paid for a full page newspaper advertisement defending their right to do so.

John Simpson is undoubtedly a fine journalist and *Unreliable Sources* demolishes any notion that Britain has a free press. However, he has celebrated his part in the invasion of Afghanistan and takes it for granted that twenty years of brutal occupation has improved the lives of the Afghans the west and its ruthless proxies haven't killed or maimed. And not only this; throughout the long century Simpson covers there have been numerous non-millionaire-owned publications, from the *Worker's Dreadnought*, through the *Morning Star* to *Socialist Worker*, willing to express alternative opinions. To ignore them is to confirm the bias at the heart of the mainstream media.

AFTERWORD

As I was completing this book the British government took the decision that we would all have to live with coronavirus. The AB-1 variant is now completely out of control and sweeping the country and I am one of the infected. It has not been said often enough that the virus is just one more consequence of global political mismanagement and a bankrupt economic system and that its effects have been made far worse by the distorted priorities of that system. In Britain the public have been treated with contempt and the pandemic has both highlighted and exacerbated the crisis in our NHS, the inequality in our society and the racism at its heart. Internationally our rulers have failed dismally to properly address devastating climate change, which will lead to conflict, famine and mass migration on a scale previously unseen.

In the past few weeks we have seen British police officers force a young black schoolgirl to strip naked on spurious grounds and the members of almost an entire police station engaged in a catalogue of racism and misogyny. The outbreak of war in Europe has led to an unprecedented increase in arms spending that can be directly compared to the dreadnought race a century ago. That madness led to entire economies being turned over to the manufacture of devices designed to violently dismember millions of men and leave millions of others mental wrecks.

While proclaiming liberty for the people of Ukraine our prime minister is prepared to shake hands with the dictator of

Saudi Arabia, who is prosecuting an even more brutal war in Yemen, and only days after Mohammed bin Salman oversaw the execution of eighty-one men in a single weekend. Our Foreign Secretary is in India attempting to recruit Narendra Modi, a proto-fascist who has orchestrated ethnic violence and pogroms, into her 'network of liberty.' The whole political class is prepared to turn a blind eye to the slow genocide of the Palestinians. P&O, a major British infrastructure provider has arbitrarily sacked eight hundred of its staff without a moment's notice. There is a spiralling cost of living crisis, further racist immigration legislation and attempts to restrict our right to protest are before parliament and members of the government have repeatedly proved themselves unable to abide by the rules they set for the rest of us. The so-called opposition is spineless, mired in jingoism and sycophancy and seeks only an opportunity to prove that it also worships money and those who have lots of it.

What other indignities must we endure before we accept our collective responsibility to get rid of the global gang of short-sighted fuckwits who regard themselves as statesmen? We have gone along with the democratic charade long enough. It is time again for the methods that brought down Tsar Nicholas, Edward Heath, Hosni Mubarak, Zine El Abidine Ben Ali, Nicolae Ceausescu and the Shah of Iran. Only then will we be able to rise above the disgusting and wasteful capitalist system that in order to survive must turn us against each other and, in the end, resort to war.

Humanity has reached an impasse. We can only advance under an entirely different management with entirely different priorities. But we have to start from where we are, not from where we'd like to be. We can't begin to dig ourselves out of the hole until we are prepared to properly accept that we are in one.

ACKNOWLEDGEMENTS

As a bibliophile who can't pass a charity shop without poking about among the murder, romance and recipes for something edifying, I am indebted to the unsung volunteers who work behind the counters in order that funds may be raised to provide what governments should provide. I also salute all those people who sit in dingy rooms writing and researching when they could be outside enjoying themselves. They are the keepers of our culture and the storm troopers of civilisation. I am also indebted to the teaching profession for arming generations of working class people with the means to understand our world. Having re-entered education later in life, before going on to teach briefly myself, I was able to appreciate just how selfless and dedicated most of those people are and I take this opportunity to recognise those I worked with and those who taught me, particularly John Cullen and Denis Shemilt. I want to thank my comrades in the SWP for completely ignoring my literary pretensions in order that I didn't become big headed. More specifically I want to thank Martin Jones for reading through the preceding text, pointing out my errors, inserting commas and full stops and writing a second introduction when I stole the content of his first one. Lastly I owe an enormous debt to my life partner for everything.

BOOKS BY THIS AUTHOR

As The Crow Flies

Cycle tour diary

Local Youth Makes Good

Poetry

The Soldier

Poetry

Car

Poetry

The Rest Is History

School teacher's diary